Welcome to

THE
EVERYTHING®
PROFILES SERIES

Welcome to the EVERYTHING® Profiles line of books—an extension of the bestselling EVERYTHING® series!

These authoritative books help you learn everything you ever wanted to know about the lives, social context, and surrounding historical events of fascinating people who made or influenced history and religious thought. While reading this EVERYTHING® book you will discover four useful boxes:

Factum: Definitions and additional information
Discussion Question: Questions and answers for deeper insights
Symbolism: Explains a concept or symbol
Fallacy: Refutes a commonly held misconception

Whether you are learning about a figure for the first time or are just brushing up on your knowledge, EVERYTHING® Profiles help you on your journey toward a greater understanding of the individuals who have shaped and enriched _____ ~ulture, and history.

Visit the entire Everything® s

D1465883

The
EVERYTHING®
Jesus Book

Dear Reader,

Like millions of children around the world, some of my earliest memories are of praying at bedtime and at mealtimes for the blessing and protection of Jesus. The earliest stories I heard were of him and his antecedents and descendants in the Jewish and Christian faiths. The moral to every story was: What would Jesus do, or what would Jesus have me do, in a similar situation? The main decision we make at every turning point depends on answering those questions, I was taught, and if something is displeasing to him, it becomes a barrier to his continued blessing. However, it was my choice as to how I lived my life, and he wouldn't interfere if I didn't ask him to.

To Christians, Jesus is the son of God and the giver of every good gift: life, a world of delight, love, meaning, and our intellects. The same questions—what would Jesus do, what would Jesus have me do—confront everyone who professes him as Savior and Lord regardless of station in life.

What follows is my quest for this Jesus in history, Holy Scriptures, and the church.

Jon Kennedy

THE
EVERYTHING®
JESUS
BOOK

His Life, His Teachings

Jon Kennedy

Adams Media
Avon, Massachusetts

dedication

This book is dedicated to my daughter, Chris; my sons, Michael and Kevin; and my grandchildren, Antony and Brandi; and their pursuit of Jesus.

• • •

Publishing Director: Gary M. Krebs
Associate Managing Editor: Laura M. Daly
Associate Copy Chief: Brett Palana-Shanahan
Acquisitions Editor: Lisa Laing
Development Editor: Jessica LaPointe
Associate Production Editor: Casey Ebert
Technical Reader: Dr. James B. Wiggins

Director of Manufacturing: Susan Beale
Associate Director of Production:
Michelle Roy Kelly
Cover Design: Paul Beatrice, Matt LeBlanc,
Erick DaCosta
Design and Layout: Colleen Cunningham,
Sorae Lee, Jennifer Oliveira

• • •

An Everything® Series Book.
Everything® and everything.com® are registered trademarks of F+W Publications, Inc.

Published by Adams Media, an F+W Publications Company
57 Littlefield Street, Avon, MA 02322 U.S.A.
www.adamsmedia.com

ISBN 10: 1-59337-712-6
ISBN 13: 978-1-59337-712-0

Printed in the United States of America.

J I H G F E D C B A

Library of Congress Cataloging-in-Publication Data
Kennedy, Jon.
The everything Jesus book / Jon Kennedy.
p. cm. -- (Everything series)
Includes bibliographical references and index.
ISBN-13: 978-1-59337-712-0
ISBN-10: 1-59337-712-6
1. Jesus Christ. I. Title.
BT203.K46 2006
232--dc22
2006019735

This publication is designed to provide accurate and authoritative information with regard to the subject matter covered. It is sold with the understanding that the publisher is not engaged in rendering legal, accounting, or other professional advice. If legal advice or other expert assistance is required, the services of a competent professional person should be sought.

—From a *Declaration of Principles* jointly adopted by a Committee of the American Bar Association and a Committee of Publishers and Associations

Many of the designations used by manufacturers and sellers to distinguish their products are claimed as trademarks. Where those designations appear in this book and Adams Media was aware of a trademark claim, the designations have been printed with initial capital letters.

This book is available at quantity discounts for bulk purchases.
For information, please call 1-800-872-5627.

Unless otherwise indicated, Scripture quotations are from The Holy Bible, English Standard Version (ESV) © 2001 by Crossway Bibles, a division of Good News Publishers.

Contents

7 His Following Multiplies 81

8 From Triumph to the Cross 95

9 The Acts and Paul 109

10 The Church, the Body of Christ 125

11 The Jesus of History 141

12 Salvation 159

13 Christian Culture 173

18 Jesus and the Culture Wars 248

19 The Jesus of the Future 263

20 Jesus as Lord and Savior 279

Top Ten Interesting Facts You'll Learn About Jesus

1. Scholars generally agree that Jesus' life is better documented than that of any other figure of historical antiquity.

2. The church at large did not celebrate the birth of Jesus, Christmas, until between three and five centuries after the church's beginning.

3. The church does not teach that Jesus' date of birth was December 25.

4. Scholars have concluded that Jesus was born about five years earlier than the beginning of the current general calendar, or about 5 B.C.

5. After a replacement was found for Judas Iscariot, all but one of Jesus' closest disciples died martyrs' deaths after keeping the faith.

6. Jesus was circumcised as all Jewish males are, as part of their covenant with God.

7. Jesus was baptized by John the Baptist, who was his second cousin.

8. In most of the Christian world, Easter is known in the local language as the equivalent word for Passover.

9. What Jesus considered the best and worst prayers are only one sentence each.

10. Thousands of martyrdoms in the first three centuries of the church are generally considered the best evidence for the truthfulness of the Gospel and the biggest impetus for the church's growth.

Acknowledgments

I want to express heartfelt gratitude to Paula Munier, Director of Product Development; my editor, Lisa Laing; and everyone else at Adams Media involved in making this book possible.

Introduction

Who was Jesus? What was the world that he was born into like? Who were his parents and ancestors? What did he teach? Who were his first followers, and how did they multiply in number to become the largest religious following in today's world?

What did Jesus mean when he told his followers they would be able to move a mountain? What did Jesus teach as necessary for salvation? Do his teachings contrast with—or complement—those of his apostles? How did we receive the Bible, and what causes orthodox Christians to believe it contains and is, in written form, the Word of God?

In today's more multicultural world, answers to such questions are no longer universally known, and with the competition of constantly increasing entertainment, educational, and information media, the Bible stories are not as widely taught to children, even if more Bibles are in the stores and in homes than ever before. Contemporary surveys of high-school-age and college-age young people have shown deep and widespread biblical illiteracy.

This book introduces Jesus from a slightly more distant perspective than that of the Bible by sharing some of the findings of Bible scholars, historians, archaeologists, and anthropologists on his life and times, his following in the church, and his impact on the world in the two millennia since his birth. The intention is to make this an easily accessible survey of Jesus, his life, his teachings, his historical impact, and more.

Chapters will give detailed accounts of the church in the first generation after Jesus ministered on earth, how persecution against Christians began and spread from Israel to the whole Roman Empire, how many of the martyrs died, and how they are considered the "seed of the church." Also looked at are the conversion of the Roman emperor Constantine and his influence on the church; and the church's influence on the emperor and, through him, on the succeeding emperors and the Roman Empire as a whole.

The Dark Ages, the Middle Ages, the Crusades, the Renaissance, the Age of Exploration, the Enlightenment, and the rise of modern democracies . . . all are surveyed in terms of their relationships with the story of Jesus, his life, and his world influence, and made easily accessible in this overview.

How is the church faring in today's generation? How big is the church in the United States, and in the world at large? How does it compare with other religions in size and the devotion of its followers? Has the Christian era peaked and started its decline, or is it poised for further growth in the world in generations to come? Who are the Catholics, Orthodox, Protestants, Modernists, and Evangelicals, and how do they relate to each other? How does the church fare alongside secular humanism in Europe, America, and the rest of the world?

Also included in this survey will be consideration of the Jesus of the future, as the Bible makes many references to the climax of history, the end of the world, the apocalypse, and the Second Coming of Jesus. What does the Bible say on these controversial topics, and what do the different churches say about those biblical teachings?

Throughout this work, references to "the traditional teaching" or "the tradition of the church" refer to the consensus of the united church before the great schism between Rome and Constantinople in 1054 (described in Chapter 11) and, especially, the defining documents and canons of the seven ecumenical councils that culminated in A.D. 787. References here to "the apostolic churches" mean those churches of the first millennium after Christ that claimed that all their bishops had been consecrated in an unbroken line of succession from the original apostles of the church (as described in Chapter 5). And consistent with this approach, though there are many theories among modern biblical scholars about the identity of the writers of the New Testament, especially Matthew and Luke, the references in this book refer to the author of Luke as "Luke," the author of Matthew as "Matthew," and so on, in the interest of simplification and clarity.

Chapter 1

Jesus of the Stable

I f the widely cited claim that one-third of the world's population identifies itself as Christian is accurate, the story of Jesus' birth is most likely the best-known account of a birth in human history, and possibly even the best-known story ever told. Even those not literate enough to read for themselves are exposed to the story through Nativity scenes, pageants, readings, and carols accompanying Christmas celebrations around the world.

Humble Beginnings

The Gospel of Luke introduces the birth portion of Jesus' story in chapter 2:1–7. These verses describe his surroundings, suggest his purpose in coming, and provide the tenor of his story by beginning the human life of the Creator and King of the universe not in a palace but in a stable, probably built into a cave in the hillside, where no one would ever expect anything of great significance to occur.

discussion question

What is the origin of the word *Christmas*?
The early church's technical name of the day set aside for observance of Christ's birth is the Feast of the Nativity. Feasts are the resumption of a regular diet after a fast such as Advent, the forty-day fast preceding Christmas. The word *Christmas* comes from the English contraction of the Roman Catholic term "Christ's mass."

Some scholars believe Luke likely received his detailed account of the birth of Jesus directly from Mary, Jesus' mother. According to church tradition, Mary was early in her childbearing years at the time she became promised to Joseph, and she lived some years after Jesus' ascension into Heaven. Biblical scholars believe Luke's Gospel and the other three Gospels were written in the latter half of the first century after Jesus' birth.

Virgin Birth

A fundamental teaching of Christianity is that Mary was betrothed but had not consummated her marriage with Joseph when Jesus was born. Without this teaching, the claim that God was Jesus' father would be disbelieved. Luke says that "in the sixth month" the angel Gabriel was sent from God to Mary in Nazareth, a town in Galilee, a region of the Israel of that time northeast of Jerusalem, to tell her God the Father had chosen her to:

... bear a son, and shalt call his name JESUS. He shall be great, and shall be called the Son of the Highest: and the Lord God shall give unto him the throne of his father David: And he shall reign over the house of Jacob for ever; and of his kingdom there shall be no end.

*Then said Mary unto the angel, How shall this be, seeing I know not a man? And the angel answered and said unto her, The Holy Ghost shall come upon thee, and the power of the Highest shall overshadow thee: therefore also that holy thing which shall be born of thee shall be called the Son of God ... For with God nothing shall be impossible (**Luke 2:31–35; 37).***

Matthew's Gospel cites the virgin birth as a fulfillment of the prophecy of Isaiah, "Therefore, the Lord himself shall give you a sign: 'Behold, a virgin shall conceive, and bear a son, and shall call his name Emmanuel'" (Isaiah 7:14; Matthew 1:23).

fallacy

It's a widespread misconception that the "Immaculate Conception" is a technical term related to Jesus' virgin birth. The doctrine of the "Immaculate Conception," taught only by Roman Catholics among the Christian communions, refers not to the conception of Jesus in Mary's womb, but of Mary's in the womb of her mother. The Immaculate Conception reinforces Mary's sinlessness. The teaching became an official Catholic dogma in 1854.

God with Us

Emmanuel is a Hebrew phrase meaning "God with us." (El, the final syllable, is short for *Elohim,* a common Hebrew name for God that appears more than 2,500 times in the Old Testament.) Most Christian interpreters hold the prophecy of Isaiah as messianic and take it to refer to a specific child to be sent by God to save his people. Matthew, whose Gospel is tailored for Jewish readers, cites this verse from Isaiah as the first of many Old Testament prophecies he uses as evidence for the divinity and messianic mission of Jesus. Jesus, which is the name both Luke and Matthew say was given to Mary for her son, is from the Greek Iesous, which in turn comes from the Hebrew Jeshua (also written as Yeshua) or Joshua, all meaning "Yahweh is salvation."

Shepherds and Angels

One indication of the humble milieu into which Jesus was born is that initially no great or powerful people were told about one of the most important events thus far in human history. But shepherds, no doubt faithful Jewish people whose major yearning was the coming of their Messiah, were let in on the news by angels they saw singing Jesus' praise in the sky over the starlit hills where they were camped. Luke devotes what now amounts to ten verses of his Gospel to the shepherds' adoration of the Christ child (the original text was not broken into verses).

Though two Gospels record details about the birth of Jesus, and some recognition of Jesus' birth is recorded in historical documents as early as A.D. 200, the Nativity does not appear in church records as an official feast of the church until A.D. 566 or 567. The slow evolution of Christmas observance probably occurred mainly because early Christians thought that in the pagan Roman practice, "only sinners' birthdays were celebrated." The first generations of Christians celebrated Jesus' baptism, as well as the adoration of the Magi, as the events that revealed him as God with us. This now-lesser feast of the Magi is known and observed to this day as Epiphany (or, in Eastern Orthodoxy, Theophany), which falls twelve days after Christmas; this is the origin of the tradition of the twelve days of Christmas.

Kenosis (Self-Humbling)

Kenosis is a Greek term for self-emptying (*ekenosen*), or self-humbling. Though it refers specifically to the later work of Jesus in going to the Cross and giving himself over entirely to the will of the Father and the vulnerability of a human death, it also describes the humble circum-stances of his birth and the gradual revelation of his godhead.

Theologians have debated whether Jesus gave up superhuman powers in this self-emptying, as some Protestant scholars have spec-ulated, or whether he merely chose not to exercise them, as Catholic and Orthodox fathers maintain. Jesus' kenosis can also apply to his submission to the parental control of Mary and Joseph, whom he depended on and obeyed despite his divine nature.

Jesus' Family Tree

In Matthew's Gospel, Jesus' genealogy, or family tree, precedes the account of his birth to make the point that he was a direct descen-dant of Abraham, whom Paul described as the "father of the faithful" (Romans 4:11; "the father of all them that believe" in the King James version), and of David, the second king of Israel and the one most highly esteemed by the nation ever after, and the king most highly regarded by God Himself. The Gospel begins with "the book of the generation of Jesus Christ, the Son of David, the Son of Abraham." It was commonly believed among the Jewish people that the Messiah would be a member of the House of David, and would be born in Bethlehem of Judea.

factum

Some Eastern European Orthodox Christians celebrate Christmas thirteen days after Catholics, Protestants, and other Orthodox do, but do not date the holiday as falling on January 7. On their calendar (introduced by Julius Caesar in A.D. 45), December 25 falls 13 days later than in the Gregorian calendar (introduced by the Pope in 1582).

Whereas Matthew traces Jesus from Abraham through his step-father Joseph, Luke traces him backward from Joseph all the way to

Adam. This evidences the different primary audiences intended by the two Gospel writers: the Jewish people in Matthew's case, who would have to see Jesus as a "Jew of the Jews," and Christians who weren't of Jewish origin in Luke's. Matthew emphasizes the royal bloodline, whereas Luke emphasizes his blood relationship with the whole race of humankind.

The Ancestors of God

The divine liturgy (worship service) attributed to fourth century Bishop St. John Chrysostom refers to the parents of Mary, in church tradition Joachim and Anna, as "the ancestors of God." Though of course the eternal God has no human forebears and cannot even be comprehended by human faculties, the church teaches that in the incarnation of the human Jesus, he is "very God of very God." For the same reason, to affirm the two natures of Christ, the fathers in the third ecumenical council, A.D. 431, called for the use of Theotokos, Greek for "God-bearer" or "Mother of God," to describe Mary and thus to underscore Jesus' fully human nature alongside his divinity. If Mary is God's mother, her parents are his grandparents or ancestors, though they all are fully human.

As mentioned previously, the genealogies of Matthew's and Luke's Gospels also trace the ancestors of Jesus. Among them are princes and kings (David, Solomon), but also ordinary people who played redemptive roles in the history of Israel, some of whom were not even ethnically Jewish (Rahab, Ruth). From this it is understood that the Gospel writers wanted to emphasize Jesus' relationship with the whole human race, "of the Jews first, and also of the Gentiles" as St. Paul repeatedly puts it.

Mary

After the shepherds came to adore Jesus in the stable, Luke says, "Mary kept all these things, and pondered them in her heart." This simple description has guided the church's impression and images of Mary since the beginning. Her traditional icon shows her holding her son. Though he is the size of an infant, he has the face of a man, which indicates his adult purpose for being born of Mary. Also in the icon she has her hand raised, pointing to him, indicating that he, not she, is the focus of the attention, not only of the icon viewers, but of human history.

discussion question

Why is Mary controversial?
Mary has been controversial, especially since the Reformation, because Protestants generally felt she got too much attention in Catholic piety, sometimes even calling Mariology "Mariolatry," or idolatry. Recently, however, some Protestants have begun asking how the angel Gabriel's prophecy that all generations will call Mary blessed is being fulfilled in their teaching and worship.

Roman Catholic teaching on Mary includes four dogmas: Mary's Immaculate Conception, which is seen as guarding her from original sin; Mary's sinlessness; Mary's perpetual virginity; and the Assumption (the ascension of her body to heaven directly after her death). Only one of these dogmas, Mary's perpetual virginity, is taught as dogma in the Eastern Orthodox Church. The Orthodox Church generally rejects the Immaculate Conception; most Orthodox believe in the Assumption but consider it not necessary to have a dogma about it, and though the Orthodox regard Mary as the most sinless natural human being ever, they feel it's not necessary to reiterate the issue of her sinlessness. As one Orthodox theologian puts it, some Orthodox writers have offered the opinion that during her lifetime, Mary probably did display some of the human foibles tracing to the fall, like impatience and anger. Protestants have a wide variety of opinions on Mary, as on most other theological issues, but in general they regard her role as a good mother to the Lord, but little else.

Joseph, the Betrothed, and James, the Lord's Brother

A Bible trivia question asks, "How many brothers and sisters—natural children of Joseph and Mary—did Jesus have?" The Bible doesn't say that Mary and Joseph had any "natural children," but the trivia question lists as its proof Mark 6:3: "Is this not the carpenter, the Son of Mary, and brother of James, Joses, Judah, and Simon? And are not his sisters here with us?" On this basis the trivia game claims that Jesus had six or more "natural" siblings. The Roman Catholic and Orthodox churches have always held that Mary had no children with Joseph (as did Martin Luther and John Calvin, generally considered the founders of Protestantism); and that Mary remained a virgin all her life. In the ancient church, Joseph has always been referred to as "the betrothed" to emphasize that though he undertook Mary's and Jesus' protection, he and Mary never consummated their marriage.

A common interpretation of New Testament references to James as Jesus' brother is that Joseph, an older man when he was betrothed to Mary, had a previous wife, James' mother, who had died. The others mentioned by Mark may have been members of Joseph's close family as cousins, or could have been Joseph's offspring by his previous marriage. To refer to close relatives this way is not unusual, as occurred when Jesus, from the cross, referred to John the Apostle, who is believed by many scholars to have been Jesus' second cousin, as Mary's new son, meaning he was being charged with her care (John 19:26).

Has the Church Forgotten?

The ancient church claims that its tradition is reliable because the church was "there" from the beginning and never was lacking in rational sense, nor was it forgetful. The early church tradition says that Mary's "perpetual virginity" was prophesied in the Old

Testament: "this gate shall be shut, it shall not be opened, and no man shall enter in by it; because the Lord, the God of Israel, has entered in by it. Therefore, it shall be shut" (Ezekiel 44:2).

factum

In most of the world, Christmas is the most celebrated day every year. Solemn adult versions of the story are told in Gospel readings and recitations in candlelight services in Catholic, Orthodox, and Protestant churches, and children's versions are presented in pageants or plays, not only in churches but even in many non-Christian schools.

That Joseph was considerably older than Mary is suggested by the fact that he had apparently died by the time of the crucifixion. That James was an older brother of Jesus, not a younger one, is evidenced by the fact that he came to believe in Jesus late in the Gospels' timeline. Some argue that younger siblings—including all the other five mentioned by Mark—would have attached themselves to an older brother of such charisma as Jesus from their childhood on, as younger siblings generally do. But although much is said about James, identified in early church records as the author of the epistle bearing his name in the New Testament, none of the other "brothers and sisters" mentioned in Mark are specifically kept in the church's tradition.

Jesus' Siblings

It's hard to imagine that the church would have forgotten those alleged stepsiblings, or that they would have had no role in the early church. Some say the offspring of Joseph and Mary after Jesus would have left a lineage that today would claim blood relationship with God. There has been considerable scholarly discussion concerning these siblings. According to Roman Catholic and Orthodox teaching, no woman whose womb had brought the very God into the world would have been used for any lesser purpose later. One theory, already mentioned, states that the siblings were stepsiblings or cousins who were already adults by the time Jesus was born. However, some scholars do believe that there is real New Testament evidence that the siblings of Jesus were his blood relatives, actual brothers and sisters.

The Star of Bethlehem

Planetariums often draw Christmas-season audiences by presenting programs built around theories about what the star of Bethlehem may have been if it was anything other than a story made up by some early disciples of Jesus. Amateur astronomer Susan S. Carroll, who has developed an extensive Web page about the star of Bethlehem, says that, although the star is mentioned only once in the Bible (in the Book of Matthew), it was likely "a genuine astronomical occurrence."

discussion question

Has Christmas always been celebrated in the United States?
No. Christmas was suppressed in Puritan New England and in Presbyterian Scotland as late as the nineteenth century. Both strict Puritans (later known as Congregationalists), in New England, and Presbyterian Covenanters in Scotland began as Calvinist denominations.

The science of astronomy studies observable events in the universe, and if the star came and went just for the Magi (the Greek word translated as "wise men" in the King James Version of Matthew's Gospel), there's nothing left to investigate or study. If we accept the ancient definition of astrology as "interpreting events in the heavens" rather than the contemporary meaning of "reading horoscopes," the Wise Men must have been astrologers, prescientific stargazers.

In their era, before the advent of astronomy as a discrete science, they can be considered the closest thing then available to scientific observers of the heavens.

Astroarchaeology

Astroarchaeology, also known as archaeoastronomy, is the study of astronomy as it was practiced in ancient times, using archaeological evidence such as Stonehenge or the Great Pyramids of Egypt. Astroarchaeologist John Charles Webb, Jr., theorizes that the Magi were the only stargazers who could see (or "discern") the star of Bethlehem, because they found it through their ancient and advanced astrological knowledge (represented, for example, by the great pyramids of Egypt, Stonehenge, and other ancient evidences of astrological knowledge that have been lost to modern science).

Unlike most astronomers' speculations on what the star of Bethlehem was, Webb rules out an alignment of several planets, appearing as a great star, as the explanation. He claims that King Herod, undoubtedly served by stargazers of his own, seemed to be unaware of any special star when the Magi brought it to his attention. According to Webb's interpretation, there must have been a representation of the event visible in the heavens to the highly trained astrological eye, because Matthew says, "the star, which they saw in the east, went before them, till it came and stood over where the young child was" (Matthew 2:9b).

Year of Jesus' Birth

Webb's charting theorizes that the star appeared on March 2, in the year 5 B.C. Other scholars had long ago concluded that the calendars put the time of Christ's birth (A.D. 0) as about five years too late, based on historical evidence for the date of King Herod's death. Earlier attempts to establish the birthdate of Jesus had concluded that it most likely occurred in the spring, but the church—though not denying the evidence—rejected that date for the Nativity Feast because it would have been too close to Easter, or the Pascal Feast.

One reason the church may have chosen December 25 for the Nativity Feast is that it was the first day after the winter solstice on which the lengthening of days could be discerned. Thus, pagans celebrated it as the rebirth day of the sun. Some speculate that even long before there was an official widely observed Nativity Feast, Christians had begun reinterpreting the pagan "Sun Festival" in a Christian perspective as the birthday of the Sun of Righteousness, one of the prophetic names for the Messiah that appears in the Old Testament. As it is written in Malachi 4:2: "But unto you that fear my name shall the Sun of righteousness arise with healing in his wings; and ye shall go forth, and grow up as calves of the stall."

factum

St. Nicholas was bishop of Myra, in what is now Turkey, in the fourth century. His legendary generosity toward poor children led to his saint's day, December 7, becoming a day for giving gifts to children. He had no direct connection with Christmas until a poem about him by divinity schoolteacher Clement Clark Moore became a seasonal favorite.

Visitors from the East

It's entirely consistent with their respective points of view that only Luke reports the visit of the shepherds to venerate the newborn Christ child, and only Matthew records the visit by the wise men. Luke's intended audience might have been more impressed to know that the child had been born and first worshipped under humble circumstances, whereas Matthew wanted to stress Jesus' divine royalty as a descendent of the house of David.

St. Matthew's recording of the visit by the "kings from the east" is consistent with his tracing of the royal lineage of Jesus. His Jewish audience would demand evidence of royal patronage or notice of the Messiah's birth. The Magi were most likely from Persia and most likely followers of Zoroaster, known as "the king of the Magi" and the founder of what is widely thought to be the world's first mono-theistic religion. The gifts the wise men brought were precious commodities, so they must have been wealthy, and even if there was only one wise man for each gift (which provides the theory that there were three of them), they most likely had a retinue providing security.

Matthew's account of the visit of the Magi is short and simple: "And when they were come into the house, they saw the young child with Mary his mother, and fell down, and worshipped him: and when they had opened their treasures, they presented unto him gifts; gold, and frankincense and myrrh" (Matthew 2:11).

symbolism

Gift giving was part of ancient feasts and celebrations, much like gifts today are given to newlyweds or graduates. Christmas gifts symbolize this universal practice and reflect the Gospel account that the Magi brought gifts of great value to the Child of Bethlehem. But pre-eminently, they recognize the Father's "indescribable gift" to us (2 Corinthians 9:15).

Scholars generally agree that the Magi arrived after the Christ child had been removed from the stable to a house, after the influx of taxpayers to Bethlehem had abated. They were most likely "kings" only in the sense that they had wealth and could move about freely in a dangerous environment. Indisputably, they are the first gentiles who worshipped Jesus.

An explanation of how the Magi found the star and the Messiah is provided by Moses in Deuteronomy, "if you shall seek the LORD your God, you shall find him; if you seek him with all your heart and with all your soul" (Deuteronomy 4:29); and the Prophet Jeremiah reiterated, "you shall seek me, and find me, when you shall search for me with all your heart," Jeremiah 29:13.

Chapter 2

The Silent Years

I t's part of natural human curiosity to want more information on the "silent years" in Jesus' life—the years between the flight into Egypt and Jesus' baptism and the beginning of his public ministry. Neither the Bible nor church tradition provides much to go on. Beginning in the early years after Jesus' lifetime, many have offered theories and have written apocryphal accounts of the thirty years about which only a few biblical verses are available.

After the Birth

Luke's Gospel records the circumcision of Jesus on the eighth day after his birth, most likely in Bethlehem while Mary was recovering from her delivery, and before the wise men had come to worship him as recorded in Matthew. In Jewish tradition, male children were named at circumcision, and Luke reports that at Jesus' circumcision "his name was called JESUS, which was so named of the angel before he was conceived in the womb" (Luke 2:21).

discussion question

What is the "purification" that Mary had to undergo after the birth?
It was a Jewish tradition required of mothers after giving birth. Experts say the purification required Mary to stay indoors for forty days, and when it was accomplished, she was then able to make the five-mile walk (or ride by donkey) from Bethlehem to the Temple in Jerusalem for the presentation.

And without referring to the wise men; the threat of Herod and the infanticide he commanded; or the flight of Mary, Joseph, and Jesus into Egypt, in the very next verse (2:22) Luke begins the story of Jesus' presentation in the Temple in Jerusalem. The Magi might have arrived to worship Jesus just before the family journeyed to Jerusalem for the presentation, though this doesn't accord with the traditional (but arbitrary) dating of the Epiphany (as mentioned previously, an early Christian feast commemorating the worship of Jesus by the Wise Men, and Jesus' baptism) only twelve days after the Nativity.

If the Magi's adoration was only a short time before the presentation, by the time Herod realized the Magi had given him the slip, he was looking for newborns in the area of Bethlehem, but Jesus may have already been in Jerusalem. It may have been there that Joseph received the angel's warning to hide out in Egypt.

symbolism

Circumcision was widely practiced as a religious ritual in biblical times, including by the ancient Egyptians, as documented in artworks dating more than two thousand years B.C. Circumcision was given to Abraham as the sign and symbol of the covenant between him and his descendants with God (Genesis 17:1), and is still practiced as a religious requirement by the Jewish people.

The Presentation

Jesus' presentation, accompanied by a sacrifice of turtledoves or pigeons, as was traditional, was marked by the appearance of a devout man named Simeon who had been told by the Holy Spirit that he would live to see the Messiah. And Luke says Simeon took Jesus "up in his arms, and blessed God, and said, Lord, now lettest thou thy servant depart in peace, according to thy word: For mine eyes have seen thy salvation, Which thou hast prepared before the face of all people; A light to lighten the Gentiles, and the glory of thy people Israel" (Luke 2:28–31).

Simeon's speech prophesies both the reason Jesus came into the world (as the expected Messiah) and his passion (suffering) and death, which Simeon describes as piercing Mary's heart (Luke 2:35). This "Canticle of Simeon" (or the *Nunc Dimittis*, as it is called in the Roman Catholic Church, based on the first two words of the verse in Latin) was a prayer sung in the liturgies of the ancient church. It is still used in the regular evening services (vespers) of Eastern Orthodox Christians.

The Prophetess Anna

Luke's story of the presentation also includes a "prophetess," Anna, who had been a widow most of her life, and had been living in the Temple, praying and fasting and, like Simeon, waiting faithfully for the Messiah. "And she coming in that instant gave thanks likewise unto the Lord, and spake of him to all them that looked for redemption in Jerusalem" (Luke 2:38).

discussion question

What is the *synoptic problem*?
It is a theological term for the seeming discrepancies among the four Gospels: Matthew, Mark, Luke, and John. For example, Matthew records the visit of the Magi and Luke records the shepherds and angels coming to the stable, but each Gospel omits the opposite accounts.

Flight into Egypt

St. Matthew continues his parallel narrative after the Magi worshipped the baby Jesus (see Matthew 2:12–18). Angels directed the Magi not to return to Herod on their way back home, and also told Joseph to flee from Israel into Egypt to escape Herod's plot to thwart any challenge of his rule over Israel by an alleged newborn king, by having all baby boys under age two killed.

Legends and Apocryphal Traditions

Anne Rice's recent bestselling novel, *Christ the Lord: Out of Egypt*, may be the latest in a long history of fictitious attempts to imaginatively recreate the childhood of Jesus. Rice's story is told from the perspective of Jesus himself, at age seven, describing events that happen as he and his large extended family make their way from Egypt to Nazareth after the angel tells his stepfather Joseph that it's now safe for him to bring the child back to Israel.

Some reviewers claim that Rice got cues for her boy Jesus from *The Infancy Gospel of Thomas*, an apocryphal Gnostic text that has been traced back to A.D. 185, when Irenaeus, bishop of Lyon, cited it. This is the source of the famous myth of the child Jesus creating clay sparrows and giving them life, but it also shows him as petulant and vengeful toward those who cross him. *The Infancy Gospel* has no connection with Apostle Thomas of the New Testament, and students of its text say that its lack of knowledge about Jewish life of the first century discounts its claim to have been written by a follower of Jesus. The Infancy Gospel of Thomas says that Jesus arrived in Egypt at age two, and after the angel gave the all clear, his family returned to Nazareth when he was seven.

Gnosis is a Greek word meaning "knowledge," but in the times of the early church, *Gnostics* referred to esoteric or hidden knowledge, which the Gnostics claimed to possess about Christ and his teachings. The Gnostics are also described as believing that matter is evil, and that therefore the goal of religion is to achieve a purely spiritual state. This contrasts with the orthodox Christian view, in which God himself took material form in the incarnation, and St. Paul's teaching that the material bodies of believers will play a vital part in their resurrection from the dead (1 Corinthians 15).

Why the Silence?

The New Testament's relative silence on the childhood and youth of Jesus is consistent with virtually all other biographies in the Bible. Jacob and Esau, Moses, Joseph, David, and Daniel are Old Testament figures whose early life is mentioned, but not with more than a few sentences.

As an infant, Moses was saved by Pharaoh's daughter after his mother and sister floated him in a reed basket on the Nile to hide him; the Egyptian Pharaoh had ordered all Hebrew babies killed. David killed a lion as a shepherd boy and killed Goliath using only a slingshot and five smooth stones before entering puberty, and was anointed as Israel's next king years before he reached manhood and the acceptance of his people. This is how the biblical stories of infancy, childhood, and youth unfold. Sketchy highlights are all that is given, in contrast to pagan and Gnostic writings that provide detailed accounts of childhood and youth.

factum

Joseph, the favorite among Jacob's twelve sons, was given the coat of many colors by his father and, because of jealousy over that favored treatment, his brothers sold him into slavery. When still in his youth, he resisted the seductions of his master's wife. And like Jesus, he saved his people, but temporally rather than eternally.

Jesus in the Koran

Interestingly, the Koran (also written Qur'an), written five to six centuries after the New Testament, has more descriptions of the childhood of Jesus than the New Testament. *The Catholic Encyclopedia* (1910) cites the Apocryphal writings (like *The Infancy Gospel of Thomas*) as the Koran's source.

The Koran affirms the virgin birth of Jesus to Mary and God's Spirit, and adds that as a baby he didn't require any teaching; he had access to all knowledge. It also refers to his making clay birds and giving them life. The Koran calls Jesus the only sinless man, but rejects his godhead, as taught in the Christian creeds and as he himself claimed. (See the Koran, Surah 3, 42–63; Surah 19 (Maryam), 16–50; Surah 4, 156–159; Surah 61, 6–9; Surah 3, 33–34, 38–39; Surah 5, 72–80.)

Settling in Galilee

Matthew's account continues by saying that an angel again appeared to Joseph to tell him Herod was dead and that it was now safe to return to Israel. Matthew also says the angel revealed that Herod Archelaus had succeeded his father, and that Joseph should take the family to Nazareth in Galilee rather than Judea (the region surrounding Jerusalem), "that it might be fulfilled which was spoken by the prophets, He shall be called a Nazarene" Matthew 2:23.

Luke relates that Nazareth had been the home city of Mary and Joseph before Jesus' birth, but it's understandable that the Holy Family may have been drawn to Jerusalem, their holy city and the center of all the action for the whole of Jewish history, knowing the promises the angels had given them regarding Jesus.

discussion question

What is the relationship of Mohammed to Christianity?
Mohammed was the prophet and founder of Islam; he was born in A.D. 570 in Mecca, the commercial and religious center of Arabia at the time. *The Catholic Encyclopedia* says that after meeting Christians and Jewish people during trade journeys, he brought monotheism to Arabia as a religious reform through the Koran, which he authored. He died in A.D. 633.

Teaching the Elders

Matthew's Gospel jumps from the Holy Family's arrival back in Nazareth to the adult ministry of John the Baptist, who is identified by Luke as Jesus' cousin, and the beginning of Jesus' public ministry. But Luke tells a few more salient facts about Jesus' formative years, saying "the child grew, and waxed strong in spirit, filled with wisdom: and the grace of God was upon him," Luke 2:40. He also reveals that the family annually went to Jerusalem for the feast of Passover and that, at age twelve, Jesus stayed behind in the Temple, teaching the teachers of the Temple, while Mary and Joseph began their return to Nazareth, assuming he was with other members of the extended family.

factum

Although people congregated in synagogues in various towns and cities to pray and study God's word, it was vital that devout Jewish people make regular pilgrimages to their Temple in Jerusalem, much the way Muslims of our time attempt to make at least one pilgrimage to Mecca in their lifetimes.

This is the closest the biblical biographies of Jesus come to the Apocryphal "petulant" boy God. But here he is precocious, not petulant, submitting to the discipline of his parents when they realized they had lost him and returned to the Temple to find him. This short passage suggests that the faithful from Galilee journeyed en masse to the great feast in Jerusalem. The procession provided security against robbers, company on the journey, and entertainment in the form of shared stories, impressions, and, no doubt, religious conversation and singing.

The Jewish World of Jesus' Childhood

From the beginning, the Jewish people were both a political (nation-forming) and a religious (God-fearing) entity. The nation was required, from the covenant between God and Abraham onward, to be a holy—that is, separated—people, not intermarrying or being otherwise corrupted by the pagan peoples around them, even those who ruled over them. As the Jewish wars and the destruction of the Temple later in the first century would demonstrate, the greatest crisis they ever faced was the Roman empire. It was in the height of this national crisis that Christ came. The Romans destroyed the Temple in A.D. 70, as part of their suppression of Jewish uprisings against Rome, and the Temple has never been restored. In Jesus' time the Temple in Jerusalem was the only lawful place where sacrifices were made for the atonement of the sins of the Jewish people, and where prescribed worship took place. And Jewish worship, without a Temple, has been incomplete ever since.

Josephus, a first-century historian from a priestly family of Jewish people, provides the best-preserved view of Jewish life, apart from the New Testament, in Jesus' time. He presents it as an era of much political upheaval, as some Jewish parties tried to mobilize revolts against Rome. At least five political groups existed in the Judaism of Jesus' lifetime: the Pharisees, Sadducees, Essenes, Zealots, and Samaritans.

Pharisees

The Pharisees were laymen who tried to preserve the Jewish faith through pious and legalistic practices, and although as a group they were strongly censured in Jesus' sermons, some of them were friends and supporters of Jesus and his disciples.

Sadducees

The Sadducees, the elite of the Jewish priesthood, tended toward less exact expressions of the faith than the Pharisees, and toward accommodating the political rulers of their time. They are described as denying the resurrection of the body, which is not specifically taught (only suggested) in the Old Testament, but which many Jewish people believed in at that time. Most of the historical information about the Sadducees, apart from the references in the New Testament, are from their critics, so historians describe them as hard to pin down.

discussion question

What is a Nazarite?
Nazarites were Jewish people who took temporary vows to abstain from wine or other strong drink, to refrain from cutting their hair, and to avoid touching the dead (see Numbers 6:2–21). They could complete their vows by performing ceremonial acts at the Temple. Acts records two instances of the Apostle Paul and others taking Nazarite vows (Acts 18:18, 21:23).

Essenes

Though Essenes are not mentioned in the New Testament, some believe that John the Baptist may have been an Essene before beginning his prophetic ministry. They are known from archaeological research (primarily from the Dead Sea Scrolls found at Qumran between 1947 and 1956) as a strict, almost monastic, sect of Jewish people who separated themselves from the Roman Empire, choosing to live in seclusion in the Sinai desert.

Zealots

Zealots were politicized Jewish people who advocated insurrection against Roman power. They were considered dangerous by the mainstream Jewish people of their time because they are thought to have tried to force the whole nation to join their rebellion, creating warlike conditions coming both from within and outside their ethnic and religious community.

Samaritans

Samaria, 35 miles north of Jerusalem and between Judea and Galilee (the region around Nazareth and bordering the Lake or Sea of Galilee), was home to another sect—Samaritans—claiming Jewish roots and faith, but not accepted by the Jerusalem establishment of that time, or any other Jewish establishment, since the nation had been taken captive by the Babylonians.

John, and Jesus' Baptism

Jesus' kinsman John, the son of Elizabeth and Zacharias (a priest in the family line of Abijah), became a highly visible symbol of the religious tumult of his and Jesus' generation by becoming a reclusive preacher of repentance in the deserts of Judea. Considered by Christians the last of the prophets of the Old Testament and the forerunner of Jesus and his New Testament, John is referred to in the Gospel of Mark as the fulfillment of Isaiah's prophecy, "I send my messenger before thy face, which shall prepare thy way before thee. The voice of one crying in the wilderness, Prepare ye the way of the

Lord, make his paths straight" (Mark 1:2–3). John baptized those of his followers who wanted to purify their bodies to symbolize their repentance of spirit.

factum

At Epiphany, the early-church feast that celebrates Jesus' baptism, water is blessed or made holy because the church teaches that in entering the Jordan, God incarnate sanctified, or made holy, all the waters of the world. Parishioners take home blessed or holy water for their use throughout the following year.

Of the Gospel accounts of Jesus' baptism by John, Matthew's is the most complete (see Matthew 3:5–17), creating a picture of Jerusalem, "and all Judaea, and all the region about Jordan" coming out to the Jordan River to be baptized by John. And when Jesus comes to John for baptism and John objects, saying, "I have need to be baptized of thee, and comest thou to me?" it is only Matthew's account that includes the detail, "And Jesus answering said unto him, Suffer it to be so now: for thus it becometh us to fulfil all righteousness."

The baptism of Jesus is the New Testament's most specific interplay of all three persons of the Trinity in one place and time. Jesus, the Son, is approved by the voice of the Father from heaven, and the Holy Spirit appears in the form of a dove above him.

Chapter 3

The Sermon on the Mount

After John baptized him, and the Father and the Holy Spirit proclaimed him, Jesus went into the surrounding wilderness to inaugurate his ministry by spending forty days and nights in prayer and fasting, and resisting the temptations of Satan. Following the baptism, John's Gospel segues directly to the calling of Jesus' first two disciples, and his ministry of healing and teaching the multitudes.

The Kingdom-of-God Lifestyle

By going into the wilderness to prepare for his public ministry, Jesus was following the example of the prophets and holy men and women of all the generations preceding him. This is probably why it is here, after Jesus had become an adult and been baptized in the presence of many witnesses, that Luke's Gospel veers off the narrative track to retrace his genealogy back to Adam, whom Luke calls "the Son of God," which Luke takes as foreshadowing the "second Adam" role Jesus had come to carry out. Matthew, Mark, and Luke all put Jesus' retreat to the wilderness immediately after his baptism, but John the Evangelist, in the fourth Gospel, tells a more personal, memoir-like account, describing events more in terms of his own impressions or what he was told, without trying to make them fit a sequential timeline.

Significance of the Wilderness

As mentioned previously, many of the prophets and other holy people performed important acts while in the wilderness. In the wilderness Moses met God in the burning bush and, atop Mount Sinai, talked with him and received The Law. Centuries earlier, Abraham had traversed the wilderness from Ur to the land of promise, and took his son, Isaac, into the wilderness to offer him up to God as a sacrifice. The nation of Israel spent forty years in the wilderness to get to the land God had promised to Abraham and his descendants forever. David the shepherd boy was tending sheep in the wilderness when he wrote the first Psalms. And it was John the Baptist—whom everyone in Jerusalem and all Judea came out to the wilderness to listen to and be baptized by—and the long line of prophets before him, that Jesus emulated in retreating to the desert before starting to preach.

Matthew and Luke have very similar versions of Jesus' retreat to the wilderness and his temptation by Satan, but Luke's version is a bit more detailed than the other Gospel accounts. Luke is the only Gospel writer who includes Jesus' reference to himself, in speaking to Satan, as "the Lord your God."

Satan uses possessions, the power to command vast lands or nations, even selected quotations from the Scriptures, to seduce, but the Word of the Lord can always best him. A widely held interpretation of this passage sees it as describing what believers go through following baptism, when they commit their lives to God. Temptation—testing—is part of the life of faith.

factum

The Apostle John, called the Beloved Apostle and the Evangelist, is not to be confused with John the Baptist. According to tradition the youngest of Jesus' twelve disciples, the Apostle John's is considered the last Gospel written, and also the most doctrinal or pedagogical of the four. He is thought to have been a leader of the church to the end of the first century.

Return to Galilee

After ending his fast and wilderness retreat, Jesus returned to Galilee (from the Judean desert near the Jordan River across from Jerusalem) to begin preaching and call his disciples. Galilee, more multicultural and less set in its doctrines than Judea, but home to numerous converts, was more likely ready to receive Jesus' message.

By now, many had heard that John the Baptist had been arrested by Herod, so the people may have been eager to hear a message like the one the baptizer was famous for. Also, since Jesus had been known in the region from his youth, it was possible that some young men there would be ready to follow him if he would only invite them. They were, and he did.

The First Called

John the Evangelist says that the first two followers of Jesus to commit to discipleship were initially followers of John the Baptist. "John, standing with some followers when Jesus walked by, said of him, 'Behold the Lamb of God!' And the two disciples heard him speak, and they followed Jesus" (John 1:35–37). One of these, John reports, was Andrew, and as the second is not named, it is believed that he was John himself, the author of the Gospel. Andrew then recruited his brother, Simon Peter, John reports, saying to Simon, "We have found the Messiah, which is, being interpreted, the Christ" (John 1: 41).

symbolism

John's calling Jesus "the Lamb of God" symbolized the Passover lamb, described in Exodus 12. God had ordered an angel to smite the firstborn of every family, man and beast, in Egypt, to force Pharaoh to release the Israelites from slavery. The angel passed over every house where his chosen people (the Jewish people) had sprinkled the blood of a Passover lamb on the doorway.

In this manner, Jesus gathered his first disciples. Luke gives additional background before the calling of the first disciples, indicating that Jesus had already begun preaching and becoming widely known in the region, first around Nazareth, and then in the north near the coast of the Sea of Galilee: "And came down to Capernaum, a city of Galilee, and taught them on the sabbath days. And they were astonished at his doctrine: for his word was with power" (Luke 4:31–32).

On the opposite end of the time spectrum from John's, the Gospel of Mark is believed by scholars to have been written first of the four evangels. Mark, though not an apostle like Matthew and John, is also believed to have been a close associate of the Apostle Peter, and some even believe his Gospel was composed under Peter's direction. Mark's is the shortest of the four Gospels, but much of its wording is repeated in one or more of the others.

Matthew provides a succinct transition from the call of the first disciples away from their profession as fishers, to fishers of men. See Matthew 4:23–25.

Jesus' actual teachings, considering the proportion of the Gospels they make up, are arguably the least known and least understood aspect of his ministry. The church in general has always said that Jesus' main teaching was that he was the Son of God, the Creator and Judge of the universe in the flesh. And, as C. S. Lewis so famously said in *Mere Christianity*, to make that claim, if it's not true, either indicates madness or a lie, and if either of those are true of him he couldn't possibly have been a "great moral teacher."

factum

Healing and miracles were marks of prophetic calling and ministry in Old Testament times, and the Gospels make it apparent that healings brought the multitudes out to see and hear Jesus. They were part of his ministry from the beginning, and they showed his power and his compassion toward the people he came to save.

The Beatitudes

Matthew's report of the Sermon on the Mount is the source of one of the most familiar teachings of Jesus, a poem that begins his sermon, known as The Beatitudes:

> *Blessed are the poor in spirit, for theirs is the kingdom of heaven.*
> *Blessed are those who mourn, for they will be comforted.*
> *Blessed are the meek, for they will inherit the earth.*
> *Blessed are those who hunger and thirst for righteousness, for they will be filled.*
> *Blessed are the merciful, for they will be shown mercy.*
> *Blessed are the pure in heart, for they will see God.*
> *Blessed are the peacemakers, for they will be called the sons of God.*
> *Blessed are those who are persecuted for righteousness' sake, for theirs is the kingdom of heaven (Matthew 5:1–10).*

The word *beatitude* is based on the Latin *beatus*, which refers to blissful happiness and, as used in religious context, implies the kind of bliss available only in being blessed or graced by God for attempting to please him. The theme of the beatitudes is humility, self-abasement, and being more other-oriented and Kingdom of God-oriented rather than self-oriented.

Hard Truths about the Kingdom of God

Jesus then says something unexpected that his hearers probably found difficult to accept, indicating that he was not there to incite revolution or the overthrow of any temporal power, but to teach and exemplify the Law of Moses (see Matthew 5:17–20). The wording suggests that Jesus' listeners may have been waiting for a new world order, a delivery from Rome's totalitarian oppression, but Jesus assures them near the beginning that he's no revolutionary or Zealot, though he advocates zeal toward the Kingdom-of-God lifestyle; in other words, fulfilling the commandments received by Moses and the prophets' teachings, for not a "jot or tittle" would be set aside.

discussion question

What is the difference between the "Kingdom Of God" and the "Kingdom Of Heaven"?
Scripture indicates that Jesus used the terms interchangeably. In Matthew 19:23 he states, "I tell you the truth, it is hard for a rich man to enter the kingdom of heaven," and in Matthew 19:24 he reiterates, "Again I tell you, it is easier for a camel to go through the eye of a needle than for a rich man to enter the kingdom of God."

In the original manuscripts, the word "jot" was "iota," one of the smallest Greek letters, and "tittle" (*keria* in Greek) was the apex of a letter. An iota was similar to our letter I, and the apexes of letters were tiny strokes. In other words, not the least appendage of the language of the law and the teachings of the prophets would be set aside or canceled out.

Jesus especially stresses that "anyone whoever shall teach men" to not keep the commandments will be regarded the lowest in the Kingdom. By citing the "righteousness" of the scribes (people who transcribed and continually studied the Torah) and Pharisees (the "strict constructionist" party of the Law of Moses), he urged his hearers to exceed the efforts to be (or appear) holy of the most conspicuous "holy classes" in the Holy City.

fallacy

The gospels teach that it was a common fallacy in the time of Jesus that the Messiah would be a political figure able to lead those waiting for him into a new secular kingdom safe from the pagan kingdoms surrounding them, and routinely taking them into various forms of captivity. Jesus' kingdom offers spiritual, not political, independence and lasting peace.

Jesus continues the sermon with warnings against holding anger or demeaning your brothers and calling them derogatory names, then emphasizes reconciliation with anyone in the community who may hold a grievance against you or against whom you hold a grievance: "if thou bring thy gift to the altar, and there rememberest that thy brother hath ought against thee; Leave there thy gift before the altar, and go thy way; first be reconciled to thy brother, and then come and offer thy gift" (Matthew 5:23, 24). This teaching referring to the altar in the Temple has generally been interpreted as being equally applicable to Christians taking Holy Communion or the Eucharist.

Obeying in Spirit

What comes next in his sermon is Jesus' interpretations of the spirit in which the commandments should be kept, and his teachings on adultery and divorce. In Matthew 5:30, Jesus states that it is better to cut off a hand that offends you rather than allow the whole body to be cast into Hell because of the sins of the hand. He continues, "It hath been said, Whosoever shall put away his wife, let him give her a writing of divorcement: But I say unto you, That whosoever shall put away his wife, saving for the cause of fornication, causeth her to commit adultery: and whosoever shall marry her that is divorced committeth adultery" (Matthew 5:31–32).

symbolism

The church has tried to apply Jesus' teachings on adultery and divorce to concrete rules or disciplines. But Jesus' teachings on these subjects can also be interpreted as metaphors or symbols of the relationship between God and his church. The church is God's bride, and when it fails to love him, it commits adultery. When it enters apostasy, as Jesus prophesies later in Matthew, it divorces him.

"Cutting off the hand and casting it away" is a metaphor for eliminating the source of temptation by excising it from one's life. And on marriage Jesus is advocating taking the extra step to make covenant relationships (marriages) work, just as earlier he emphasized that Kingdom-of-Heaven lifestyle requires going the extra mile to make peace with those who have grievances and to bear others' burdens.

Oaths Prohibited

The next section prohibits using oaths to establish your truthfulness. The church has generally interpreted this as pertaining to casual conversation, in which disciples are not to invoke God or something else holy to establish the reliability of their word, but the teaching is that it does not include formal situations in which an individual's word may not be good enough because his or her reputation is not known. "Let your yes be yes and your no, no" (Matthew 5:37) means that if you become known as a reliable and truthful person, you will not need to swear to everything. This is likely an extension, by Jesus, of the Old Testament's strict application of "you shall not take the name of the Lord your God in vain." The extension is, don't use any name in vain.

The generally accepted interpretation of the next paragraph, teaching his disciples not to use force to oppose evildoers, has been that it applies to individuals in one-to-one situations but not to civil authorities, who have social obligations to keep order (for example, a police officer cannot forgive a lawbreaker on the basis of his personal ethics, but must act on behalf of the government or the whole society). In other words, don't be a bully, and turn the other cheek rather than use violence, but keep civil order. St. Paul has more to say about this later in the New Testament.

Love Your Enemies

In Matthew 5:43–46, Jesus turns the "common-sense wisdom"—that we love our neighbors but hate our enemies—upside down: "But I say unto you, Love your enemies, bless them that curse you, do good to them that hate you, and pray for them which despitefully use you, and persecute you; That ye may be the children of your Father which is in heaven: for he maketh his sun to rise on the evil and on the good, and sendeth rain on the just and on the unjust.

"For if ye love them which love you, what reward have ye? do not even the publicans the same?" (Matthew 5:44–46). Jesus acknowledges that it is very easy to love those who are already your friends and who love you in return. Here Jesus is asking his followers to undertake the much more difficult task of loving those who they would not naturally be inclined to love, and who do not love them.

Jesus' reminder that God's rain falls on both the just and the unjust could be extended to natural disasters: his hurricanes, tsunamis, and earthquakes befall the good and the evil both, and they are not meant as judgments of anyone's merit. Jesus then wraps up the first portion of his sermon with the simple, easier-said-than-done rule: "be perfect even as your Father in heaven is perfect" (Matthew 5:48).

Prayer for the Glory of God

The next section of the sermon teaches that alms must be given secretly, not openly for recognition; prayer is to be between you and God, not out in public for the notice of others; and "when you pray, do not use vain repetitions, as the heathen do, for they think that they shall be heard for their much speaking. Do not be like them, for your Father knows what you need before you ask him," (Matthew 6:7, 8). In other words, be confident that God hears prayer. And though he later teaches that persistence in prayer is a good thing, he is here condemning insincere, vain repetition (or babble) for its own sake. Then Jesus goes on to give the multitude his famous exemplary prayer, known as the Lord's Prayer or the "Our Father."

Forgiving others their debts or trespasses as God forgives ours is an extension of many of the previously stated precepts Jesus is preaching. In this context he interprets it by illustrating his own meaning: reach out and love someone who, by your standards, is unlovable, and you'll begin approaching the Kingdom-of-God lifestyle. "Lead us not into temptation" refers to the kinds of temptation he had just recently withstood from Satan; that part of the prayer could be rephrased as "Father, don't test us beyond our spiritual strength to withstand." And the three-fold conclusion of the prayer is a reminder that the glory is not to be ours, but to be reflected back to God and that all is to be undertaken, and prayed for, for his sake, not our own.

After Jesus recites the Lord's Prayer he returns to the earlier theme: don't do your spiritual obligations for show, but for the Father only, applying the point this time to fasting. Then follows one of the most famous passages in the sermon: "Lay up your treasure in heaven, where neither moth nor rust corrupt and where thieves do not break in to steal. For where your treasure is, there will your heart be also," (Matthew 6: 20–21).

factum

It's a recurring theme of Jesus' teaching that doing things for show or to impress others is hypocrisy, and that this is a sure shortcut to failure in the spiritual life. "Judge not" is a key to overcoming superior attitudes that lead to a great fall.

Exhortations to Holiness

The conclusion of the sermon comes in Matthew 7, the highlights of which include do not judge, that you not be judged, and with what standards you use to judge shall be used by God when he judges you. Jesus tells his listeners, don't try to pull a "mote," or tiny splinter, out of another person's eye before first removing the "beam" or post from your own eye. In other words, don't be a hypocrite.

Jesus tells his listeners not to give holy things to dogs or cast pearls to swine. Then he says, "Ask, and it shall be given you; seek, and ye shall find; knock, and it shall be opened unto you: For every one that asketh receiveth; and he that seeketh findeth; and to him that knocketh it shall be opened. Or what man is there of you, whom if his son ask bread, will he give him a stone? Or if he ask a fish, will he give him a serpent?" (Matthew 7:7–10). Here he is reiterating the Old Testament teaching that anyone who truly seeks the Lord will surely find him, for God wants to give his best to his children.

He also compares good trees and their good fruits with corrupt trees that produce evil fruit; "wherefore by their fruits ye shall know them" (7:20). Jesus ends the sermon with the parable of the man who built his house on a rock and it withstood the ravages of life's storms, and the man who built his house on the sand and it was quickly demolished by the wind. He ends by saying that those who hear his sayings and act accordingly are like the wise man, and those who hear but fail to act accordingly are the foolish ones.

Jesus' Authority and the New Covenant

Matthew writes that when Jesus had ended these sayings, the people were astonished at his teaching, for he taught them as one having authority, and not as the scribes. All of the true prophets, including John the Baptist, also taught as though they were speaking the very words of God, because telling the truth with boldness was the mark and the sign of a prophet.

discussion question

What was meant by "taught as one having authority"?
One commentator says the scribes taught by invoking various theories and experts, but refusing to take a position themselves, whereas his followers saw Jesus as speaking as though he was, himself, authoritative about the Kingdom of Heaven and the requirements to fulfill the law and the teachings of the prophets.

Though it has only been partially revealed thus far, the point of Jesus' authoritative speaking is that he was there to impart, and even to personify, a whole new covenant between God and his people. From Law to Grace is the general theme of the New Testament and the life of Jesus Christ. By setting out the necessity of fulfilling the Old Covenant (the Law) in the Sermon on the Mount, Jesus is setting the stage for disclosing the new grounds on which his believers will meet God.

Chapter 4

Jesus the Miracle Worker

The matter-of-fact way in which the Gospels treat the healing aspects of Jesus' ministry suggests that Jesus' listeners expected healing power from someone who offered a prophetic ministry and who could be the Messiah. The church teaches traditionally that holiness and godly authority are bound up with power over physical infirmities. In other words, spiritual perfection overrides natural limitations. In a time when medicines were primitive, what is now generally called faith healing was a major treatment for all ailments.

A Leper Cleansed

The first healing specifically described in Matthew's Gospel is the cleansing of a leper who worshipped Jesus and said that if Jesus chose to do so, he could make him clean. "Uncleanness" was the Law's way of describing those with leprosy. Jesus replied, "I will be thou clean" while touching him (something prohibited in the Law of Moses, Leviticus 7:21). And immediately the man was "cleansed" of the leprous spots over his body. Thus Jesus demonstrates—immediately after sermonizing that the smallest letter of the Law of Moses should not be abrogated but must be fulfilled—that he is the Lord of the Law, not its slave.

factum

Though it is widely believed that the healings were done mainly to demonstrate his messianic claims and to verify his teaching, Jesus performed many healings upon his arrival in Galilee, before choosing his first disciples and giving his most important teaching sermon.

Though Jesus had access to all power, the power he is demonstrating here is similar to powers earlier prophets also used. His attitude here in the early days of his ministry is "come and see." And as the passage says, large crowds chose to go along, wanting to see more wonders and hear more encouraging words. Anyone who advocated the Golden Rule, as Jesus did, could not avoid the imperative to use any power he had to help those humbly asking for help. Compassion and mercy were the keystones of his ministry, not optional virtues.

Paralysis Reversed

The second healing Jesus accomplished was the reversal of paralysis that, in the King James translation, is called palsy. As Jesus entered the city of Capernaum, a centurion (an officer in the Roman legion) approached him and told him his servant lay sick at home with paralysis. When Jesus offered to go to the officer's home to heal the afflicted man, "the centurion answered and said, Lord, I am not worthy that thou shouldest come under my roof: but speak the word only, and my servant shall be healed." To this, the gospel says, Jesus, "marvelled, and said to them that followed, Verily I say unto you, I have not found so great faith, no, not in Israel." Read the whole account in Matthew 8:5–13.

discussion question

What do the churches make of Jesus' unqualified acceptance of the centurion?
The preponderance of church teaching has interpreted Jesus' not questioning or judging the centurion's military occupation, as part of the oppressing Roman army, as evidence that Jesus was not advocating pacifism. The personal and interpersonal peace he advocated and offered was qualitatively different from peace among factions and nation-states.

The centurion, a Roman military officer who commanded over a hundred men, was a gentile, the first since the Wise Men to recognize Jesus for who he was. Galilee is said to have been home to many such non-Jewish seekers after God, but Jesus is prophesying when he says this gentile is prefiguring multitudes of others who will eventually follow him, while most of the Jewish multitudes ("children of the kingdom") will turn aside. His saying that "I have not found so great faith in Israel" refers to the centurion's humility by opening with "I am not worthy."

A Second Paralytic Healed
A second account of a paralytic being healed also takes place in Capernaum, the city that Jesus chose as his headquarters while

ministering in Galilee (see Matthew 9:1–8). This time, it was the crowd that marveled at Jesus' words, because instead of telling the man to rise and walk, he said, "your sins are forgiven." And scribes (scholars in the Old Testament teachings) who were there murmured that he had blasphemed by presuming to forgive sins, which power belongs to God only.

symbolism

As mentioned previously, healings in prophetic ministries like Jesus' were symbolic of godliness on the part of the healer. To accusers who said Jesus healed through satanic powers or black arts, he retorted that Satan cannot cast out Satan; the tree is known by its fruits. He used healings of human afflictions to demonstrate his power to heal the sickness we all suffer unto death, sin.

In the accounts in Mark's and Luke's Gospels, this event is even more dramatic; it's added that because of the crowds, the paralytic's friends lowered him down through an opening they made in the roof of the house to get to Jesus. The presence of scribes on the scene of his healings suggests that Jesus' fame had become so significant that the scribes felt they had to check up on him by lurking around the fringes to get whatever goods they could get on him.

Sins Forgiven

Knowing what the public's reaction would be, Jesus reveals that he used the phrase, "your sins are forgiven" intentionally to get his mission noticed, to inaugurate the kind of controversy that was bound to follow, and to get people wondering, what manner of man, prophet, or messiah is this? And Jesus lets the people know that he can read the thoughts of their hearts even though they had not uttered them.

Infirmities Alleviated

Healings of varied infirmities are next described, beginning with the healing of Simon Peter's mother-in-law of fever, described in Matthew 8:14–15. The Bible records thirty-eight specific healings and miracles, as well as numerous healings mentioned only in general terms (for example, Matthew 4:24).

Healings and Miracles in the Gospels

Event	Matthew	Mark	Luke	John
Leper cleansed	8:1–4	1:40–45	5:12–19	
Centurion's servant cured	8:5–13		7:1–10	4:46–54
Peter's mother-in-law cured of fever	8:14–15	1:29–31	4:38–39	
Storm on lake of Galilee calmed	8:23–27	4:35–41	8:22–25	
Demons cast out into herd of swine	8:29–34	5:11–17	8:26–39	
Paralytic cured in Capernaum	9:2–8	2:1–12	5:18–26	
Resurrection of Jairus' daughter	9:18–26	5:22–43	8:40–56	
Woman with a hemorrhage cured	9:20–22	5:24–34	8:43–48	
Two blind men cured	9:27–31			
Mute demoniac healed	9:32–34			
Water turned into wine				2:1–11
Catch of fish multiplied		5:1–11	21:1–14	
Demoniac cured		1:23–28	4:33–37	
Sick man at Bethesda cured				5:2–15
Man's withered hand restored	12:10–13	3:1–5	6:6–10	
Resurrection of the son of widow of Nain			7:11–16	
Blind and dumb demoniac cured	12:22–23			

Event	Matthew	Mark	Luke	John
Feeding of the five thousand	14:13–21	6:34–44	9:11–17	6:2–14
Walking on water	14:22–33	6:47–51		6:16–21
Gentile's daughter exorcised of demons	15:22–28	7:24–30		
Deaf-mute healed		7:32–37		
Feeding of the four thousand	15:32–38	8:1–9		
Blind man healed at Bethsaida		8:22–26		
The transfiguration	17:1–8	9:1–8	9:28–36	
Demon-possessed boy exorcized	17:14–21	9:17–29	9:37–42	
Shekel taken from a fish's mouth to pay tax	17:24–27			
Blind man healed		10:46–52	18:35–43	9:1–38
Many crippled, blind, and mute healed	15:30–31		7:21–22	
Woman healed on the Sabbath			13:10–17	
Resurrection of Lazarus				11:1–44
Man with dropsy healed on the Sabbath			14:1–6	
Ten lepers cleansed			17:11–19	
Two blind men healed at Jericho	20:29–34	10:46–52	18:35–43	
Fig tree cursed to not bear fruit	21:18–22	11:12–14		
Ear of High Priest's servant restored	*	*	22:49–51	*
Resurrection	28:1–10	16:1–8	24:1–12	20:1–18
Ascension		16:19–20	24:50–53	

*All four Gospels record the ear's being severed; only Luke reports it being restored.

In the healing of the leper, Jesus used touch; in the healing of the centurion's paralytic servant, he used only his word. Jesus uses touch again to heal Peter's mother-in-law. Later, a woman is healed by simply touching the hem of his robe as he passes. In each case, the faith of the ones healed is the key.

Mastery over the Weather

One of the most dramatic accounts of a miraculous event in Jesus' early ministry is the calming of a storm on the lake where his first disciples were fishing. The disciples were frightened of the storm and begged Jesus to save them (see Matthew 8:23–27).

factum

Geographers say that the Lake of Galilee is highly susceptible to sudden strong storms, as the mountainous terrain around it causes extreme changes in high and low barometric pressure. These changes produce winds that blow down onto the lake, making it treacherous to anyone in a small craft of the type used by fishermen of the time.

Some interpreters have proposed that not only did Jesus subdue the storm; he also may have summoned it in the first place to give the disciples an unforgettable teachable moment. Though this account is presented in the Gospels as a real event, it has parable-like aspects that many have cited: when believers or the church are "tempest tossed," Jesus is only a prayer away.

Feeding the Five Thousand

The feeding of the 5,000 is the only miracle Jesus performed before his followers that is recorded in all four Gospels (see John's account in John 6:2–13).

The disciple Andrew seems to have become familiar enough with Jesus' modus operandi to be hoping against hope that the five barley loaves and two small fishes might be used to feed the multitude. Some interpreters say the 5,000 "men" does not include a large population of women and children who would have also been fed. And one commentator has been quoted as saying the miracle wasn't all it has been thought to be; perhaps they were just five very large loaves and two big fishes.

Walking on Water

Jesus walking on water is reported by the Gospels of Matthew, Mark, and John, but Matthew is the only one who tells of Peter's joining him on the lake's surface (see Matthew 14:22–33). It seems apparent that Jesus wanted to test and to strengthen his disciples' faith when, as Matthew records, he sent them across the lake before him. Peter's faith has long and often been characterized as the most impetuous of all the disciples, which is demonstrated here, but it could also be called the most robust, as he was willing to test his own limits. And Jesus' invitation to him to join him on the water can be seen as symbolizing his desire that his disciples become more like him by being willing to try previously impossible feats, through growing faith.

Feeding of the Four Thousand

Matthew's and Mark's Gospels both record this second mass feeding miracle just a few paragraphs after describing the feeding of the 5,000 (see Mark 8:1–10). This miracle was performed on the other side of the lake from the first, where most of the residents were gentiles. And Matthew specifies in his account that this time there were 4,000 men, plus women and children. The large crowds who were attracted to Jesus and experienced his miracles no doubt made up the core of early members of the church, which spread quickly after Pentecost, as will be discussed in Chapter 9.

Exorcising Demons

Jesus and his disciples again crossed the Lake of Galilee for Jesus' next demonstration of power, this time over demonic spirits. Matthew 8:28–34 tells the story of their visit to the Gergesenes on the eastern shore of the Lake of Galilee. There, Jesus and his companions met two men possessed by "fierce devils" who lived in a cave. Jesus cast out the demons, who asked permission to go into a herd of swine that was feeding nearby. Jesus granted their request, but the swine leapt off a cliff into the lake, and drowned. The people in the city who came out to meet him were more angry than impressed. It was the economic effect of losing the swine, not the personal salvation or the healing of mental disease or demon possession, that mattered most to the Gergesenes, and their feelings led them to reject Jesus and his miraculous works. Swine were unclean to Jewish people, but keeping the animals was without doubt a livelihood to their gentile keepers. What effect the death of the swine had on the demons isn't specified, but it seems apparent that they were no longer able to work in that locale.

Power of God, or Power of Satan?

Matthew 12:22–29 gives another account of Jesus casting out a demon, this time from a blind and mute man. The people witnessing the miracle were amazed, but Matthew says that when "the Pharisees" heard of it, they accused Jesus of casting out demons by the power of "Beelzebub the prince of the devils." Jesus replies with the logical syllogism that a house divided against itself cannot stand, so how could the prince of devils be interested in casting out devils?

Luke relates that after appointing the twelve disciples (which is discussed in more detail in Chapter 5), Jesus had appointed a second level of disciples, "the seventy," whom he commissioned to go out and preach, heal, and cast out demons in his name (see Luke 10:17–22). When they return rejoicing in their power over demons, Jesus tells them that he witnessed Satan being cast out of heaven "like lightning," and that it would be better for them to rejoice that they are accounted worthy of the kingdom of heaven rather than in their power over evil spirits, and that they can withstand scorpion stings and venomous snakebites without harm. Literal-minded snake handlers have interpreted the previous passage as suggesting that the faithful should take up venomous snakes to prove they have received the power of the Holy Spirit. But such demonstrations seem counter to the spirit in which Jesus performed his miracles, and also seem to contradict the statement "rejoice not in your power but in having your names being written down in heaven."

discussion question

What is the unforgivable sin?

Jesus gave a solemn warning in Matthew 12: "blasphemy against the Holy Spirit shall not be forgiven" In the story of Jesus casting out a demon from a blind and mute man, the "offense against the Holy Spirit" is attributing the Spirit's works to Satan, which Jesus is saying is what these Pharisees have done.

Miracles vs. Stunts

Jesus' works of power or miracles are not publicity stunts, as shown by his frequent injunctions that the recipients of healing not broadcast that he has healed them. Moreover, any attempt to demonstrate God's power would seem to prove more vanity and pride on the claimant's part, rather than holiness and power. Though later disciples and holy followers of Christ are able to survive venomous snakebites (as in Acts 28:3–7), the metaphor here is that despite the tremendous power of Satan and his minions, Jesus' followers have greater power to overcome them.

Water into Wine

The Apostle John describes Jesus' turning water into wine in the wedding in Cana as the beginning of his miracles (see John 2:1–11).

When the host of the wedding ran out of wine, Jesus' mother, Mary, told him of their plight. He objected, "Woman, what have I to do with thee? mine hour is not yet come," but undeterred, she told the servants to do whatever he said, and Jesus told them to fill six stone water pots, holding two or three firkins each, with water. That done, he then directed them to take some of the contents of the water pots to the governor of the feast, who, in turn, sent some to the bridegroom. Usually, everyone sets out the best wine in the beginning, with the poorer quality beverage saved for later, he declared, but this time the best has been kept for last; the water had turned into wine of the best quality.

factum

A firkin is said to be nine gallons, and there are four firkins to a barrel. Though hard evidence is no longer available for the location of Cana in New Testament times, tradition identifies it as located in the same site as the modern-day Israeli village Kefr' Kenna, approximately four to five miles from Nazareth.

Many have observed that God is always turning water, in the form of rainfall and irrigation, into wine by nature's turning the juice of grapes into wine. But the creator of the grape can bypass a few steps to make it happen more expeditiously when necessary.

Some take Jesus' words in response to Mary's request as suggesting a distancing between himself and his mother. But considering that he fulfilled her request exactly as she made it, by providing wine for the wedding, the whole miracle can be seen as a reward of Mary's faith. In that, she becomes the first of the believers in Jesus to bring about a miraculous event through her requests. And by seeing how Mary's faith was rewarded, the other disciples realized they could call forth similar power over nature, and by doing so confirm their faith.

Resurrections

Resurrections from the dead are rare in the Bible, even in the ministry of Jesus, who is described as restoring life to three whose loved ones sought his intervention. Though he became incarnate in order to be the resurrection and the life (John 11:25) it is apparent that even his earthly adoptive father Joseph had passed away and was not restored to life before Jesus launched his ministry. And the three who returned under his ministration from the other side of the veil between life and death still faced the penalty of sin.

The First Resurrection

The first resurrection performed by Jesus is recounted in all three of the synoptic Gospels, Matthew, Mark, and Luke. Matthew 9:18–27 records the event. A certain ruler (identified by both Mark and Luke as Jairus, a ruler of the synagogue) told Jesus that his daughter was already dead, but that if he were to lay his hand on her she would revive. Jesus and his disciples joined the man on the way to his home. On the way, "a woman diseased with an issue of blood twelve years" touched the hem of Jesus' robe, believing that act would heal her. Sensing the power go out of him, Jesus turned to her and said "Daughter, be of good comfort; thy faith hath made thee whole."

On arriving at the ruler's house, minstrels were already playing mourning music, but Jesus said the maid was only sleeping, which elicited macabre laughter from the mourners. But Jesus "went in, took her by the hand, and the maid arose." On his way out of the neighborhood, Jesus was importuned by two blind men seeking healing.

Second Resurrection

The second resurrection is recounted only in Luke 7:11–17. As Jesus and his disciples approached the gate of Nain, a town in Galilee south of Nazareth, they met a funeral party carrying a dead man on a bier, his widowed mother mourning with many townspeople. Jesus "had compassion on her, and said unto her, Weep not. And he came and touched the bier: and they that bare him stood still. And he said, Young man, I say unto thee, Arise. And he that was dead sat up, and began to speak. And he delivered him to his mother." This miracle so impressed the witnesses that its word spread as far as Judea, the region around Jerusalem, beyond Samaria from Galilee and Nain.

Resurrection of Lazarus

The final resurrection miracle performed by Jesus was the raising of his friend Lazarus, which immediately preceded Jesus' passion week, which will be taken up in Chapter 8.

These "temporary" resurrections all pale beside the resurrection of Jesus himself, in which he returned from the grave in a totally renewed, "spiritual body," which was permanent and indestructible (see 1 Corinthians 15). These resurrections demonstrate the power of the Creator and the Lord of Life but those who witnessed these miraculous events had seen little compared to the resurrection to come.

Blindness Cured

Several incidences of blindness being cured are recounted in the Gospels. The most illuminating one is given in the Gospel of John, Chapter 9. The whole chapter tells the story of a man who had been born blind but was restored to sight by Jesus, who made clay of dust and spittle, put it on the man's eyes, and directed him to wash his eyes in the pool of Siloam, which he did, receiving his sight.

The account of this miracle affirms several significant bits of good news (the meaning of "Gospel"). First, the Jewish teaching affirmed by Jesus, by the blind man who regained his sight, and even by the Pharisees trying to prove Jesus was healing through satanic power, was an established tradition: that a measure of spiritual purification was a prerequisite of wonder-working power. Second, those who think themselves able to see are blind (deluded), and those who consider themselves lacking insight ("poor in spirit") are given sight. Those who have their own light have no need from the Light of the World that Jesus came to bring and to be.

discussion question

How does Jesus' healing relate to Moses?
Though the Pharisees who opposed Jesus professed to be followers of Moses, not "this fellow," all of the healings of Jesus are typified in the ministry of Moses in the wilderness journey from Egypt to the Promised Land, where God called himself "Yahweh, Rapha," the Lord your healer.

Through Moses, God promised, conditionally, not to bring sicknesses on the Israelites. "If you will diligently listen to the voice of the LORD your God and will do what is right in his sight, and will hear to his commandments and keep all his statutes, I will put none of these diseases upon you that I have brought upon the Egyptians: for I am the LORD who heals you" (Exodus 15:26).

Chapter 5

Choosing the Twelve

After Jesus recruited as disciples John, the son of Zebedee, and Andrew, (with help from John the Baptist, whose disciples they had first been), Andrew recruited his bother Simon Peter, and John's brother James was quickly added. To this initial core of four disciples, eight more were added to become the Twelve, ordained as the inner circle, the ones to whom Jesus would entrust the full disclosure of the Gospel of the Kingdom and, later on, the establishment of his church.

Fishermen Made Fishers of Men

Matthew 4:18–22 recounts the famous story of Jesus choosing his disciples: Jesus saw the brothers Simon Peter and Andrew, and said, "Follow me, and I will make you fishers of men." Next he called brothers James and John, the sons of Zebedee, likewise. They all answered the call without hesitating. Mark's account is virtually the same, but it is preceded with a reference to Jesus being spurred by the arrest of John the Baptist to declare the time right for the introduction of the Gospel of the Kingdom.

Difference in Perspective

The difference between Matthew's and Mark's accounts, and that of John's Gospel (as given in Chapter 3, which begins with John's and Andrew's call from the very side of John the Baptist), reflects a difference in perspective between John and Peter. John was there, on the scene and, most likely being the youngest of the fishermen, was probably more strongly impressed by all the new events and the incredible charisma of John the Baptist and Jesus. Peter, many believe, told his story the way he remembered it in Mark's presence, and Matthew may have got his outline of details from Mark's account.

factum

In *Fox's Book of Martyrs* (1563), John Fox refers to James and John, the sons of Zebedee, as relatives of Jesus "for [their] mother Salome was cousin-german to the Virgin Mary." Cousin-german is an old English term for first or full cousin, a child of your uncle or aunt.

Neither Matthew nor Mark was on the scene when Jesus called the fishermen. This is not to say it didn't happen; only that it happened a little later than when Simon Peter and Andrew were first tapped to be followers of Jesus. The first "call" may have been understood by brothers Andrew and Simon Peter as a one-time short enlistment, maybe for one evening event, but when Jesus came to their boat to call them again, it finally sank in that he was calling them to a permanent change of life. They would still continue fishing for a livelihood, as other events already discussed (like Jesus walking on the water to join them on their fishing vessel) confirm, but that kind of fishing would be—from this call onward—their secondary vocation. Both sets of brothers (Simon Peter and Andrew; James and John) now had a higher calling.

The Third Calling and the Other Eight

The synoptic Gospels Matthew, Mark, and Luke all have similar versions of the selection of the Twelve to the higher calling of apostles. The four first called to be followers are still listed as the first four disciples, but it's clear that the additional eight now being ordained for special ministry were considered from a larger pool of followers, most of whom may have followed Jesus during his ministry and even on into the beginning of the church. It's instructive that with all his power and knowledge, Jesus still spent a whole night in prayer—what later monastics call a vigil—seeking the Father's direction on the choosing of the Twelve. This choosing of the Twelve for apostleship is the basis for the ordination processes followed by most Christian communions and denominations today.

discussion question

What have the modern churches learned from Jesus' discipleship process?
Many ministries have discipleship programs concentrating on cementing loyalty to the ministry by having senior and junior ministers spend great amounts of time in one-to-one interaction. Some of the world's largest congregations are built on a cell model, in which tiny groups are instructed by intensive fellowship and training.

The word *apostle*, from the Greek *apostello*, means "sent" or "sent out." At this point, the Twelve are not yet ready to be sent out, but they have now been put on what today's generation might call a fast track leading to the mission field. Their "ministry graduate school"—theological seminary—was the most intensive 24/7 crash course the church has ever known.

Mark 3:14–15 adds that Jesus ordained twelve apostles to be with him, so that he might send them out to preach, and empower them to heal infirmities and cast out demons. Matthew 10:1 specifies that Jesus gave them power to cast out unclean spirits and to heal all kinds of disease.

Simon Peter

Called "the rock" by Jesus (Cephas or Kephas, in Aramaic) and commonly known as Peter (from Petros, the Greek equivalent of Cephas), Simon (also called Simeon) Bar-jona (son of Jona) is the first-named apostle and was the first to declare that Jesus was "the Christ, the Son of the living God." To that dramatic confession, Jesus gave a response that has been controversial for much of the church's next two millennia: "Blessed are you, Simon Bar-jona, for flesh and blood have not revealed this to you, but my Father who is in heaven. And I say also to you, you are Peter, and upon this rock I will build my church; and the gates of hell shall not prevail against it. And I will give to you the keys of the kingdom of heaven so that whatever you shall bind on earth shall be bound in heaven and whatever you shall loose on earth shall be loosed in heaven" (Matthew 16:16–19).

The Catholic and Orthodox Churches have held that, from the beginning, Jesus' choice to lead his church was Peter. But Peter received the strongest rebuke from his Master of any disciple, in response to Peter's protesting to Jesus foretelling the fate he would suffer from the leaders of the Temple. "Get behind me, Satan," Jesus tells him. "You are an offence to me, for you don't prefer the things of God but those of man" (Matthew 16:23). As with the incident of Peter's wanting to join Jesus on the surface of the lake, his impetuosity got ahead of his better judgment. But the most critical moment in Peter's time under Jesus' teaching is found in Luke 5:3–10 where, in response to Jesus performing a miracle by filling their nets with fish, Peter "fell down at Jesus' knees, saying, Depart from me; for I am a sinful man, O Lord." But Jesus replied, "Fear not; from henceforth thou shalt catch men."

factum

Catholic scholar J. Macrory suggests that Mark was Peter's interpreter in Rome in the latter days of Peter's ministry and life. Having heard all of Peter's memories many times, Mark felt compelled to write them down after Peter's death as the first written Gospel. Peter was born in Bethsaida, on the Lake of Galilee, where, it's reported, the house he lived in is still preserved beneath a church.

In this moment Peter's humbling was complete, and his redemption had been won. The lesson could not have been more transparent. Compared with fishing for men, fishing Lake Galilee is no big thing.

discussion question

What is "the Petrine office"?
The Roman papacy is also known as "the Petrine office," or the office of Peter as first Bishop of Rome. According to Catholic theologians, the Roman Papacy has authority over all other church leaders. The Orthodox churches agree that Peter was bishop of Rome and, as Rome was the center of the empire, that office was first to receive honor, but it does not have ruling authority over other leaders of the church.

John

The younger son of Zebedee and Salome (called Mary Salome by some Bible scholars) and the brother of James the Greater calls himself the disciple "Jesus loved" (John 13:23) and is generally called "the beloved disciple." As previously mentioned, he is also called John the Evangelist because he is the writer of the fourth Gospel ("Evangelium" in Latin), and he also is believed to be the author of three short New Testament epistles (1–3 John) and the Apocalypse, or Book of Revelation.

Luke's account of the raising of Jairus' daughter from the dead says John was one of the three members of Jesus' inner circle: "he did not allow any man to go with him, except Peter, James, and John." At several other key moments in Jesus' ministry (as will be shown) these were the only disciples invited as witnesses.

The New Testament records James as the first apostle to die (martyred by King Herod Agrippa I in A.D. 44, Acts 12:2). The Catholic and Orthodox tradition, also affirmed by the Protestant author John Fox in his *Book of Martyrs*, indicates that his brother John was the last of the Twelve to die, having ministered, by one account, for sixty-eight years after the Passion of Jesus. A Roman Catholic source puts his death in about A.D. 100, and a Greek Orthodox one puts it at A.D. 104.

Andrew and James

Simon Peter's brother, Andrew Bar-jona, was first a disciple of John the Baptist, who was with John the Beloved when John the Baptist said of Jesus, "behold the Lamb of God." With John the Beloved, Andrew immediately began following Jesus. He rushed to tell Simon that they had found the Messiah, and later it was he who told Jesus that a boy in the crowd of 5,000 had five barley loaves and two small fishes. Andrew, thought to be a common name at the time, is Andreia, in Greek, meaning manly boldness or valor.

James the Greater, son of Zebedee and Salome and brother of John the Beloved, was a fisherman on the Lake of Galilee on his father's ship. He is said to have been dubbed "the Greater" to distinguish him from the other James among the Twelve, called "James the Less," possibly because the latter was of shorter height. Jesus referred to both of the sons of Zebedee as Boanerges, "sons of thunder" (Mark 3:17). James is *Yakob* in Hebrew and *Iakobos* in New Testament Greek.

symbolism

Baptism symbolizes washing, bathing, and new life. The Apostle Paul calls it being buried with Jesus and being raised in newness of life (Romans 6:4). Churches and theologians disagree about baptism's power to affect new life (baptismal regeneration). But all say it symbolizes desire to receive new life and identify with Christ and that, unaccompanied by sincere faith, it effects nothing.

The fact that James' mother, Salome, is believed to have been the cousin of the Virgin Mary may be pertinent to James and John being included in Jesus' inner circle, and also connected to a plea and Mark's Gospels, to "Grant that these my two sons may sit, the one on thy right hand, and the other on the left, in thy kingdom."

Jesus asked if the Apostles were prepared to drink from his cup and partake in his baptism, which they agreed they were. Then he replied that the decision was not his, but his Father's, to make. Drinking from his cup and participating in Jesus' baptism, the Apostles shared in the suffering and death he would be required to endure.

Philip and Nathanael Bartholomew

Apostle Philip is listed fifth in the three lists of Apostles in the synoptic Gospels. Like John and Andrew he was also an earlier follower of John the Baptist. After Jesus asked Philip to follow him, Philip recruited Nathanael (John 1:43–51). A Jewish man from Galilee, Philip's Greek name is taken by some to have been given in honor of Philip the Tetrarch, who had been credited with making positive reforms in Philip's family's area under his administration.

Nathanael is thought by many to be another name for Bartholomew, his full name being Nathanael Bar-tholomew, meaning Son of Tolmai. John's Gospel identifies Nathanael as a friend of Philip, but all three of the other lists of disciples pair Philip and Bartholomew, omitting the name Nathanael. Bartholomew is likely his more formal name.

John also attributes a widely quoted line from the New Testament as coming from Nathanael, a reply to Philip's telling him that they have found the prophesied Messiah, Jesus of Nazareth: "Can there any good thing come out of Nazareth?" But after meeting Jesus and hearing him call Nathanael "an Israelite indeed, in whom is no guile!" because Jesus had earlier noticed him under a fig tree (possibly praying), Nathanael was so impressed that he exclaimed, "Rabbi, thou art the Son of God; thou art the King of Israel."

Thomas

Although there is a persistent history of claims that Thomas was the apostle to India, and there is a Mar Thoma Church (St. Thomas Church) there that claims him as its founder, very little hard historical evidence is available about Thomas beyond his mention in the lists of apostles in the synoptic Gospels, four anecdotes in John's Gospel in which he plays key parts, and the "doubting Thomas" sequence in John 20, which will be taken up in Chapter 9.

John's Gospel gives its first brief look at Thomas in Chapter 11, where Thomas responds to Jesus' sorrow about the death of Lazarus: "Then Thomas, who is called Didymus, said to his fellow disciples, 'Let us also go, that we may die with him.'" Though less specific than Peter's and Nathanael's confessions ("truly you are the Son of God"), this displays deep faith in Thomas, who puts his fate entirely in the Master's hands.

John's next glimpse of Thomas comes in another well-known passage on Jesus' divinity and his way of salvation, chapter 14:1–7.

Jesus describes his intention of creating "many mansions" in his Father's house for his disciples, and says they know where he goes and how. But Thomas interrupts to say, "Lord, we know not whither thou goest; and how can we know the way?" To which Jesus replies that he is the way, the truth and the life; no man comes to the Father except by him. This is probably the most specific declaration in the Bible by Jesus of being the exclusive way of eternal salvation.

fallacy

There is much Gnostic apocryphal literature bearing Thomas' name (including *The Infancy Gospel of Thomas*), and some of it purports to be his biography. However, the claim in one of these accounts that he was the twin brother of Jesus himself indicates that the Apostle Thomas is most likely not the author of these documents.

Matthew, Also Known as Levi

Matthew, also known as Levi, despite being author of the Gospel bearing his name, is mentioned only four times in the New Testament, excluding the lists of the apostles. His call to discipleship, however, is described in more personal terms than that of the others in the latter half of the lists. In his own Gospel, that event is described in these words: "And as he went out, he saw a man named Matthew sitting at the receipt of custom, and he said to him, 'Follow me.' And he arose, and followed him" (Matthew 9:9).

Matthew seems to be too humble to mention his own parts played among the followers of Jesus, because while his Gospel alludes to their going into a house for a dinner, it is only in Luke's Gospel that we are told that Matthew (Levi) made a great feast "at his own house" for Jesus and his disciples, with many other publicans being invited to join in (Luke 5:29). And the reaction among the scribes and Pharisees to this event turned it into a signifi-cant teachable moment in Jesus' ministry. They accuse him, to put it in modern parlance, of partying with his disciples too much for a holy man of God. To which Jesus replied, "Can ye make the chil-dren of the bridechamber fast, while the bridegroom is with them? But the days will come, when the bridegroom shall be taken away from them, and then shall they fast in those days." Here Jesus is pre-viewing the understanding of the church as bride of Christ, which he will make clearer toward the end of his time with his disciples. His eating and drinking with people considered vulgar and unholy by the pillars of religious society is consistent with his being born among farm animals and being worshipped by shepherds rather than introduced with fanfare and splendor in the Temple.

factum

Matthew was labeled a publican (public tax collector), and for that the Pharisees, who held all publicans in contempt, despised him. This may be why Jesus recruited him, to show that none is beyond the reach of the Father's grace, and that man's superficial stan-dards for judging are not God's standards.

James the Less, Thaddeus, and Simon of Canaan

As previously mentioned, James, the son of Alphaeus, as Matthew and Luke identify him (Matthew 10:3, Luke 6:15, and Acts 1:13) is better known as James the Less to distinguish him from James, the son of Zebedee, or James the Greater. The Less, or Minor, can mean in Latin either smaller of stature or younger. Though there are many opinions about the various Jameses in the New Testament, the con-sensus seems to be that there were four principal ones: James, the brother of the Lord (described earlier as the son of Joseph by a previous marriage), who was the first bishop of Jerusalem and the author of the Epistle of James; the two apostles named James (Greater and Less); and James, the son of Cleopas and another Mary (Mark 15:40, Luke 24:10). Some Roman Catholic writers conflate James, the brother of the Lord, with James, the son of Cleopas.

Thaddeus

The Apostle Thaddeus is also known as Jude, Judas the brother of James, and "not Iscariot" (Luke 6:16 and John 14:22), and Lebbaeus (Matthew 10:3, which calls him "Lebbaeus, whose surname was Thaddeus." Mark 3:18 refers to him simply as Thaddeus). His speaking is recorded only once in the New Testament when, in John 14:23, he asks Jesus, "Lord, how is it that you will manifest yourself to us and not to the world?"

Simon of Canaan

Also called Simon Zelotes, Simon the Zealous or Simon the Zealot, Simon of Canaan is believed by some to have been the bridegroom at the wedding in Cana where Jesus turned water into wine. Though some believe he was a member of the party known as the Zealots who advocated violent overthrow of the Roman oppressors in Israel, a Roman Catholic source says the better reading of Zelotes is "Zealous," as in zealous for the faith and Jewish teachings.

symbolism

The Roman Catholic Church assigns symbols to each apostle. Those associated with Simon the Zealous are a saw (by which tradition says he was martyred by being cut in two) and a book. A scroll and a key represent Simon Peter. Peter's brother Andrew is represented by a decussate cross, the type on which he was crucified.

As Jesus early dispelled any hopes some may have had that he would lead a revolution, it is likely that if Simon was ever a member of the Zealots, he was converted into a zealous apostle of his newfound Lord. An apocryphal *Acts of Simon and Judas* (Thaddeus) maintains that after the establishment of the church Simon and Thaddeus preached the Gospel in Persia.

Judas Iscariot

The only one of the Apostles set off by himself in the lists is Judas Iscariot, who is traditionally remembered as the betrayer (Matthew 10:4; Mark 3:19; Luke 6:16) who sold his Master for thirty pieces of silver (Matthew 26:15). Iscariot is said to refer to his birthplace, Iscariot being a Hebrew phrase "man from [the town of] Kerioth or Carioth." Judas is the Greek form of the Hebrew Judah.

John's Gospel in Chapter 6 describes a point at which many of Jesus' disciples abandoned him. "Will you also go away?" Jesus asked the Twelve. To which Simon Peter answered, "Lord, to whom shall we go? You have the words of eternal life and we believe, and are certain, that you are the Christ, the Son of the living God." In reply, Jesus, speaking of Judas Iscariot, said, "Have I not chosen you twelve, one of whom is a devil?"

Matthew's account says that Judas, after realizing how wrong he had been in setting up his Master for crucifixion through betraying him into the hands of the Temple leaders, first threw away the pieces of silver he'd been paid in the Temple, then hanged himself in despair. The Temple leaders used the silver to buy a potter's field to "bury strangers in" (Matthew 27:3–7).

But Peter, in a sermon quoted by Luke in Acts 1:18, says that "this man purchased a field with the reward of iniquity and, falling headlong, he burst asunder in the midst, and all his bowels gushed out." Catholic writer W. H. Kent suggests that by returning the pieces of silver to the Temple leaders, Judas "indirectly" paid for the field that Matthew says the Temple leaders bought for use as the potter's field.

Chapter 6
Parables and Other Teachings

In addition to his sermons, Jesus is famous for another kind of teaching: the telling of stories with moral points, called parables, the general theme of which is the Kingdom of God and how to attain it. The Gospels record approximately four dozen parables, depending on how you calculate the overlap among the accounts. Several parables also appear in the Sermon on the Mount. Another type of teaching Jesus used, as recorded in the Gospels, is prophecy, which can be described as "foretelling while forth-telling."

Hidden Wisdom

Matthew's Gospel says "Jesus spoke to the multitudes in parables; and didn't speak to them without a parable, in order to fulfill the saying of the prophet, 'I will open my mouth in parables; I will utter things that have been kept secret from the foundation of the world'" (Matthew 13:34–35, referencing Psalm 78:2).

It seems obvious from Jesus' teaching that he is pacing himself. Usually, he seems to be trying to avoid an argument by posing propositions as riddles or in ambiguous wording so detractors will have a hard time pinning him down through accusations. But at other times, he speaks directly, as if to confront his detractors, even by reading their negative thoughts and disclosing his power to do so (as was shown in Chapter 4).

discussion question

Why are the parables' meanings not always clear?
The parables have a sense about them that they will be understood better after Jesus' listeners have the whole picture. This may have led to the academic discipline of systematic theology or dogmatics; Jesus instilled in his listeners a need that resounds even now: to comprehend the big picture of God's plan for his world and its capstone, the human community.

Some of his parables, short of being stories, are simple similes, like "The Parable of the Treasure Hidden in a Field," that requires only one verse in Matthew: "Again, the kingdom of heaven can be likened to treasure hidden in a field which, when a man found it, kept to himself and, in joy, went out and sold all he had to buy" (Matthew 13:44). The moral is that anyone finding how to attain the Kingdom of Heaven should put aside anything necessary in order to do it.

Mysteries of the Kingdom

When Jesus' disciples asked him about why he spoke in parables, he replied, "It is given to you to know the mysteries of the kingdom" but to those among the crowds gathering to hear him teach who reject him and his Kingdom, "it has not been given . . . I speak to them in parables because they do not see when seeing, and do not understand when hearing" (see Matthew 13:10–17, Mark 4:10–12, and Luke 8:9–10). This information is sandwiched between each of the evangelists' recitation of Jesus' Parable of the Sower and his explanation to the disciples of its meaning.

As with most events in his ministry, Jesus' parables are ordered in different sequences from one Gospel to the next, and some appear in some Gospels, or in only one, but not in all, as the following table illustrates.

Parables in the Gospels

The Parable of	Matthew	Mark	Luke	John
1. The bread of life				6:30–59
2. New patch on an old garment	9:16	2:21	5:36	
3. New wine in old wineskins	9:17	2:22	5:37,38	
4. The sower and the soils	13:3–13	4:2–20	8:4–15	
5. Lamp under a bushel	5:14–16	4:21,22	8:16,17/ 11:33–36	
6. The seed that grows up		4:26–29		
7. The wheat and the tares	13:24–30			
8. Wicked tenant vineyard keepers	21:33–45	12:1–12	20:9–19	
9. Prophecy of the fig tree	24:32–44	13:28–32	21:29–33	
10. The watchful doorkeeper		13:33–37		
11. Wise and foolish men's houses	7:24–27		6:47–49	

The Parable of	Matthew	Mark	Luke	John
12. Kingdom compared to a mustard seed	13:31,32	4:30–32	13:18,19	
13. Leavening yeast	13:33		13:20,21	
14. Treasure hidden in field	13:44			
15. Pearl of great price	13:45, 46			
16. Both good and bad fish caught in the net	13:47–50			
17. Scribe like a householder	13:52			
18. The lost sheep and the 99	18:12–14		15:3–7	
19. Forgiven servant who doesn't forgive	18:23–35			
20. Hired laborers for vineyard	20:1–16			
21. Sons and the father's will	21:28–32			
22. Guests for wedding feast	22:2–14		14:16–24	
23. Wise and foolish virgins	25:1–13			
24. Talents	25:14–30		19:11–27	
25. Debtors and forgiveness			7:41–43	
26. The Good Samaritan			10:30–37	
27. Friend in need persists			11:5–13	
28. The foolish rich farmer			12:16–21	
29. Watching servants			12:35–40	
30. Servants unprepared for master's return	24:45–51		12:42–48	
31. Barren fig tree spared			13:6–9	
32. The shepherd and sheep				10:1–30

The Parable of	Matthew	Mark	Luke	John
33. Highest and lowest seats			14:7–11	
34. The cost of building and of making war			14:25–35	
35. Lost drachma coin			15:8–10	
36. The prodigal son			15:11–32	
37. Scheming manager			16:1–13	
38. Rich man and Lazarus			16:19–31	
39. Unworthy servants			17:7–10	
40. The widow's persistence			18:1–8	
41. The prayers of a Pharisee and a tax collector			18:9–14	
42. The vine and the branches				15:1–27

The Sower

Luke's version of the parable of the sower who sowed seeds on varied soils is the most concise of the three takes on it in the New Testament. Asked by the disciples to explain the parable's meaning, Jesus said the seed is the word of God, those by the wayside are those who hear; the devil comes and takes away the word out of their hearts.

The seeds that land on rock and have no roots are those who hear and receive the word of God, but do not follow it. And the seed that fell among thorns represents listeners who, when they hear, get choked with cares, riches, and pleasures of this life, and bring no fruit to perfection; in other words; they don't attain the Kingdom of God. The seed that falls on the good ground represents those who, hearing the word, keep it, and bear fruit through persevering.

symbolism

Bringing "fruit to perfection" is presented here as the key to attaining the Kingdom of God, and it is won only by struggling for it and persevering in the place where the believer takes root.

The Good Samaritan

Though the Good Samaritan is one of the best known and widely preached parables in Jesus' repertory, it appears only in Luke's Gospel, where Jesus gives it in answer to a question meant to ensnare him when "a certain lawyer" asked him what he would have to do to inherit eternal life. When Jesus asked him how he reads the Law on that question, the man replied, "Thou shalt love the Lord thy God with all thy heart, and with all thy soul, and with all thy strength, and with all thy mind; and thy neighbour as thyself." But, he asked when Jesus concurred, "who is my neighbor?"

The Spirit of the Law

Jesus replied by telling the story of a man traveling on the road to Jericho being attacked, stripped, robbed, and left injured on the roadside. A priest and a Levite going that way saw him lying in great pain but passed by without offering aid. But a Samaritan, a member of the untouchable class in the midst of Israel, seeing the man, stopped, dressed his wounds, put him on his donkey and took him to an inn for additional treatment and time to recuperate, telling the innkeeper he would take care of any additional charges that might be accrued the next time he passed that way. The road from Jerusalem to Jericho, though ancient and long traveled, was notoriously dangerous both by the terrain it crossed through treacherous passes, and because of highwaymen like those who beset the victim in Jesus' story.

The priest and Levite fell short of the spirit of the Law. The Samaritan, a member of a sect that claimed to be Jewish but was shunned because they were considered apostate by the orthodox, showed more of the Law's spirit than its representative main advocates in Israel.

The Woman at the Well

John writes that in order to return to Galilee from Judea (from the area of Jerusalem to that of Nazareth and Capernaum) Jesus "had to go through Samaria." And there he stopped at a well, a center of community life, to rest and get a drink while his disciples went into town to get something for lunch, it being around the sixth hour, which in the way of reckoning in that era meant noon, or about six hours after daybreak.

Jesus didn't have anything to use to draw water from the well, so he waited until a woman from town approached to get her household water, and asked her for a drink. She was taken aback: "How is it that you, a Jew, ask me for a drink, seeing I am a woman of Samaria and the Jews have no dealings with the Samaritans?" To this, Jesus replied that if she knew who it was who was asking, she would be asking him for a drink which, once drunk, would quench her thirst forever. And he also revealed that he knew her very heart by describing her sinful past, though they had not met before.

factum

So powerful was Jesus' Good Samaritan parable that, even in today's parlance, a Good Samaritan refers to a stranger who offers help to someone in need. The origins of the Samaritan ethnic and religious minority in Israel have been studied for centuries. DNA tests made on what remains of ethnic Samaritans show that their genetic lines go back to both Jewish and Assyrian ancestors.

The Samaritan woman at the well was so amazed at what Jesus said that she ran to bring the men of her household to meet him, something that the disciples were scandalized to see when they returned. (Presumably it was okay to buy food from the Samaritans, but not to be sociable with them.) Jesus' radical departure from the customs of his generation is in line with his eating with publicans and touching lepers to heal them.

The Rich Farmer

The parable of the prosperous farmer who tried to plan his life without taking into account God's will for it seems—compared with the story of the Good Samaritan—more like an imaginative story than an account of actual events. Like the Samaritan story, it was offered in response to a question from a man who approached Jesus to ask something of him. Luke 12:13–21 has the account. The request this time was, "Master, speak to my brother, that he divide the inheritance with me." Jesus replied that he was not a judge between people. And he warned, "beware of covetousness . . . a man's life doesn't consist in abundance of things and possessions."

Then he told the story of the farmer who had such a good harvest he had to build bigger barns to make room for storing it. He told himself he had enough goods "laid up for many years" so it was time to eat, drink, and be merry. "But God said unto him, Thou fool, this night thy soul shall be required of thee." And Jesus concluded, "so is he who lays up treasure for himself and is not rich toward God."

As Psalms 14:1 and 53:1 say, "The fool has said in his heart, There is no God." Jesus is saying that anyone who doesn't realize his accountability to God is a fool.

The Great Supper

As he sat with his disciples at mealtime, Jesus told the story of a man who put on a dinner party but could not find people to share it with him (see Luke 14:15–24). Everyone he invited to the dinner started making excuses, and when none on his guest list accepted, he told his servant, "Go out quickly into the streets and lanes of the city, and bring in hither the poor, and the maimed, and the halt, and the blind." This done, the servant said there was still room and food for more, so the host told him to go out in the street and "compel" anyone who would join them to come and fill the house. And those on the guest list who had refused to come would not be allowed to partake of his feast, he said.

This parable shows how God invites everyone to his house, but only those poor enough in spirit to realize they need his generosity will receive it and, as a result, only they will be awarded a place at his banquet. Nothing takes precedence over an invitation from the Lord, though it is human nature to say, when distracted by the busyness of every day, "Please excuse me this time."

The Talents

Both Matthew and Luke recount Jesus' parable of the talents (a talent in this context is a large amount of money), though the two versions of the parable vary somewhat in the details. Matthew 25:14–30 probably provides the text of more sermons, and therefore Matthew's version of the parable is more familiar than Luke's version. In it, Jesus likens the kingdom of heaven to a man traveling to a far country. He called his servants to him to entrust his assets to them, giving five talents to one, two talents to a second, and one to a third.

fallacy

The church taught for centuries that Jesus prohibited lending at interest. Though Jesus isn't advocating market investing and speculation, this parable has more recently been used to support lending and investing at interest, which, over the centuries, has virtually obliterated the earlier church teaching that charging interest on loans or paying dividends on investments constitute the sin of usury.

The first two servants managed to double their assets on the master's behalf, but the third buried his share of the money. When the master returned after a long time and reckoned with them, he said "well done thou good and faithful servant" to each of those people who doubled their funds and promised to entrust them both to many more assets in the future.

But when the third servant boasted that he had not lost his talent but buried it to keep it safe, the master said, "Thou wicked and slothful servant, thou knewest that I reap where I sowed not, and gather where I have not strawed: thou oughtest therefore to have put my money to the exchangers, and then at my coming I should have received mine own with usury. Take therefore the talent from him, and give it unto him which hath ten talents. For unto every one that hath shall be given, and he shall have abundance: but from him that hath not shall be taken away even that which he hath."

Though many sermon illustrations have rung interpretations on this parable related to financial stewardship and wise investment, as well as making the most of the "talents" God has given you, the parable's weight is directed to faith and grace. To the person who has faith, God will give more, and to the one who lacks trust and obedience, God will not give faith or grace to believe, so even his doubts will harden into disbelief.

The Pharisee and the Tax Collector

The parable of the Pharisee and the publican, or tax collector, has influenced the church's understanding of prayer and the state of the heart in which prayer originates. Luke 18:9–14 provides the only account of this parable, introducing it as being intended for "certain who trusted in themselves and their own righteousness, and despised others." A Pharisee and a publican went to the Temple to pray. The Pharisee prayed, "God, I thank thee that I am not as other men are, extortioners, unjust, adulterers, or even like this publican. I fast twice in the week, I give tithes of all that I possess. And the publican, standing afar off, would not lift up so much as his eyes unto heaven, but smote upon his breast, saying, God be merciful to me a sinner." Jesus concludes that "this man went down to his house justified rather than the other: for every one that exalteth himself shall be abased; and he that humbleth himself shall be exalted."

The publican's prayer, slightly altered as "Lord have mercy on me a sinner," is the basis of the Jesus Prayer, which is the subject of one of the most widely read books of the modern era, the nineteenth-century Russian anonymous novel (or what some believe is a nonfiction biographical account), *The Way of the Pilgrim*, and also is a focal point in J. D. Salinger's novel, *Franny and Zooey*. The most common enlarged version of the Jesus Prayer is, "Lord Jesus Christ, Son of God, have mercy on me a sinner."

factum

In *The Way of the Pilgrim*, the protagonist tours Czarist Russia asking spiritual people how it's possible to "pray without ceasing," as recommended in 1 Thessalonians 5:17. The Pilgrim discovers the Jesus Prayer and the technique monastics used for centuries, internalizing the Jesus Prayer as a continuous state of prayer at an almost subconscious level referred to as praying from the heart.

Also of interest in this short parable is the insight it provides into the spiritual practices of pious first-century Jewish people, such as two days of fasting each week. And Jesus' summation, "he who humbles himself shall be exalted" is considered a keystone of the spiritual life, words to live by as an antidote to the first deadly sin of pride.

The Prodigal Son

Alongside the parable of the Good Samaritan, the story of the Prodigal Son is another of the best-known parables of Jesus, and as a story it has the most fully developed characters, motivations, settings, plot, resolution, and emotional impact. Some lists of Jesus' parables refer to it as the parable of the two sons, because of the contrast drawn between two of the three central characters. Reminiscent of the stories of Cain and Abel, and Jacob and Esau in Genesis, the story has served as inspiration for some of the great works of literature, including Shakespeare's *The Merchant of Venice*, John Steinbeck's *East of Eden*, and for movies including *Legends of the Fall* and *Boogie Nights*.

The Child Who Rebels

Like the Good Samaritan, only Luke recounts the parable of the Prodigal Son. In current speech, a prodigal son refers primarily to any child who rebels and becomes a new kind of person, especially if he or she openly rejects father and family and later returns with his tail between his legs. But Jesus' parable contrasts the rebellious son who leaves with a good and loyal son, who stays.

After asking for his inheritance from his father early to leave and make his own way in the world, the younger, rebellious son spirals from liberation into debauchery until eventually, broke and jobless, he ends up tending a herd of pigs for the privilege of being able to eat any of the pigs' food they miss.

Nothing would seem more demeaning to a good Jewish son than to have fallen so far. Finally, in desperation, the younger son sees the error of his ways, and returns home to offer to take a job as one of the household servants, just to be able to live on the family's farm again. The father, seeing him approaching "from afar," welcomes him with great fanfare by running to embrace him and order that he be given new clothes, a ring, and a feast featuring the family's fatted calf as the entrée. "For this my son was dead, and is alive again," the father says, "he was lost, and is found. And they began to be merry."

Sibling Rivalry

Everyone was overjoyed . . . except for the older, loyal, son who realized that if his rebellious brother is again taken back into the family, part of the inheritance he was expecting to receive is going to be diminished by the portion the brother has already squandered. "And he said to his father, 'All these many years I have served you, and I have never disobeyed your commandment. Yet you never gave me a kid [a young goat], so I might make merry with my friends. But as soon as this son came back who devoured your substance with harlots, you have killed the fatted calf for him.'"

symbolism

The theme of something that is lost and is found again is a repetitive one in Jesus' parables (a lost coin, the lost sheep). Its point is that repentance is the most important and indispensable way to the Kingdom of God. Even if one gets "lost" (commits a sin), one can repent and be "found" again by the grace of God.

The father's response is one of the most dramatic and touching in the New Testament:

"Son, you are always with me, and all that I have is yours. It was proper that we should make merry and be glad, for this your brother was dead, and is alive again; was lost, and is found" (see Luke 15:11–32).

Prophetic Teachings

Prophecy is central to the ministry and the life of Jesus, as the Apostle Matthew, especially, documents in his Gospel. Not only does Matthew cite scores of passages from the prophets from centuries before Jesus' birth to support his messianic claims, but also he emphasizes, more than any other New Testament writer, the prophetic utterances of Jesus himself concerning the future of the church and the world. Matthew describes Jesus' teachings as peppered with prophecies about his own suffering, crucifixion, and resurrection, as well as allusions to the future of the church, like his reaction to Peter's confession that Jesus truly was the Son of God ("on this rock I will build my church," Matthew 16:18), and the sending of the Holy Spirit to be the church's Comforter.

Prophecies in Matthew

It is widely known that the Book of Revelation (also called The Apocalypse) is the major prophetic book in the New Testament, especially when it comes to things that are widely believed as not yet fulfilled. But it's not as well known that Jesus gave long-term prophecies that occupy much of two chapters of Matthew's Gospel. The first prophecy is his prediction that the Temple of Jerusalem would be destroyed: "There shall not be left here one stone upon another, none that shall not be thrown down" (Matthew 24:2). This was fulfilled in A.D. 70, less than forty years after he said it. Some scholars claim the "prophecy" proves that Matthew's Gospel was written after the event.

The action in Chapter 24 of Matthew takes places at the Mount of Olives, where Jesus and the disciples retreated to get away from the crowds, and it seems that the disciples were in a mood to hear more prophecy. "Tell us, when shall these things be?" they asked. "And what shall be the sign of your coming and of the end of the world?"

Jesus replied:

> *Beware so no one deceives you. Many shall come in my name, saying, I am Christ; and shall deceive many. And you shall hear of wars and rumors of wars; don't let that trouble you, for all these things must come to pass, but the end is not yet. Nation shall rise against nation, and kingdom against kingdom; there shall be famines, pestilences, and earthquakes in various places. All these are the beginning of sorrows. Then they shall deliver you up to affliction and shall kill you. And you will be hated of all nations for my name's sake (Matthew 24:4–9).*

Past or Future

Traditional church interpretations of these prophecies see them as referring to things that will take place when Jerusalem and the Temple are destroyed by Rome in A.D. 70, still the future when Jesus was speaking. Matthew indicates these lengthy prophecies of Jesus were given just two days before the Passover that culminated in his betrayal and crucifixion, making these the last teachings the disciples received from him.

factum

Mark's Gospel has a shorter passage, in Chapter 13, with parallels to chapters 24 and 25 in Matthew. Luke also recounts much of the same scenario, but more briefly, in Chapter 21, with this dramatic climax: "When these things start to occur, look up and lift your heads to see that your redemption draws near" (Luke 21:28).

These passages predict many attempts to deceive the church and pull it away from its first love to Jesus (many Bible scholars refer to this deception as the apostasy), the great tribulation, and "the abomination of desolation" of the Temple, followed by "the end." In this section, many Protestants believe, he speaks of taking his faithful away from the tribulation through "the rapture" (though that word does not appear, it has been applied to the predicted mysterious "taking" of many of his followers).

Chapter 7

His Following Multiplies

I n the apostolic churches the woman at the well in the parable of the Good Samaritan is known as St. Photini, meaning "the enlightened one." Tradition holds that she traveled to far parts of the Roman Empire to evangelize pagans. None of this is mentioned in the New Testament, and historical documentation is sparse, but Photini is representative of multitudes of early converts, largely unknown, whose names have been lost but who surely must have existed in order for the church to grow as quickly as it did.

Mary Magdalene

From the New Testament itself, it seems safe to say that Mary Magdalene was the leading woman convert and follower of Jesus. She is mentioned in only twelve verses in the Gospels—three times in Matthew (27:56 and 61, and 28:1), four in Mark (15:40 and 47; 16:1 and 9), two in Luke (8:2 and 24:10), and three in John (19:25; 20:1 and 18)—but these suggest a zeal for the Kingdom and a special love for Jesus, who healed her.

Delivered from Demons

Luke is the only evangelist who establishes Mary Magdalene's background and conversion: "He went throughout every city and village, preaching and showing the good news of the kingdom of God, with the company of the twelve [apostles] and certain women who had been healed of evil spirits and infirmities: Mary called Magdalene, out of whom seven demons were cast; Joanna, the wife of Chuza, Herod's steward, and Susanna, and many others, who ministered to him of their substance" (Luke 8:2–8).

This passage suggests that such women may have been Jesus' and the other disciples' major financial supporters, or at least that they contributed by getting meals and other essential support, a bit of historical trivia that can easily be missed in a casual reading of Luke's Gospel. It's likely that Jesus' and the disciples' having women as part of their retinue was something of a scandal in that time, as well.

Not a Prostitute

Pope Gregory the Great referred in a sermon in A.D. 591 to Mary Magdalene as a converted prostitute, conflating into one person Mary of Magdala (from which Magdalene is derived), Mary of Bethany, and an unnamed woman in Luke 7:37, called "a sinner," who, like Mary of Bethany, anointed Jesus' feet.

Much of the contemporary fascination with Mary Magdalene is rooted in Gnostic gospels, including a Gnostic *Gospel of Mary*, purportedly written by Mary Magdalene, only fragments of which have survived. That apocryphal gospel pits Mary against Simon Peter and the male disciples, and claims that the men, out of jealousy over

Mary's closeness to Jesus, conspired to exclude her from a position of recognized leadership in the church. Traditional Christian scholars, however, recognize only the twelve apostles mentioned in the New Testament.

fallacy

There is no support for the claim that Mary Magdalene was a prostitute in the New Testament or in the Orthodox Church tradition, and in 1969 the Vatican amended its documents to represent the two women as separate persons. The image persists, however, and was perpetuated in the 1973 rock musical *Jesus Christ Superstar*, where Mary Magdalene is presented as a would-be lover of Jesus.

The New Testament does not hide Mary Magdalene's central role in first discovering Jesus' empty tomb and meeting the resurrected Christ in the garden. On the contrary, Mark and Luke state that the disciples did not believe Mary's report about Jesus' rising from the dead. Mark says, "Now when Jesus had risen early the first day of the week, he appeared first to Mary Magdalene, out of whom he had cast seven demons. And she went and told them who had been with him, as they mourned and wept. And they, when they had heard that he was alive and had been seen by her, did not believe it" (Mark 16:9–11). And Luke's statement of the disciples' disbelief is even more pointed: "It was Mary Magdalene, and Joanna, and Mary the mother of James, and other women who were with them, who told these things to the apostles. And their words seemed to them as idle tales, and they did not believe them" (Luke 24:10–11).

Joanna and Susanna
Joanna is mentioned only one more time in the New Testament, again in Luke's Gospel, when she is one of the women who goes to the sepulcher on the morning of the Resurrection with Mary Magdalene,

and is with her when she reports the news of the empty tomb to the disciples. Though Susanna is not mentioned again, in Orthodox tradition she was with the others who followed Jesus from Galilee to Judea, and was a witness to the Crucifixion and Resurrection. Both women are called saints in the Orthodox churches, and both are cited by advocates of the ordination of women to the priesthood as examples of early women leaders in the church who were considered on par with the apostles.

The Greek tradition says that Mary Magdalene became a companion of Mary, the Mother of Jesus, and lived with her in her latter years in Ephesus, in Asia Minor (modern Turkey). Gregory of Tours (538–594), in his time the highest-ranking churchman in Gaul (modern France) supports the claim that Mary spent her later years in Ephesus, and makes no claim that she lived in Gaul. But a strong French Catholic tradition holds that Mary Magdalene spent her later life in Marseilles, France, where she was instrumental in evangelizing Provence.

discussion question

What are saints?
Protestants consider all followers of Jesus saints, citing the Apostle Paul, who called believers "saints," and Protestants have no canonization process. In Roman Catholicism, exceptionally holy people are declared saints through lengthy examination by church courts. In Orthodoxy, popular acclaim and veneration of a holy example can lead to canonization. Moreover, many uncanonized persons are considered saints.

Lazarus, Mary, and Martha

John 11:5 describes Lazarus, Mary, and Martha of Bethany as close friends of Jesus. Luke is probably referring to this same Martha and Mary when he records a visit of Jesus and his disciples: "as they went, he entered into a certain village and a woman named Martha received him into her house. And she had a sister, Mary, who also sat at Jesus' feet, and heard his word. But Martha, encumbered with the work of serving their guests, came to him and said, 'Lord, do you not care that my sister has left me to serve alone? Ask her to help me.' But Jesus replied, 'Martha, Martha, you care and are troubled about many things. But one thing is needful, and Mary has chosen that good thing, which will not be taken away from her.'"

Mary had found the only thing really needed in life, the top priority: loving and serving her savior. The next encounter with Martha and Mary is recorded in John's Gospel, in chapter 11, where an emissary of the sisters tells Jesus that Lazarus, "he whom you love, is sick." But Jesus says the sickness "is not unto death but for God's glory" and he stays on in Jerusalem several days longer. His disciples, meanwhile, urge him to return to Judea because the opposition to him in Jerusalem is getting intense.

Lazarus Asleep

"Our friend Lazarus is sleeping," he replies "but I'm going to awake him from his sleep." The disciples replied, "Lord, if he's asleep, he'll do well." But Jesus was speaking of his death, though they thought he had meant taking rest in sleep. Then said Jesus plainly, "Lazarus is dead. And I am glad for your sakes that I was not there, so that you may be caused to believe. Now, let us go unto him" (John 11:3–15). Jesus is making certain that the disciples know that he waited before going to Lazarus to demonstrate his power over death. And this miracle will seal Jesus' fate with his enemies in Jerusalem who seek to have him put to death.

Martha and Mary Speak to Jesus

When they arrived at Bethany, only about two miles from Jerusalem, they were told that Lazarus had been in the tomb for four days already, and when Martha met Jesus on his arrival, she said, "Lord, if you had been here, my brother would not have died. But I know that even now, whatever you will ask of God, God will give it to you." To which Jesus replied, "Your brother shall rise again."

Martha said, "I know that he shall rise again in the resurrection at the last day." But Jesus replied, "I am the resurrection and the life. Whoever believes in me, though he is dead, shall yet live. And whoever lives and believes in me shall never die. Do you believe this?"

"Yes, Lord," Martha replied. "I believe that you are the Christ, the Son of God, who should come into the world." And having said this, Martha left and called Mary, her sister, privately, saying, "The Master is here and calls for you."

factum

Traditionally, these events are considered to have taken place on the Sabbath before the Crucifixion. This Saturday, the day before Palm Sunday, is a prelude to Holy Week in Orthodoxy, where it is called Lazarus Saturday.

Jesus is taken to the tomb of Lazarus, and seeing that his friend is dead, he weeps for him and his skeptical followers are impressed, saying, "See how he loved him." He orders the stone sealing Lazarus' grave removed, and after praying, "'Father, I thank you that you have heard me. I know that you always hear me, but because of the people who stand by I said it, so they may believe that you have sent me.' And when he had spoken, he cried with a loud voice, 'Lazarus, come forth.' And he who was dead came forth, bound hand and foot with grave clothes and his face bound with a napkin. Jesus said to them, 'Loose him, and let him go.'"

The next day, six days before Passover, Jesus goes to a dinner hosted in his honor by Simon of Bethany, a leper whom he had healed. And when Jesus' enemies saw Lazarus there with Jesus, they added Lazarus to their list of people to kill to end Jesus' claims to being the Messiah, and the human Son of the Eternal God.

It was at the dinner at Simon of Bethany's house that Mary of Bethany anointed Jesus' head with oil and washed his feet with her tears and precious perfume. This is considered an indication of Mary's consummate faith in Jesus, and her recognition of what the disciples were refusing to receive, that his death was near.

Roman Catholic tradition says that Lazarus was shipped out of Israel and became the first bishop of Marseilles, in what is now France. Orthodoxy records him as the first bishop of Kition, Cyprus, and commemorates him each year on the Saturday before Palm Sunday. The tradition also says that Mary and Martha lived with him in Cyprus and spent the rest of their lives there. The ancient liturgical hymns describe Lazarus' resurrection as a preview of the general resurrection of the believers in Christ.

Zaccheus

The story of Zaccheus is known by every Sunday school child who has sung the chorus about the "wee little man" who climbed the sycamore tree to see Jesus pass by because he was too short to see over the taller people in the crowd around him. Those who don't recall the chorus can find the whole record in Luke's Gospel, 19:1–10. The Gospel says he was both rich and the chief among the publicans. Because of his short stature, he ran ahead of the parade accompanying Jesus' procession through Jericho, to climb the tree to get a good look at this much-talked-about preacher of the Kingdom. "And when Jesus came to the place, he looked up, and saw him, and said unto him, Zaccheus, make haste, and come down; for today I must abide at thy house."

Zacchaeus seems to have been looking for approval from a religious figure, because Luke says he "made haste" to come down and joyfully received Jesus and took him to his home. Some were scandalized that, again, a publican was being treated as worthy of God's grace. But Zaccheus was so impressed and moved that he said "the half of my goods I give to the poor; and if I have taken anything from any man by false accusation, I restore him fourfold."

And Jesus said unto him, "This day is salvation come to this house, for he also is a son of Abraham. For the Son of man is come to seek and to save that which was lost."

fallacy

The women described earlier as supporters of Jesus' ministry are like Zaccheus in that they are all affluent disciples. According to Jesus, it is the love of riches, or making them an end in themselves, that gets in the way of sanctification.

Though, in another incident, Jesus called upon a rich young man to give all that he had to the poor in order to gain the Kingdom of God (Luke 18:18–23), he made no such demand on Zaccheus. Knowing the hearts of both men, Jesus understood that his wealth would be an impediment to the rich young man, but that Zaccheus had already become poor in spirit, meaning he was aware of the vacuity of his riches. In other words, Zaccheus understood that his wealth was meaningful only if used to make the lot of less fortunate better.

Joseph of Arimathea

Joseph of Arimathea is also an affluent follower of Jesus. And though he is mentioned in all four Gospels, each names him only one time, and in each case it is to mention that it was he who asked Pilate for permission to remove Jesus' body from the cross and bury it in his own private sepulcher.

Mark calls Joseph "an honorable counselor" (meaning, most likely, a lawyer); Luke calls him a Jew who was waiting for the Kingdom of God, and John says he was a secret disciple of Jesus "for fear of the Jews," meaning the Temple leaders who sought to destroy Jesus, of course, not all Jewish people. Catholic writer Francis E. Gigot says that there's evidence that he was a member of the Sanhedrin, the ruling council of the Jewish people, which would shed light on his access to Pilate.

Extra-biblical Texts

But unlike Zaccheus, for whom no extra-biblical legend is found, there is more nonbiblical legend about Joseph of Arimathea than in the Gospels. One text attributes to apocryphal sources a legend that the Apostle Philip led Lazarus, Mary Magdalene, Joseph of Arimathea, and others to Marseilles, in Gaul, and thence Philip and Joseph continued north, over the English Channel, to what was then the Roman province of Britain.

Joseph might have been a trader in metals, a business that may have taken him to Britain even before the crucifixion of Jesus. Even the Arthurian myth includes a passage saying that Joseph of Arimathea arrived in Britain in the middle of the first century A.D.

Nicodemus

Nicodemus is mentioned in connection with Joseph of Arimathea's request to take the body of Jesus. He, too, is identified as a rich member of Israel's Sanhedrin, and a Pharisee, and is the man who came to Jesus by night and asked him the often-cited question, "How can a man be born when he is old? Can he enter the second time into his mother's womb, and be born?" (John 3:4). This was his response to Jesus telling him, "Truly, truly, I say to you, unless a man is born again, he cannot see the kingdom of God."

The *Catholic Encyclopedia* of 1911 says that in his night visit to Jesus, Nicodemus "[was] a learned and intelligent believer, but timid and not easily initiated into the mysteries of the new faith. He next appears (John 7:50–51) in the Sanhedrin, offering a word in defense of the accused Galilean; and we may infer from this passage that he embraced the truth as soon as it was fully made known to him. He is mentioned finally in John 19:39, where he is shown co-operating with Joseph of Arimathea in the embalming and burial of Jesus."

The latter passage in John says Nicodemus "brought a mixture of myrrh and aloes weighing about a hundred pounds" to the burial, which would indicate a rather serious commitment. An Orthodox source contrasts Nicodemus' courage in openly taking the body of Jesus when the apostles had all gone into hiding, and calls the hundred pounds of myrrh and aloes "a symbolic number exalting the dignity of Christ as King."

factum

A later apocryphal *Gospel of Nicodemus* is considered orthodox (in the sense that it doesn't counter the general teachings of the church), but it is believed to have been first published centuries after the church's beginning, and after Nicodemus's lifetime.

The Seventy

Luke is the only evangelist who records the appointment of seventy disciples by Jesus, saying that he "sent them two and two before his face into every city and place, which he himself planned to visit" (Luke 10:1). The Seventy could be compared with the "advance teams" that visited America preceding the arrival of John Wesley and George Whitfield and the Great Awakening (a widespread revival of religious fervor) in the eighteenth century, and the public relations-trained specialists who Billy Graham used in his crusade days, and others like him still do.

The Seventy were to prepare the cities for the coming of the Master, who ordered them to travel shoeless, not stop to kibitz on the way, take no personal effects along, and accept hospitality wherever they could find it.

Eusebius' Reference

Eusebius, c. A.D. 260–341, the bishop of Caesarea and the father of church history, says that he knew of no comprehensive list of the Seventy, but he lists Barnabas, Cephas, Sosthenes (later bishop of Caesarea), Matthias, Thaddeus, and "the Lord's brother" James among those commonly believed to have been among them.

Some manuscripts render the figure of this second flank of disciples as seventy-two rather than seventy, and St. Jerome chose the seventy-two figure for his Vulgate translation of the Bible into Latin. Many prefer seventy, however, as it comports well with other uses of seventy as a significant figure in biblical history, such as Moses' appointing seventy leaders of the twelve tribes of Israel, the Psalmist proclaiming the lifespan of a man as three score and ten, the seventy nations of the world established after the flood of Noah, and the requirement to forgive adversaries "seventy times seven."

Barnabas

Among those listed by Eusebius, the most prominent is Barnabas, a native of Cyprus and a member of the Jewish tribe of Levi, the priestly tribe. Some believe he may have met Paul before the latter's conversion (when Barnabas was known as Joseph, and Paul was known as Saul), when they both studied under Gamaliel, the best-known Jewish teacher of their generation.

The disciples renamed Joseph Barnabas, meaning "son of consolation," in recognition of his gift of healing hurting hearts. He joined Paul after the latter's conversion, and they traveled widely together but parted company when Paul did not want to include Barnabas' cousin, Mark, as an additional team member, though the three men later worked together after the initial rift. Tradition says that Barnabas was the first disciple to take the Gospel to Rome, but he was martyred in his native Cyprus and was buried by Mark in Salamis.

Titus

Another prominent member of the Seventy, Titus was also highly educated (in Greek philosophy), but upon reading the Prophet Isaiah began looking for more information and traveled with some fellow natives of Crete to Jerusalem. Here he became a convert to Jesus and, later, an esteemed companion of Paul, by whom he was baptized. Paul refers to him in epistles as a son (Titus 1:4) and a brother (2 Corinthians 12:18). Titus is believed to have been a witness to Paul's martyrdom by beheading in Rome, and to have returned to Crete to serve as the bishop there for the rest of his life.

Partial lists of lesser-known members of the Seventy have included Tychicus (referred to in Acts and several times in Paul's epistles); Aristarchus, who became bishop of Apamea, Syria, and is mentioned by Paul (Philemon 24), as a "fellow laborer"; and Simeon (see Matthew 13:55 and Mark 6:3), a son of Cleopas and a nephew of Joseph, Jesus' stepfather, and therefore a full cousin of James, "the Lord's brother."

Mark

John, as he was known in Hebrew, had Marcus added to his name and is known more commonly as Mark, the writer of the second Gospel in the New Testament. He is also known as the son of a prominent woman follower of Jesus, as a friend of Simon Peter in Jerusalem, and as the cousin of Barnabas.

discussion question

What is Mark's connection with Simon Peter?
Mark is believed to have been Peter's interpreter in Rome. From that experience, having often heard Peter's accounts of the life of Jesus, he wrote his Gospel, which many believe to have been written first of the four.

Though an early source says that Mark was not himself a follower of Jesus (joining the apostles later), others feel the source is mistaken. Some believe that Mark is alluding to himself in his Gospel, 14:51–52, when soldiers come to Gethsemane in the night to arrest Jesus: "And there followed him a certain young man, having a linen cloth thrown around his naked body; and when the young men laid hold on him he left the linen cloth and fled from them naked."

Luke

As the author of a Gospel and the book of Acts, Luke is one of the most significant of the early church evangelists who were not among the Twelve, yet little historical data survives about him other than a few references to him in Paul's writing, which describes him as a "dear and beloved physician." Catholic scholars have concluded that he was born in Antioch and was born a Greek, not a Jew, both of which facts seem to explain the partiality to gentiles and the city of Antioch that appears in his writings.

The origin of Luke's faith in Christ is not recorded. An ancient source speculates that he was a companion of Cleopas on the walk to Emmaus on the evening after the Resurrection. However, Luke's knowledge of the Septuagint (the Jewish Bible translated into Greek, which was the widely circulated version of the Bible in the first century) suggests that he may have been a convert to Judaism, though he could have also studied the Jewish Bible through his association with Paul and other apostles.

factum

Reading between the lines in Luke's writings, referencing things that show knowledge both medical and nautical, some speculate that he may have worked as a shipboard physician, sailing the Mediterranean Sea.

Luke's association with Paul is introduced in Acts 16:8–12, which relates Paul's "Macedonian call" to take the Gospel to Asia, and where the narrative point of view becomes the second-person "we," rather than the more distanced third-person reporting style before this point. Though Luke's method of gathering the information on the life and ministry of Christ is less dramatic than Mark's method, the introduction to his Gospel is fairly specific about his method and his purpose: "Forasmuch as many have taken in hand to set forth in order a declaration of those things which are most surely believed among us, Even as they delivered them unto us, which from the beginning were eyewitnesses, and ministers of the word; It seemed good to me also, having had perfect understanding of all things from the very first, to write unto thee in order, most excellent Theophilus, That thou mightest know the certainty of those things, wherein thou hast been instructed" (Luke 1:1–4).

discussion question

Who was Theophilus?
There is some debate over whether the Theophilus Luke addresses is a real person or a figure he invents to represent the faithful, since the Greek term Theophilus means "lover of God."

Though Luke's esteemed mentor Paul was not a disciple during Jesus' ministry, he received a divine revelation in the form of a vision set in heaven itself, which may have revealed facts and intentions of the Gospel that the eyewitnesses at the time missed or tended to ignore. Without seeming to boast, Luke is establishing his credentials as a scholar, saying that he has set out to establish all that could be learned about Jesus and the Gospel.

There is also a hint in this introductory passage that Luke was an eyewitness, "having had perfect understanding of all things from the very first." But this could mean "from the very first hearing about them." His stress that his account is "in order" suggests that he believes the events he describes are in the chronological sequence in which they happened, something that is missing from Mark's Gospel.

Chapter 8

From Triumph to the Cross

The raising of Lazarus in Bethany so impressed Jesus' followers and the public that it led to Jesus' triumphal entry into Jerusalem a day or two later, and a week of preaching in the Temple. But both Lazarus' raising and his triumphal entry fueled growing opposition to Jesus among most of the Temple leaders, and culminated in his being arrested on a charge of blasphemy, scourged, and executed on a cross. His enemies used his claim of divinity as proof he blasphemed their God and insulted their religion.

The Transfiguration

The Transfiguration comes at the climax of Jesus' public ministry. Just after speaking to his disciples about his coming death at the hands of his enemies in Jerusalem, Jesus led the inner core of the Twelve—Peter, James, and John—from the town of Caesarea Philippi (miles to the north from the Lake of Galilee) up a high mountain. And there he was transfigured before their eyes; his facial look changed, he literally glowed with white light, and his clothes turned as white as snow. Moses, representing the Law, and Elijah ("Elias" in Greek), representing the Prophets, joined him. The disciples could hear the three discussing Jesus' impending arrest and suffering.

And while Jesus, Moses, and Elijah were speaking, a dark cloud settled down over the mountaintop, and a voice thundered from the cloud, "This is my beloved Son; hear him." Mark says that the disciples were terrified by the transcendent vision, and Peter characteristically offered to build tabernacles over the spots where the three men had sat glowing. Matthew and Mark say that after the cloud dispersed, Moses and Elijah were gone as suddenly as they appeared.

As they started down the mountain, Jesus commanded that they speak nothing about this "until the Son of Man has risen from the dead," a new conception to the disciples that they speculated about. After they regained their courage, the disciples asked Jesus specifically, "Why do the Scribes say that Elijah would come before the Messiah and declare his coming?"

John the Baptist Was Elijah

Jesus said Elijah, in fact, was to come first, and restore all things written about the Son of man, and that Jesus must suffer many things, and be put to death. "But I say to you, Elijah did indeed come, and they did to him whatever they liked, as it was written of him" (Mark 9:12–13). Matthew, only, adds, "Then the disciples understood that he was speaking to them of John the Baptist" (Matthew 17:13).

Matthew also says earlier in his Gospel, quoting Jesus: "Truly I say to you, among those born of women not a greater one has come than John the Baptist, notwithstanding he who is least in the kingdom of heaven is greater than he." Jesus continued, "For all the prophets and the law prophesied before John. And if you will receive it, this is Elijah, who was to come. Let him who has ears to hear, hear" (Matthew 11:13–15).

discussion question

What does Jesus say about the use of violence?
Matthew quotes Jesus as saying, "from the days of John the Baptist until now the kingdom of heaven has suffered violence, and the violent take it by force." This "violence" refers to forcing oneself to do the right thing, to keep the faith despite all opposition. It is a spiritual, not physical, violence.

John the Baptist Was Not Elijah

But elsewhere the Apostle John, one of the three disciples who witnessed the Transfiguration and participated in the discussion with Jesus while they descended the mountain, says of John the Baptist: "this is the record of what John [the Baptist] did when the Jews sent priests and Levites from Jerusalem to ask him, 'Who are you?' And he did not deny; but confessed, 'I am not the Christ.' And they asked him, 'Then who? Are you Elijah?' And he said, 'I am not.'" And when they pressed him, John the Baptist said, "I am the voice of one crying in the wilderness, 'Make straight the way of the Lord, as said the prophet Elijah'" (see John 1:19–21).

The explanation of the apparent contradiction between Jesus' words and John the Baptist's is found in the angel's appearance to the father of John the Baptist, as recorded in Luke's Gospel: "your wife Elisabeth shall bear a son who you shall name John. . . . And he shall go before him in the spirit and power of Elijah, to turn the hearts of the fathers to the children, and the disobedient to the wisdom of the just; to get the people ready for the Lord" (see Luke 1:13–17).

symbolism

Jesus' Transfiguration to a being of light reconfirmed his divinity claims—as "true light of true light," as the Nicene Creed puts it. It also revealed John the Baptist was at a higher level than Jesus' disciples, for he now says no prophet ever surpassed him, and that all the prophets formed a succession that led to his appearance.

The Disciples' Wondering

Those who asked John if he "was" Elijah were trying to see if he would claim to be a reincarnation, something the Old Testament prohibits believing in. He was not Elijah reincarnated, but he was Elijah come back "in spirit and power." This is what Jesus meant when he qualified his affirmation of John as Elijah with "if you will receive it, this is Elijah." Jesus' cryptic statement about taking the kingdom of heaven by violence "and the violent take it by force," has been interpreted traditionally as referring to John's heroic asceticism, "neither eating or drinking" (fasting and abstaining from strong drink).

Lazarus Saturday

The early Catholic Church observed the Saturday before Palm Sunday as Lazarus Saturday, a preview of the resurrection of believers before the last day of judgment. As mentioned previously, the Orthodox Church still observes this day. As was seen in the section on Lazarus in Chapter 7, Jesus' followers saw Lazarus' rising from the dead after four days in the grave as an amazing wonder. This phenomenon, coupled with the plotting of those seeking to silence Jesus by having him put to death, got greater Jerusalem in a buzz just a few days before the beginning of the greatest feast of Judaism's liturgical year, Passover.

After Lazarus rose from the tomb, to impede the growth of the Jesus movement, Jesus' enemies added him to their list of those to be put to death. And later, whether the same evening or the next, Lazarus and Jesus attended a dinner in Bethany put on by Jesus' friend Simon, a leper. The morning after that dinner, Jesus and his companions started making their way to Jerusalem. Jesus sent two of the disciples to "Go into the village, and . . . find an ass tied, and a colt with her. Loose them and bring them to me. And if any man asks about it say, 'The Lord needs them,' and he will let them be taken." And the disciples went and did what Jesus commanded (see Matthew 21:1–6).

discussion question

What is liturgical worship?
Liturgical worship, unlike freeform worship, is a service of prayer led by the clergy following a script, with choir and congregational responses. Both the Temple in Jerusalem and the synagogues followed liturgies, drawing mainly from the Psalms and other prayers from the Torah, which the first churches adapted to their services. Liturgy means "the people's work."

Triumphal Entry (Palm Sunday)

John's Gospel (12:10) says "the chief priests consulted that they might put Lazarus also to death" because his resurrection had caused another wave of people to believe in Jesus. And the next day, the people heard that Jesus was coming to Jerusalem from Bethany, so they "took branches of palm trees" and met him, crying "Hosanna, blessed is the King of Israel who comes in the name of the Lord." And those who had witnessed Lazarus' coming out of the grave "bore witness. . . .For this cause the people also met him, for that they heard that he had done this miracle."

The Pharisees began to think that their efforts to dissuade the people from following Jesus were coming to nothing, saying among themselves, "the world is gone after him." John then interjects that "certain Greeks among them" came up to worship and asked Philip, knowing him to be from Bethsaida of Galilee, how they could meet Jesus. So Philip told Andrew, and they together went and told Jesus. "And Jesus answered them, saying, 'The hour is come, that the Son of man should be glorified'" (John 12:23).

factum

Based on John's Gospel, most Bible scholars agree that this is the third Passover recorded in the Gospel accounts of Jesus' ministry, indicating the end of his ministry's third year, though some dispute that number. Regardless of how many years he and the disciples ministered together, there is no doubt that this was the last Passover they observed together on earth.

Matthew says, "when he came into Jerusalem, all the city was moved, saying, 'Who is this?' And the multitude said, 'This is Jesus the prophet of Nazareth of Galilee'" (Matthew 21:10–11).

The reference to the Greeks who wanted to see Jesus, the crowds coming out to welcome Jesus with palms, the cries of Hosanna, and (as Matthew and Luke add) the people putting down their garments on Jesus' path as a virtual carpet to follow into the city paint a picture of the festive air that filled the Jewish capital city before the holiday.

Jesus Glorified

All three synoptic Gospel writers—Matthew, Mark, and Luke—specify that the triumphal procession brought Jesus all the way to the Temple, and there children and other followers continued worshipping him, incurring the wrath of the chief priests and Temple leaders. But despite this, Luke says Jesus continued preaching in the Temple every day that first Holy Week.

Only John's Gospel describes Jesus' glorification as the climax of his triumphal entry. After saying he was going to die, like a "corn of wheat" that falls into the ground and dies to be raised up and yield fruit, Jesus prayed, "'Father, save me from this hour: but for this cause came I unto this hour. Father, glorify thy name.' Then came a voice from heaven, saying, I have both glorified it, and will glorify it again. The people that stood by and heard it said that it thundered: others said, An angel spake to him. Jesus answered, This voice came not because of me, but for your sakes. Now is the judgment of this world: now shall the prince of this world be cast out" (John 12:23–31). The grain-of-wheat simile refers to the body being buried and decaying, so that the resurrection body can rise from it as a spiritual body.

Moneychangers Routed

Later on this first Holy Week, Jesus threw the moneychangers out of the Temple, saying they had turned his house into a "den of thieves." He spent the night after that event back in Bethany, and on the way back to the Temple the next morning, he looked in the branches of a fig tree along the way for some breakfast fruit, and finding it barren, "said to it, 'Let no fruit grow on you ever again,' at which the fig tree immediately withered away. And when the disciples saw that, they marveled, 'How soon is the fig tree withered away!' Jesus answered to them, 'Truly I say to you, if you have faith, and doubt not, you shall not only do this that was done to the fig tree but also if you shall say to this mountain, "Be moved and be cast into the sea," it shall be done'" (Matthew 21:19–21).

Interpreters often see the fig tree as representing the Jewish established leaders, who, that week, would reject him and be quickly replaced in God's reckoning by his church. And if that's so, some propose that the mountain represents the pagan Roman Empire that would fall from its pinnacle of power in Rome, to be recreated under Christ's dominion in Byzantium. The word that the apostles and their successors had to say to "move the mountain" was the good news of the Gospel.

Also that week, the Temple priests tested Jesus with questions like "under whose authority do you teach these things," to which he replied, "tell me first whether John the Baptist and his baptism were from God," which they refused to answer, knowing John was revered by the multitude who considered him a prophet from God. So Jesus didn't answer their questions, either.

factum

Some theologians call Jesus' week of preaching in the Temple and throwing out the moneychangers his "occupation of the Temple." Josephus, the Jewish historian, says that Pharisees in the Temple asked the people to throw lemons at him and his followers to expel them.

Crowd Pleaser

But Jesus continued teaching the multitudes at the Temple that week (in the courtyard areas inside the walls, but under the sky), with the people waiting for their Passover feast and basking under the power of the master teacher.

Matthew recorded one of Jesus' most controversial teachings:

"Did ye never read in the scriptures, The stone which the build-ers rejected, the same is become the head of the corner: this is the Lord's doing, and it is marvellous in our eyes? Therefore say I unto you, The kingdom of God shall be taken from you, and given to a nation bringing forth the fruits thereof. And whosoever shall fall on this stone shall be broken: but on whomsoever it shall fall, it will grind him to powder." And when the chief priests and Pharisees had heard his parables, they perceived that he spake of them. But when they sought to lay hands on him, they feared the multitude, because they took him for a prophet **(Matthew 21:42–46).**

In exasperation, the Pharisees conspired to take him, and found their opportunity in his one skeptical disciple, Judas Iscariot. John 13:21–30 begins the account of Judas' betrayal at the Last Supper, when Jesus hosted his disciples in one last and everlastingly sig-nificant meal somewhere in Jerusalem. There Jesus cryptically revealed that Judas would give him into his enemies' hands. After the meal ended, Judas slipped out to the Temple and sold the chief priests and Pharisees the information about where Jesus might be found later that night. In exchange for this information, Judas gained another thirty pieces of silver for the disciples' treasury.

Good Friday

After Judas left the room where Jesus and the other disciples were finishing their supper, John says Jesus took advantage of their last, fleeting, sociable moments together to teach more truths: "A new commandment I give you, that you love one another as I have loved you, so should you also love one another. By this shall all men know that you are my disciples, if you love one another" (John 13:34–35).

"And when they had sung a hymn, they went out into the Mount of Olives," Matthew says. The mood is tired and drowsy after the supper, and the disciples' voices are clear but seem distant or ethereal as they walk in the dark out of the city to the place called Gethsemane. Holy Land geographers describe Gethsemane as an area in "the Kidron gully," a narrow valley or arroyo (as they are called in the American southwest, Spanish for "dry creek") that runs adjacent to the Mount of Olives and continues out of the city all the way to the Dead Sea.

factum

Gethsemane is now the site of many Jewish, Christian, and Muslim cemeteries. Perhaps there were burial grounds there then, too, which may be the origin of the place being called "the garden of Gethsemane," even though it is barren, rocky, and desert-like. But there were also olive trees, including some that botanists believe were already a thousand years old by the first Good Friday.

Though it was still Thursday night when they left the room where the Last Supper took place (as the Jewish calendar reckons one day to the next from sunset to sunset), it was already Good Friday. And though the Passion of the Christ is mainly thought of in terms of his trial before Pilate in the morning, along with the whippings by the Roman arresting officers, and Jesus carrying his own cross out to Golgotha, another view is that the real Passion was the final hours he spent that night with his disciples praying in Gethsemane.

The Passion of Christ

Jesus' "dark night of the soul" is, like the Transfiguration, recounted in all three synoptic Gospels, with an especially detailed listing of his Gethsemane prayers in John's Gospel. As at the Transfiguration, Jesus invites only his three core apostles—Peter and the sons of Zebedee, James and John—to share it with him. But what a contrast this night is with the night he and his core disciples went up the Mount of the Transfiguration. Then he was filled with light and met Moses and Elijah, and his three closest disciples were terrified by the display of God's power.

On this night, Jesus "began to be sorrowful and very heavy and said to them, 'My soul is overly full of sorrow, even unto death. Wait here and watch with me.' And he went a little farther, fell on his face, and prayed, 'O my Father, if it can possibly be, let this cup pass from me. Nevertheless, not my will, but yours be done.' And he came back to the disciples and found them sleeping" (see Matthew 26:37–40).

Jesus' Vigil

Matthew's and Mark's Gospels repeat this pattern three times and end it with Jesus rousing his vigil-breaking disciples because his betrayer and the mob have arrived. Luke adds these most dramatic details: after Jesus prays "'nevertheless, not my will but yours be done,' an angel appeared to him from heaven, strengthening him. And being in agony he prayed more earnestly, and his sweat was, as it were, great drops of blood falling down to the ground. And when he rose up from prayer he came to his disciples, whom he found sleeping for sorrow, and said to them, 'Why do you sleep? Rise and pray, lest you fall into temptation'" (Luke 22:43–46).

Jesus Leaves His Disciples

Jesus, with Peter, James, and John, met up again with the other disciples just as the mob organized by the chief priests of the Temple came looking for him. Judas came along "with a great multitude carrying swords and staves," and kissed Jesus on the cheek to let the officers know whom to arrest. Jesus asked who they were looking for. "Jesus of Nazareth," they replied, and he told them, "I am he." He asked why they had to come looking for him with swords and staves when he had been preaching daily in the Temple. Peter, agitated, cut off the ear of the High Priest's servant, but Jesus quickly healed the wound and told his followers not to take up swords in his defense.

The Crucifixion

The story of Jesus' trial before Pilate, his transportation to Herod, the attempts of both political leaders to wash their hands of the matter of "Jesus the accused blasphemer," his scourging, the long trudge to Golgotha, and the crucifixion is so well known that most people can recite the main points.

discussion question

Why did Jesus entrust Mary to John?
As the beloved disciple, John was the closest thing Jesus had to a full brother. From the cross, Jesus beheld John, kinsman of Mary and himself, and his mother standing by, and said, "Mother, behold your son," and to John, "behold your mother." It was Jesus' last will and testament.

The mob from the Temple bound Jesus, and after consulting among the Temple leaders, took him to the palace of the Roman governor, Pilate. The disciples slunk to the background. Peter warmed his hands over a fire behind the palace, and, when asked if he hadn't been with Jesus, denied it, three times. And when the rooster crowed, it reminded him of his protestation the previous evening that he would never deny his Lord and Master. Then he wept.

All four Gospels tell the crucifixion sequence. Read John's account in John 18:16–37. John warrants to all who read his Gospel that he witnessed it all by his own eyes, and has written in his own words, "that you might believe."

The Resurrection

All four Gospels tell the story of the resurrection of Jesus, with John's being much more detailed than the others. The accounts vary in details, differing according to the perspective of the source who told it to the evangelists. (John's account varies from the others' because he was a Gospel writer who was also an eyewitness.) But the main outline is that at dawn following the Sabbath, myrrh-bearing women made their way to the tomb where Jesus had been interred, sealed by a huge stone.

When they got near, they saw the stone rolled away, and an angel glowing like lightning greeted them and told them Jesus was not there, but had risen as he had foretold. The angel also said they should tell the Eleven (Judas having hanged himself after realizing the gravity of his sin in betraying his Lord), and should return to Galilee, where he would come to them.

Some skeptics point out that the resurrection and its aftermath get fewer verses in the Gospels than many other events, including the crucifixion, to suggest that this may be an addition to the story of Jesus appended later. The church's traditional answer to this doubt is two-fold. First, Jesus' resurrection was foretold many times in the other sections of the Gospels; the prophesies about Jesus' life and passion were fulfilled when he arose. And second, the raising of Jesus was the precursor of the raising of his other, larger, body, the church, which was the point of all of his stories or events.

The Ascension and Great Commission

Jesus made appearances among his disciples for forty days after the resurrection, the first day being celebrated by the church as Easter or Pascha (Greek for Passover) and the last, Ascension Day. According to St. Paul in his first epistle to the church in Corinth, probably written earlier than any of the Gospels, Jesus also appeared in his resurrection body to a congregation of "five hundred brethren" at one time (1 Corinthians 15:6).

factum

John records a miracle he performed, bringing many large fish into the disciples' nets, and Jesus also "restored" Peter to leadership among the disciples by giving him three opportunities to rescind his three-times denial on the morning before the crucifixion. Peter's blessing came at a price; Jesus also predicted the persecution and violent death he would face years later.

Matthew's and Mark's Gospels record the "Great Commission" as the last instruction Jesus gave his followers. Matthew ends with this rendering: "Then the eleven disciples went away to Galilee, to a mountain Jesus had appointed to meet them. And when they saw him, they worshipped him: but some doubted. And Jesus spoke to them, saying, "All power is given to me in heaven and in earth. Go, therefore, and teach all nations, baptizing them in the name of the Father, and of the Son, and of the Holy Spirit, teaching them to observe all that I have commanded you. And, lo, I am with you always, even to the end of the world. Amen" (See Matthew 28:16–20). Mark and Luke add that after that teaching he rose up out of their presence into heaven.

Chapter 9

The Acts and Paul

ating from about four or five decades after the Ascension (A.D. 75–85), Acts is the earliest conscious attempt to chronicle the history of the fledgling and struggling church. The book is divided mainly between the leadership of Peter in the beginning, and of Paul later on. It also follows the companions of Peter and Paul and their interaction with other apostles when Luke was an eyewitness, or when others told him their stories.

Acts of the Apostles

From its beginning, it's apparent that the Book of Acts is a continuation of the Gospel of Luke. The writing style in Acts will strike any reader of Luke's Gospel as familiar. He opens with a one-sentence thesis statement:

> *The former treatise have I made, O Theophilus, of all that Jesus began both to do and teach, until the day in which he was taken up, after that he through the Holy Ghost had given commandments unto the apostles he had chosen: To whom also he shewed himself alive after his passion by many infallible proofs, being seen of them forty days, and speaking of the things pertaining to the kingdom of God, and, being assembled together with them, commanded them that they should not depart from Jerusalem, but wait for the promise of the Father, which, saith he, ye have heard of me* **(Acts 1:1–4).**

The "former treatise" is the Gospel that Luke also addressed to Theophilus, whether that is an actual person or a collective name for all the lovers of God (as mentioned previously, the literal translation of Theophilus) likely to read his books. Note the King James Version's use of "passion" as Luke's word for the suffering and death of Jesus, if any wonder about the origin of that term. Also note that the forty days' sojourn of Jesus with his disciples after the resurrection compares with the forty days he was tested by Satan in the wilderness before beginning his ministry. What the disciples were to wait for in Jerusalem was the coming of the Holy Spirit and the official birthing of the Church of Christ at Pentecost.

Unlike Matthew and Mark, Luke didn't include the Great Commission in his Gospel, but recaps it at the beginning of Acts as a transition to Pentecost. "You shall receive power when the Holy Spirit comes upon you. And you will witness to me in Jerusalem and in all Judea, Samaria, and to the end of the earth" (see Acts 1:8). Luke also elaborates a bit on the Ascension: "And when he had spoken these things, while they watched, he was taken up. And a cloud received him out of their sight. And while they stood gazing toward heaven as he went up, two men in white apparel stood by them and said, 'Men of Galilee, why do you stand gazing up into heaven? This same Jesus who has been taken up from you into heaven shall come in like manner as you have seen him go into heaven'" (Acts 1:9).

Christian Pentecost

Luke says that when the fiftieth day after Passover had fully come, the disciples were all gathered in one place, waiting as the Lord had instructed. Then there was a sound like a rushing strong wind coming into the house and the room they occupied. And they saw "tongues" of fire, one hovering over the head of each person in the room. They began speaking in other languages "as the Spirit gave them utterance." The people who were crowded into Jerusalem for the Pentecost feast, after hearing the noise of the wind at that place and of the people speaking in tongues, gathered around them and "marveled" at what they saw, people who were of all one dialect speaking in many different languages. The account says that "Parthians, Medes, Elamites, dwellers in Mesopotamia, and in Judea, Cappadocia in Pontus, and Asia, Phrygia, and Pamphylia in Egypt, and in the parts of Libya about Cyrene, and foreigners from Rome, Jews and proselytes, Cretes, and Arabs" all heard their own languages coming from these Galilean Christians.

factum

Moses instituted Pentecost to end the Passover season, fifty days after Passover Sabbath. Originally the "feast of the harvest of first fruits," the name used by Greek-speaking Jewish people (*pentekonta* being fifty in Greek) was common in the first century. These Jewish Christians continued to worship in the Temple and observe holy days, fasts, and hours of prayer (see Acts 3:1).

Many marveled, Luke said, but some mocked, attributing the miracle of the tongues to "new wine." Peter answered, "these are not drunk, as you suppose, as it is only the third hour of the day," or 9 A.M. Then Peter began a sermon, fulfilling the prophecy that when the Spirit came on the disciples they would receive power to witness for Jesus and his Gospel to all nations. Luke records Peter's sermon, the first evangelistic sermon in Christian history, in Acts 2: 16–24. Peter then showed how the prophesies concerning the Christ (Messiah) as the descendant of David the great king, pertained to Jesus. And then Peter showed those who wanted to repent how to be saved (see Acts 2:36–47).

The First Megachurch

Not only was a megachurch, as congregations of several thousand members are called today, reportedly founded in Jerusalem on Pentecost, but most likely dozens, possibly scores, of churches were created by members of the crowd who were in Jerusalem for the feast, heard Peter's sermon, were baptized, and returned home to tell the news to friends and relatives. Presumably, those with the gift of tongues that day were interpreting Peter's words in all the languages represented.

Memories Still Fresh

Many of these people had been in Jerusalem for Passover just more than fifty days earlier and had seen Jesus being hailed on what Christians now call Palm Sunday, his preaching in the Temple, and his being crucified, and it's likely his passion was a topic of conversation at the time. The seed that had been planted had sprung up and already was having its first fruits, on this the festival of the first fruits of harvest. Not only would Passover become the most important feast in the new church (as Easter is called in most non-English-speaking churches), Pentecost would also be adopted from Judaism to be commemorated everywhere Christians established congregations and received the Holy Spirit.

The New Church

The leadership Jesus had assigned to Peter, and that Peter had par-tially assumed when traveling with Jesus and the Twelve, was quickly confirmed at Pentecost. And the next time we see Peter in Acts, his acts are even more impressive. While walking into the Temple with John for the prayers of the ninth hour (3 P.M.), he is accosted by a lame beggar asking for alms. Peter utters the famous line, "Silver and gold have I none; but such as I have give I thee. In the name of Jesus Christ of Nazareth, rise up and walk." And the man not only makes an effort to get up, he also leaps and runs around the Temple porch, calling out like a man who has just met his Savior.

Such is the ruckus the healed man stirs up that a large crowd gath-ers around him, Peter, and John, asking how the man they had known as a lame beggar all his life was now whole and praising God.

Church Growth

Peter's response is similar to the one he made at the feast when the Holy Spirit had given the disciples the gift of tongues. He tells them the Jesus they had crucified is living again, and he is the one God had promised through all the prophets and had even said would be persecuted by those he came to redeem, "all the prophets from Samuel and those that follow after, as many as have spoken, have likewise foretold of these days. You are the children of the prophets, and of the covenant God made with our fathers. For he said to Abraham, 'And in your seed shall all the peoples of the earth be blessed.' Unto you first God, having raised up his Son Jesus, sent him to bless you, in turning away every one of you from his iniqui-ties" (see Acts 3:24–26).

Then, Luke says, the rulers of the Temple sent the captain of the temple (a high-ranking official charged with maintaining order in the temple precinct), who arrested Peter, John, and the man healed from lameness, and put them in a cell for the night. But even despite this, "many who heard the word believed;" and this time, "the num-ber of the men who believed was about five thousand."

Witnessing to their Enemies

The next morning the chief priests and leaders of the Temple put Peter and John "in their midst" and asked them, "by what power, or by what name, have you done this?" And Peter, Luke says, "filled by the Holy Spirit," started witnessing to these same men who had delivered Jesus to Pilate for crucifixion: "Let it be known to all of you and to all the people of Israel that by the name of Jesus Christ of Nazareth, whom you crucified, who God raised from the dead, even by him does this man stand here before you whole. This is the stone that was set aside as nothing by you builders, and has become the head of the corner. Neither is there salvation in any other: for there is no other name under heaven given among men, whereby we must be saved." (See Acts 4:10–12.)

Free Speech Prohibited

The accusers marveled at Peter's and John's boldness and, consulting among themselves, privately admitted that a verifiable miracle had been performed by the accused on the formerly lame man. And fearing repercussions if they punished Peter and John, they commanded them not to speak any longer in Jesus' name. But again the lead apostles were fearless: "Whether it's right in the sight of God to obey you more than God, you can judge. But we cannot do other than speak the things we have seen and heard." So after the accusers had further threatened the apostles, they let them go (see Acts 4:19–21). Peter's fame spread so much that people tried to position themselves in line with his shadow, thinking that being touched by his shadow would heal them.

Solomon's Porch

The apostles continued to preach in Solomon's Porch (inside the Temple walls), to the great displeasure of the Temple rulers, so much so that the rulers eventually threw the apostles back into the Temple jail cell. But while the apostles were incarcerated, an angel released them, and told them to return to Solomon's Porch early the next morning and continue teaching the Word as they had been.

discussion question

What was behind the apostles' new "holy boldness"?
Though Peter had addressed the lame man with what seems to be doubt about his own power to cure him, the man's healing was a miracle that confirmed that power and pushed the mushrooming church from 3,000 new members the first day to 8,000 the next, and similar miracles followed everywhere the apostles went, with even more growth occurring with every new event.

After they continued teaching, they were taken before the council, and when the council was about to punish them, a Pharisee and "learned teacher," Gamaliel, rose to the apostles' defense, concluding, "If this is of men, it will come to nothing, but if it is from God, we can do nothing to stop it." So the council agreed to ignore the apostles a while longer, and they continued to teach in the Temple.

factum

Gamaliel was a teacher of Saul, who became Paul; and Joseph, who became Barnabas. Historians say Gamaliel was a son of Simeon and a grandson of the famous Rabbi Hillel, whose teachings are still widely used in Jewish synagogues.

Throughout this growth period, Luke inserts facts about the internal working of the new church. The newly baptized shared among themselves their property and a common purse, for example, and Luke describes the need of some members for more personal ministry and help, for which reason the apostles appointed the first deacons. Among the deacons, the first named is Stephen, "a man full of faith and of the Holy Spirit."

The First Martyr

Stephen is described as doing many miracles, but because his zeal attracted opposition in several of the synagogues, his opponents conspired to have him executed by stoning, thus making him the first martyr of the church: "They threw him outside the city and stoned him: and the witnesses laid down their clothes at a young man's feet, whose name was Saul" (Luke 7:58).

Writing after the fact, of course, here Luke foreshadows the rise of Saul/Paul by noting his presence at the stoning of Stephen. For although Luke records in the first chapter of Acts the replacement of Judas Iscariot by casting lots among names of disciples close to but not part of the Twelve, God seemed to have another apostle in mind to round out the select core of the founding church. Saul, converted from persecutor of the church and ranking "official" witness to Stephen's martyrdom, becomes the Apostle Paul in the second portion of Acts, and the main influence on the direction the church would now take, away from Jerusalem.

Stephen's sermon occupies the whole seventeenth chapter of Acts and shows the same kind of power from the Holy Spirit as Peter's sermons. It may have been because Stephen spoke in a less central location when he testified of the resurrected Christ and where converts were not yet numerous that he was executed, while Peter and John were able to escape that fate.

From Persecutor to Apostle Extraordinaire

Luke said that Saul was consenting to Stephen's death. And, he adds, there was a great persecution against the church at Jerusalem, and all the Christians, except the apostles, scattered throughout the regions of Judea and Samaria. Devout men buried Stephen, "and made great lamentation over him." As for Saul, he made havoc of the church, entering into individual houses and arresting men and women and committing them to prison (see Luke 8:1–3).

The persecution in Jerusalem, by scattering the less-active apostles and converts, affected the rapid growth of the church in outlying areas. For example, Philip preached in Samaria and found the people ready to receive his message.

discussion question

What did Jesus teach were the worst and the best prayers?
The worst was "Thank you, God, that I am not like this sinner"; the best, "Lord have mercy on me, a sinner."

God directed Philip to go into the Gaza desert beyond Jerusalem, where he found a high-ranking Ethiopian sitting in a chariot reading the Prophet Isaiah. So Philip approached him and preached the Word by way of the prophesies in Isaiah and forthwith baptized him into the faith. Sub-Saharan Ethiopia is by all historical evidence one of the first distant countries to receive the Gospel, its evangelization probably inaugurated by this early convert.

Saul's Conversion

Saul asked the high priest of the Temple to give him a letter of introduction to synagogues in Damascus, Iturea (as it was called in the Roman Empire, Syria in modern times), so that he could have Jewish converts to Christ there arrested and returned to Jerusalem (a long journey) for trial.

But on the way to Damascus, a bright light blinded Saul, and he heard a heavenly voice that identified its speaker as Jesus, "whom you persecute." Saul's companions heard the voice but saw no source for it, and when Saul's eyes were reopened, he found himself sightless and had to have his companions guide him on to Damascus, leading him by the hand.

A disciple of the Lord in Damascus, Ananias, one of those no doubt Saul wished to persecute, had a vision from the Lord telling him to seek out Saul on the "Street called Straight" and heal his blindness. But Ananias told the Lord he had already heard of the letters Saul had received from the high priest to persecute Damascus' Christians. "Go on your way," the Lord replied, "for he has been chosen by me to carry my name to the Gentiles, and kings, and the children of Israel, for I will show him how great things he must suffer for my name's sake" (see Acts 9:15–16).

Paul Proves His Conversion

Like Ananias, the Christians in Damascus were reluctant to receive Saul, their persecutor. But when he began preaching in the synagogues and making converts, the Christians were soon convinced of his true conversion, and the people who opposed the converts became Paul's enemies and tried to arrest him.

He escaped by being lowered out the city wall in a basket by night, and returned to Jerusalem to join the apostles. But he was again rebuffed because they feared him, until his old acquaintance from student days under Gamaliel, Barnabas, was convinced and took Paul to vouch for him before the apostles.

After Paul began openly preaching the Word of Jesus in Jerusalem, he became targeted for death, and when he was secretly shipped back to his hometown of Tarsus, Luke says there was a time of peace for the churches in Judea, Samaria, and Galilee. In the meantime Peter's ministry continued to flourish, and he healed a paralytic, and raised Tabitha, also called Dorcas, from the dead at Joppa.

An Angel Visits a Gentile

Cornelius, a god-fearing gentile and devout centurion (a Roman military officer with command of a hundred men), was visited in Caesarea by an angel, who told him to call Peter from Joppa and invite him to visit Cornelius at his home. At the same time, Peter had a vision in which the Lord told him to eat animals considered unclean under Jewish dietary law, which God was showing him being lowered from the sky on a sheet.

factum

Although it looks like a contradiction in terms, the phrase "Jewish Christian" is not an oxymoron. Jewish Christians were people who believed in Jesus, but continued to follow the Laws of Moses and to observe the Jewish rituals and holy days. This term is used to describe the followers of Jesus in the early days of the Christian movement, before Christians began to be expelled from Jewish temples (some time in the A.D. 80s).

Cornelius' invitation was waiting for Peter when he came out of his vision-trance, and after a four-day journey, he arrived in Caesarea where he met a "large company" waiting for him in Cornelius' house. And he said, "You know it is an unlawful for a Jewish man to keep company or come to one of another nationality, but God has shown me that I should not call any man common or unclean. Therefore, I came to you without hesitation, as soon as I was sent for. I ask therefore for what intent you have sent for me?"

And after Cornelius explained his visitation from the angel, Peter preached Christ to the people at the house, many of whom received the Holy Spirit as Peter spoke, the gentiles even demonstrating the gift of tongues to the astonishment of those "of the circumcision." After he finished, Peter baptized those who believed in Christ, again to the astonishment of the Jewish Christians.

A Turning Point

This was a great turning point for the church, as for the first time the disciples started preaching to gentiles who had not first become Jewish through proselytism and circumcision. But it did not become "official" church practice until a council, called among the apostles in Jerusalem, debated and decided that circumcision was not necessary to become a Christian. They put their finding in a letter to Barnabas and Paul at the church in Antioch, about 300 miles from Jerusalem. When Judas, Barnabas, and Silas, the disciples appointed to take the letter to Antioch, got to their destination and presented the letter to the large congregation gathered there, the congregation rejoiced (Acts 15:28–31).

discussion question

Why does the church emphasize sexual purity?
One source of this policy is the apostles' letter to Barnabas and Paul and the church in Antioch, which said, "it seemed good to the Holy Spirit, and to us, to lay upon you no greater burden than these necessary things: That you abstain from meats offered to idols, from blood and from things strangled, and from fornication. If you keep yourselves from these you shall do well. Fare ye well."

First Church Council Teaching

This decision that a person did not have to be circumcised to become a Christian created a permanent separation of Christians with the Old Testament ceremonial and moral laws. Christians are not required to keep Jewish ceremonial laws (including circumcision, abstaining from "unclean meats" like pork and shellfish, mixing meat and dairy foods, and many other rules given under Moses), while they are still held to the moral laws of Moses.

Born Out of Time

Most of the rest of the book of Acts is coverage of Paul's three missionary journeys. In 1 Corinthians 15:8, Paul recites the evidence for Jesus' resurrection, citing the many eyewitnesses who saw him after his death, and adds, "And last of all he was seen by me also, as one born out of due time." This is more than an expression of regret that he was "born too late" to have been in the first group named as apostles. It's closer to Paul's confession elsewhere that he is the least of the apostles, and the chief of sinners.

Some of this humility may be repentance for the role Paul played in the stoning of Stephen and the persecution of the church before his conversion, but more likely it is Paul's adoption of the Beatitudes discussed in Chapter 3, in other words, taking on the self-effacing meekness that puts oneself last in order that Christ can come first.

But in other cases Paul boasts of his sufferings for Christ and of his apostleship. As an apostle he became one of the key leaders of the first-generation church, despite not having been there when the original Twelve were chosen, or when Judas Iscariot's official successor was chosen by lot.

The First Foreign Missionary and Itinerant Preacher

Paul made three major missionary journeys that Luke covers between chapters 13 and 28 of Acts. The first, described in Acts 13 and 14, took Paul and Barnabas from Antioch in Cilicia (in modern-day Syria), to Antioch in Pisidia (modern-day Turkey), by way of Seleucia; Salamis, and Paphos, Cyprus; and Perga and back via Iconium, Lystra, Derbe, and Attalia.

discussion question

What is an itinerant preacher?
Paul preached in one place for a while, and went on to another. Thus he became the first itinerant preacher (in other words, a traveling preacher). This job title was common in American colonial and frontier times, where congregations were too small to support full-time ministers, and parishioners were so scattered that constant travel was often a central item of a preacher's job description.

The second missionary journey, during A.D. 49–52, is covered in Acts 15–18. It took Paul and Silas from Jerusalem to Antioch, Derbe, Lystra, Troas, Neapolis, Philippi, Amphipolis, Apollonia, Thessalonica, Berea, Athens, Corinth, Cenchreae, Ephesus, and Caesarea. The third journey, from A.D. 53 to 57, is recorded in Acts 18:23 through 21:16. In it, Paul went from Antioch to Ephesus, Thessalonica, Corinth, Philippi, and Toras, and back by way of Assos, Mitylene, Miletus, Tyre, and Caesarea to Jerusalem.

Paul's epistle to the church in Rome, Romans, is especially theological, often described as the inspiration for most major renewal periods in church history from St. Augustine on. Hebrews, also, is highly doctrinal, but its authorship has been disputed, as its style seems Paul-like, but its language and tone do not quite sound like his.

Paul's Interpretation of the Gospel

Paul expounds on grace and its free provision by Christ, and emphasizes the emancipation of the Christian from "the law" so forcefully that he is sometimes thought to have been at odds with Jesus' emphasis on the fulfillment, rather than the abrogation, of the law. But the apparent contradiction is resolved in Romans 15:13: "May the God of hope fill you with all joy and peace in believing, so that you may abound in hope by the power of the Holy Spirit." Paul consistently teaches that one should be willing to suffer for one's testimony to the Gospel by resisting temptation and not yielding to coercive attempts to force disobedience to Christ (as the Roman persecutors of the early church did, overtly and persistently). But he says it is "all joy and peace" (Romans 15:13) to be freed from sin, and in that freedom there is no "law," no sense of coercion, because the desire to do what Christ requires wells up from the willing heart that he has given second birth.

factum

Paul wrote more books of the New Testament than any other early church leader, though Luke's two books may contain as many words as Paul's. Twelve of the twenty-eight books are his epistles, if Hebrews is not counted. And his epistles are the foundation of most orthodox Christian theological study, as they speak to specific problems congregations faced.

The Epistles to Timothy and Titus

Timothy was a steadfast follower of Paul and a leader in the Thessalonian and Corinthian churches. Being young, he was besieged by teachers of various innovations in the young church's doctrine, and Paul may have written his epistles as much to bolster Timothy's positions as to teach him things he didn't already know. It's a safe assumption that a congregation of that generation would have been willing to settle many disputes with just a word on the subject from an apostle of Paul's stature.

Titus was a gentile convert of Paul who worked with Paul and Barnabas at Antioch and journeyed with them to Jerusalem, where the Twelve agreed that he did not have to be circumcised to become a church leader. Paul used him as his emissary to the church in Corinth and wrote to him about overseeing the church in which he was Paul's personal representative (but not, yet, a bishop himself). In the conclusion of this letter Paul asks Titus to meet him in Nicopolis.

fallacy

It's a myth that Paul himself chose to "take over" the fledgling Jesus movement. Jesus told Ananias in his vision, "Saul has been chosen by me to carry my name to the Gentiles, and kings, and the children of Israel, and I will show him how great things he must suffer for my name's sake."

Pharisee to Martyr

Sources outside the New Testament record Paul's death as an execution under orders from Nero in Rome somewhere between A.D. 64 and 67. From Paul's studying under Gamaliel to be a Pharisee, he became what many believe is the most important founder of the Christian religion other than Jesus Christ himself. Many commentators have expressed the opinion that the fledgling church may have faded out had Paul not come along and solidified its doctrines, reached and supported scores of struggling congregations, and written many of its most closely reasoned documents.

Chapter 10

The Church, the Body of Christ

After Luke's history, spanning roughly the first thirty years of church history, the work of Josephus, who chronicled Roman and Jewish history about the same time the New Testament was being written, is the first external historical documentation of Jesus' life and impact. Ignatius, the bishop of Antioch who was a child in the time of Jesus, and Eusebius, the bishop of Caesarea in Palestine in the time of Constantine the Great, were the next recorders of some aspects of church history.

The Early Jesus Movement

Apart from the New Testament itself, the best historical documentation of Jesus' life and influence, and of the infant church surviving from ancient times, comes from Flavius Josephus, A.D. 37–101, a historian in the courts of several Roman emperors. Though Josephus was Jewish and of a priestly lineage, some Jewish people have considered him suspect because he tried to sustain a middle ground between paganism and orthodox Judaism. But since Josephus' writings date from the same period as the writing of the New Testament, historians generally consider them the most reliable general records of those times. His writings deal widely with Israel, Judah, Palestine, Rome, and (briefly) the new sect called Christians. Josephus' main description of Jesus and the church is this passage, from a section on Herod the Great from his twenty-volume work, Jewish Antiquities (Book XVIII):

> *About this time lived Jesus, a man full of wisdom, if indeed one may call him a man. For he was the doer of incredible things, and the teacher of such as gladly received the truth. He thus attracted to himself many Jewish people and many of the Gentiles. He was the Christ. On the accusation of the leading men of our people, Pilate condemned him to death upon the cross; nevertheless, those who had previously loved him still remained faithful to him. For on the third day he again appeared to them living, just as, in addition to a thousand other marvelous things, prophets sent by God had foretold. And to the present day the race of those who call themselves Christians after him has not ceased.*

Josephus' Jewish Antiquities recapitulates the Torah and tries to tell the whole history of the Jewish people, from which the excerpt just provided about Jesus and the church, is just one paragraph.

It is curious that Josephus wrote so positively about Jesus and the Christians, as Christianity was considered an illegal religion in Rome at the time, and was opposed by the Jewish establishment.

Some scholars believe his positive treatment of Jesus came not from him, but from additions made by later Christian editors.

factum

Josephus wrote in Greek, the language of scholarship in the era of the emperors under whom he served (Vespasian, Titus, Domitian, and Trajan). His works were translated in the common language of the empire at the time, Latin, and were widely read and circulated throughout the churches.

Missions to Pagan Rome and the Gentiles

The Roman Empire of the time of Jesus and the early church dates from the Roman emperor Octavian's reorganization of the Roman Republic in 31 B.C. Octavian added Egypt to the collection of territories, like Greece and what is now called the Middle East, that were part of the previous Roman Republic.

discussion question

What does "fullness of time" mean?
Many biblical commentators have suggested that the Apostle Paul, in referring to his era as "the fullness of time" in which God chose to send the Messiah and establish his church, was suggesting that the Roman Empire was the right place at the right time for the Gospel (see Galatians 4:4 and Hebrews 1:2).

Octavian became Caesar Augustus, the first Roman emperor and the one still in power when Jesus was born, as recorded in

Luke's Gospel: "there went out a decree from Caesar Augustus, that the entire world should be taxed" (Luke 2:1). Augustus was the most powerful world ruler since Alexander the Great, who had conquered the known world (from Europe to India) 300 years earlier.

Like Greece four centuries earlier, Rome was devoutly pagan, with mythological deities renamed and resized to fit the Roman ethos from their earlier Grecian reigns, and a cult of the emperor as the divine lord. Pertinent to the church's growth is a look at the social conditions paganism fostered, which the population increasingly rejected as inhumane or morally defective as the Christian minority grew.

factum

The New Testament did not exist at this early date. Epistles like Paul's, Peter's, and John's, and individual Gospels and Acts appeared one by one and were sent around congregations. Reading aloud from these, as well as Old Testament passages, was part of worship in the early church, which was modeled after worship in the Jewish Temple and synagogues.

The early Christians' charity and compassion for their neighbors commended the Gospel to large segments of the population. One writer observes that when a plague decimated the population of the empire early in the church's history, the only people caring for both their own families and their neighbors, rather than running from the infectious population centers, were the Christians.

Paul's Definition of Apostle

Most of Paul's thirteen epistles begin by establishing his credentials as an apostle, specifically as the apostle to the gentiles (ironically, as he was trained as a Pharisee, an especially strict group among orthodox Jews). Paul claims he became an apostle through the will of God. In his first epistle to the church in Corinth, he explains the importance of his apostolicity most completely: "Am I not an apostle? Am I not free? Have I not seen Jesus Christ our Lord? Are not you my work in the Lord? If I am not an apostle to others, still without doubt I am one to you, for you are the seal of my apostleship in the Lord" (see 1 Corinthians 9:1–2).

Missionary

The word *apostle* means "sent one," a synonym for "missionary." Yet from Jesus' way of selecting and commissioning the Twelve (as discussed in Chapter 5), he was using the word *apostle* as an office apart from and above others in the church. And Paul in Corinthians reinforces this meaning and undoubtedly elevated its understanding to the early church. Moreover, his words, which follow, leave little doubt that he considered the apostolic office the church's highest after the Ascension of its Founder and Head:

"And God has set some in the church, first apostles, secondarily prophets, thirdly teachers, after that miracles, then gifts of healings, helps, governments, diversities of tongues. Are all apostles? Are all prophets? Are all teachers? Are all workers of miracles?" (1 Corinthians 12:28–29).

Apostolicity the Seal

Even Protestants who broke from authoritarian church hierarchies in the Reformation considered being an apostle the seal of God, as referred to earlier in the formula, "Apostolicity was the norm of canonicity," meaning that when the New Testament books were collected in one volume and given the church's seal as the Word of God, those written by apostles or companions of apostles were in, and the many other books of the time that dealt with Jesus and early church leaders were out.

Though the twenty-seven books that now make up the New Testament were all written, according to tradition, by A.D. 100, they were not declared to be the official New Testament until near the end of the fourth century. In one way, it is remarkable it took so long for the church fathers to recognize their New Testament as the Word of God. The New Testament itself constantly cites the Old Testament as the church fathers knew it in its widely circulated version in their generation, The Septuagint (a Greek version of the Old Testament dating from the third century B.C.).

discussion question

Who canonized the New Testament?
In 382, a council in Rome, not an ecumenical one (an ecumenical one would have delegates from all corners of the known church with which its conveners had communion), agreed that the twenty-seven books that are now considered the New Testament were the only ones to be included.

Paul, for example, writes to Timothy: "From childhood you have known the holy scriptures, which are able to make you wise unto salvation through faith in Christ Jesus. All scripture is given by inspiration of God and is profitable for doctrine, for reproof, for correction, for instruction in righteousness in order that the man of God may be perfect, thoroughly equipped to all good works" (see 2 Timothy 3:15–17).

Persecutions Multiply

The success of the church in its first generation, having established congregations from Ethiopia in Africa to India in Asia, and to Rome, Gaul, and Britain in Europe, unfortunately led others to persecute Christians. Some early Christians escaped the persecutions recorded in Acts with the martyrdom of Stephen and the scattering of the Jerusalem flock, only to find themselves persecuted in the pagan Roman empire. The people of the Roman empire initially thought this new Jewish sect curious, then bizarre, then fair game for use in sports spectacles in their coliseums, and, finally, a threat, as their growth in numbers and unflagging loyalty to Christ made Jesus more beloved and worshipped by more people than the current Caesar.

The Book of Martyrs

John Fox (or Foxe), 1517–1587, a brilliant English scholar, and master of biblical languages and history of the early church, compiled the most definitive study of the persecution of Christians under the Caesars between Nero and Constantine (A.D. 54–313). Also containing chapters on later persecutions of Christians, the book is described by James Miller Dodds thus: "After the Bible itself, no book so profoundly influenced early Protestant sentiment as the *Book of Martyrs*. Even in our time it is still a living force."

Fox begins with the crucifixion of Jesus, followed by the martyrdom of Stephen, adding to the details in Acts that Stephen's time of death is believed to have been the Passover following the crucifixion, and that "about 2,000" suffered martyrdom during this persecution in Judea.

The Second Martyr

"The next martyr we meet with, according to St. Luke in the History of the Apostles' Acts," Fox writes, "was James the son of Zebedee, the elder brother of John . . . ten years after the death of Stephen, [James'] martyrdom took place; for no sooner had Herod Agrippa been appointed governor of Judea than . . . he raised a sharp persecution against the Christians . . . by striking at their leaders.

"Thus did the first apostolic martyr cheerfully and resolutely receive that cup, which he had told our Savior he was ready to drink. Timon and Parmenas suffered martyrdom about the same time; one at Philippi and the other in Macedonia" in A.D. 44.

Fifteen Others

Fox records another fifteen apostles and disciples who died as martyrs:

- Philip "suffered martyrdom at Heliopolis, in Phrygia. He was scourged, thrown into prison, and afterwards crucified, A.D. 54."
- Matthew was martyred in Ethiopia, "slain with a halberd in the city of Nadabah, A.D. 60." (A halberd is an ax with a long, pointed spike.)
- James, the Lord's brother and bishop of the church in Jerusalem, "at the age of ninety-four was beaten and stoned . . . and finally had his brains dashed out."
- Matthias, elected to succeed Judas Iscariot, "was stoned at Jerusalem and beheaded."
- Andrew, Simon Peter's brother, "on his arrival at Edessa, was taken and crucified on a cross, the two ends of which were fixed transversely in the ground. Hence the derivation of the term, St. Andrew's Cross."
- Mark, companion of Peter and author of the Gospel bearing his name, "was dragged to pieces by the people of Alexandria . . . ending his life."
- Peter, bishop of Rome, was crucified upside down, because he thought he was unworthy to be crucified in the same way as the Lord.
- Paul died at the hands of Nero's soldiers, who "came and led him out of the city to the place of execution, where he, after making his prayers, gave his neck to the sword."
- Jude, author of the epistle bearing his name and "the brother of James, and commonly called Thaddeus, was crucified at Edessa, A.D. 72."
- Bartholomew, said to have translated the Gospel of Matthew into an Indian language and to have preached it there, was "cruelly beaten and then crucified."

- Thomas, the twin famous for doubting Jesus' resurrection, "preached the Gospel in Parthia and India, where exciting the rage of the pagan priests, he was martyred by being thrust through with a spear."
- Luke, author of the Gospel bearing his name and of Acts, "is supposed to have been hanged on an olive tree, by idolatrous priests of Greece."
- Simon "Zelotes, preached the Gospel in Mauritania, Africa, and even in Britain, in which latter country he was crucified, A.D. 74."
- John was cast into a cauldron of boiling oil, but miraculously escaped without injury. He was the only apostle who escaped a violent death.
- The death of Barnabas, one of the Seventy, erstwhile companion of Paul, "is supposed to have taken place about A.D. 73."

John Fox summarizes the list of the martyrdoms of the church's first generation of leaders with: "notwithstanding all these continual persecutions and horrible punishments, the church daily increased, deeply rooted in the doctrine of the apostles and of men apostolical, and watered plenteously with the blood of saints."

discussion question

Why was John the only apostle allowed a natural death?
The Bible doesn't say, but some relate it to his being Jesus' "beloved disciple." His being entrusted with the care of Jesus' mother from the Cross, some speculate, led to a relatively peaceful life as an earthly reward for that. Ironically, John's brother James was the first apostle who was also a martyr.

The Ten Persecutions
Fox documents ten waves of persecutions in Imperial Rome.

Nero (Roman Emperor A.D. 54–68)
Nero ordered Rome burned, and it was in flames for nine days, killing thousands. Afterward he blamed the fire on the Christians and started persecuting them. "Nero even refined upon cruelty, and contrived all manner of punishments for the Christians that the most infernal imagination could design. In particular, he had some sewed up in skins of wild beasts, and then worried by dogs until they expired; and others dressed in shirts made stiff with wax, fixed to axletrees, and set on fire in his gardens, in order to illuminate them. This persecution was general throughout the whole Roman Empire; but it rather increased than diminished the spirit of Christianity. In the course of it, St. Paul and St. Peter were martyred." Fox mentions that Nero martyred members of "the Seventy," including Erastus, Aristarchus, Trophimus, Joseph Barsabas, and Ananias, bishop of Damascus.

Domitian (Roman Emperor A.D. 81–96)
Fox describes emperor Domitian as "naturally inclined to cruelty," having executed his own brother and some members of the Roman Senate, "some through malice and others to confiscate their estates." Under his rule, many Romans turned in their Christian neighbors for persecution and martyrdom. Paul's coworker Timothy, bishop of Ephesus, was among the many martyrs from this period.

Trajan (Roman Emperor A.D. 98–117)
Fox says that under Trajan's reign, "Pliny the Second, a man learned and famous, seeing the lamentable slaughter of Christians, and moved to pity, wrote to Trajan, certifying him that there were many thousands of them daily put to death, of which none did anything contrary to the Roman laws worthy of persecution."

fallacy

Many have the impression that Protestants deny that Peter was ever the Bishop of Rome, but Fox includes the martyrdom of Ignatius as occurring under Trajan. Himself an early Protestant reformer, Fox affirms the tradition that Ignatius was second bishop of Antioch, after Peter had moved to the same position in Rome.

Trajan was succeeded by Adrian. "About this time Alexander, bishop of Rome, with his two deacons, were martyred; as were Quirinus and Hernes, with their families; Zenon, a Roman nobleman, and about ten thousand other Christians."

But when Adrian died in A.D. 138, he was succeeded by Antoninus Pius, "one of the most amiable monarchs who ever reigned, and who stayed the persecutions against the Christians."

Marcus Aurelius Antoninus (Roman Emperor A.D. 161–180)

Marcus Aurelius instigated the fourth wave of persecutions. Polycarp, bishop of Smyrna and a father of the church, is one of the most famous martyrs of this period. When guards came to arrest him, he prepared a feast for them and asked them for an hour in which to pray, and his prayer was so fervent that "his guards repented that they had been instrumental in taking him. He was, however, carried before the proconsul, condemned, and burnt in the market place." Fox also reports that especially harsh persecution flared up in Lyon, France, at this time.

Severus (Roman Emperor A.D. 193–211)

Though Fox says that Severus was inclined to relieve the persecutions, the people at this time had come to fear the Christians because of the explosive growth in the churches, so they pressured the government to have the older laws against the Christians enforced. "Tertullian," Fox says, "who lived in this age, informs us that if the Christians had collectively withdrawn themselves from the Roman territories, the empire would have been greatly depopulated." Fox lists scores of martyrs in Rome, Africa, and Lyon during this period, including that of the celebrated bishop of Lyon, Irenaeus, a father of the church and author of a book considered a classic in Christian literature, *Against Heresies*.

Maximinus Thrax (Roman Emperor A.D. 235–238)

During this sixth wave of persecution, some of the martyrs were members of the Roman Senate, as the church continued to make inroads in the society and culture of Rome. Fox writes, "During this persecution, raised by Maximinus, numberless Christians were slain without trial, and buried indiscriminately in heaps, sometimes fifty or sixty being cast into a pit together, without the least decency. When the tyrant Maximinus died in A.D. 238, he was succeeded by Gordian, during whose reign, and that of his successor Philip, the church was free from persecution for the space of more than ten years."

Decius (Roman Emperor A.D. 249–251)

Decius, who hated Philip (who was rumored to be a Christian), again turned up the campaign against the church. By now, the pagan temples were being abandoned and churches were bulging, but, Fox reports, factions were beginning to appear in the church as well. The rack, which stretched the bodies of the victims before they were beheaded, was put into use at this time.

Valerian (Roman Emperor A.D. 253–260)

The eighth persecution began in A.D. 257 and continued for three and a half months. "The martyrs that fell in this persecution were innumerable, and their tortures and deaths as various and painful." During this time the government ordered the execution of the clergy in Rome. "In Africa the persecution raged with peculiar violence; many thousands received the crown of martyrdom, among whom" was Cyprian, bishop of Carthage. "At Utica . . . three hundred Christians were, by the orders of the proconsul, placed round a burning limekiln. A pan of coals and incense being prepared, they were commanded either to sacrifice to Jupiter, or to be thrown into the kiln. Unanimously refusing, they bravely jumped into the pit."

Diocletian (Roman Emperor A.D. 284–305)

The ninth wave of persecutions began with Aurelian (Roman Emperor A.D. 270–275), and was continued by Diocletian, his successor. Under Diocletian, the most severe campaign against the Christians began with an imperial order to destroy all churches and their Scriptures. "The persecution became general in all the Roman provinces, particularly in the east; and as it lasted ten years it is impossible to ascertain the numbers martyred, or to enumerate the various modes of martyrdom. Racks, scourges, swords, daggers, crosses, poison, and famine, were made use of . . . to dispatch the Christians."

After the executions "became tiresome," some of the provincial governors petitioned for relief, and the executions were changed to bodily mutilations and other means of making the lives of the Christians miserable. "The persecution of Diocletian began particularly to rage in A.D. 304, when many Christians were put to cruel tortures and the most painful and ignominious deaths."

Constantius and Galerius

Diocletian was succeeded by Constantius (Roman Emperor A.D. 305–306) and Galerius (Roman Emperor A.D. 305–311), who divided the empire into two provinces: eastern (ruled by Galerius) and western (ruled by Constantius). In the east Galerius continued the persecutions just as severely, while in the west Constantius was much more benign and tolerant of the Christians.

Miracles Continue

The church of the imperial era considered the martyrs to be instant saints, inheritors of the Kingdom of Heaven by virtue of earning the martyr's crown. And as the persecutions spread and Christians told their stories everywhere, martyrdom seemed to take on some appeal, as though it were a shortcut to eternal bliss. Whether the persecutions culminated in execution or "only" physical tortures or mutilations, they were means of grace that set the suffering Christians of this era apart from their neighbors, who didn't have to suffer.

Accounts of miracles like the deliverance of St. John the Beloved from a cauldron of oil continued, and most hagiographies (biographies of saints) of the period are full of similar reports. But in most cases the martyrs may have stayed their execution by a miracle, only to be killed soon after by another method, usually beheading.

Fox Recounts Miracles

Fox's *Book of Martyrs* recounts several notable miracles of this type. "Some of the restless northern nations having risen in arms against Rome, the emperor marched to encounter them. He was, however, drawn into an ambuscade, and dreaded the loss of his whole army. Enveloped with mountains, surrounded by enemies, and perishing with thirst, the pagan deities were invoked in vain; when the men belonging to the militine, or thundering legion, who were all Christians, were commanded to call upon their God for help.

"A miraculous deliverance immediately ensued; a prodigious quantity of rain fell, which, being caught by the men, and filling their dykes, afforded a sudden and astonishing relief. It appears that the storm which miraculously flashed in the face of the enemy so intimidated them, that part deserted to the Roman army; the rest were defeated, and the revolted provinces entirely recovered."

Lions in the Coliseum

Another account of miracles is typical of wonders seen when Christians were being executed by lions in the Coliseum:

> "Blandina, on the day when she and her three other champions were first brought into the amphitheater, was suspended on a piece of wood fixed in the ground, and exposed as food for the wild beasts; at which time, by her earnest prayers, she encouraged

others. But none of the wild beasts would touch her, so that she was remanded to prison.

"When she was again brought out for the third and last time, she was accompanied by Ponticus, a youth of fifteen, and the constancy of their faith so enraged the multitude that neither the sex of the one nor the youth of the other were respected, being exposed to all manner of punishments and tortures. Being strengthened by Blandina, he persevered unto death; and she, after enduring all the torments heretofore mentioned, was at length slain with the sword."

Presbyters, Bishops, and Martyrs

As described previously, the office of apostle was considered a conduit of the will and word of God from the heavenly realm to the congregations on earth. The office of apostle was so important that the apostolic church developed the doctrine of apostolic succession as a standard for ordaining bishops.

discussion question

What is a bishop?
Bishops (*episcopos* in Greek), comparable in rank to high priests of the Jewish Temple, were the senior pastors in the church's multiple congregations in metropolitan areas. This is why metropolitan is another name for bishop in Eastern Orthodoxy. *Priest*, an old English rendering of the Greek word *presbyter*, or minister, is comparable to the priests of the Jewish Temple.

The idea of apostolic succession is simple: Catholic and Orthodox teaching claims that all of the bishops were appointed first by an apostle, as in the case of Timothy, who was appointed bishop of the church in Ephesus by Paul. Most metropolitan sees of the ancient church trace their bishops from the beginning of the church, as in Antioch, where, as mentioned earlier, Simon Peter is traditionally recorded as the first, and Ignatius the second, having succeeded in Antioch while Peter was still overseeing the congregations in Rome. After this first generation, all subsequent bishops, to be considered legitimate in the whole church, were appointed by bishops that had been selected by apostles.

The same Ignatius, writing just before his martyrdom in A.D. 107, says "your bishop presides in the place of God." But although the bishops of the ancient churches, including the Anglicans, claim to be successors of the apostles, they do not to claim to have been given the direct communication channels from God the original apostles had. Though they were often godly and holy men, and many of them worked wonders in their time, the bishops of the early church also confessed to being sinners, and less than infallible.

To be a bishop in the pre-Constantinian Roman empire, as Fox's *Book of Martyrs* indicates, was often a sentence of death, especially in Rome, where the first martyr in another wave of persecution mentioned by Fox is often "the bishop of Rome."

Chapter 11

The Jesus of History

The martyrdom of thousands in the first three centuries of the church who were willing to face death rather than burn incense to Caesar or a pagan idol, is the strongest evidence for the truth of the claims of the New Testament. Men who had recently been afraid to be seen with Jesus when he hung on the cross on Golgotha were willing to bet their very lives on the conviction that he was raised from the dead and that his victory had procured their own hope for life beyond death.

Western History Begins with Him

Though there has been effort for some years to redefine the western calendar as divided between B.C.E. (before common era) and C.E. (common era) rather than B.C. (before Christ) and A.D. (Anno Domini, or year of our Lord), there can still be little doubt about the dividing line between the "before" and "after"; it is the approximate birth of Jesus, the God whose incarnation marks, for Christians, the watershed between lost and found, between law and grace, old and new, the world that was perishing and the world being renewed.

The Calendar Is Established

In western civilization, all history is anchored to this event. However, although the general sense is that A.D. 1 was Jesus' first birthday, in the Roman empire of the caesars the calendar was restarted every time a new emperor was installed. Dionysius Exiguus (translated as Dennis the Small) changed the Julian calendar's revision method, under direction of the Latin side of the church, in the sixth century. As this was long before the Gregorian calendar was introduced in 1582, but also long after Christianity was recognized as a religion tolerated by the Roman Empire in 313, Dionysius Exiguus' calendar had to be redacted back into historical records.

discussion question

How accurate were Dionysius Exiguus' calculations?
Later scholarship found that the death of Herod the Great had taken place about five years earlier than Dionysius Exiguus' year 1, so his calendar is about five years off (since Herod was ruling when Jesus was born, according to Matthew's Gospel).

Dionysius Exiguus' calendar reform was the first time Jesus' estimated year of birth was officially fixed as the permanent beginning of the new era, though by that time many historians had already been referring to it as the great watershed of history.

Some Unconvinced

Despite the biblical evidence confirming Jesus and his ministry, some still dispute whether there ever was such a person as Jesus of Nazareth who preached his own advent as the Jewish Messiah. And since the Enlightenment (1700s), there have been theologians who feel the Bible is unreliable, so their duty is to strip off the religious testimony about Jesus and research the historical evidence about him to determine the elusive truth.

The Historical Jesus Debates

Since 1985, much mainstream media coverage of Christianity has focused on the work of the Jesus Seminar, a group of scholars convened by the Westar Institute, a nonprofit "educational institute dedicated to the advancement of religious literacy." The purpose of the Jesus Seminar is described as being to "renew the quest of the historical Jesus and to report the results of its research to more than a handful of gospel specialists."

This purpose assumes that the historical figure of Jesus has eluded popular, and much of scholarly, comprehension. The Institute's intention of making its research known to the general public, rather than just the academic community, is promoted through its public-relations efforts. This PR has helped the Institute gain a PBS network series, much coverage on major television network news programs, where religion is seldom considered news, and exposure in major newspapers and magazines throughout the United States.

Operating Assumption

At its meetings, the Seminar fellows present scholarly papers on aspects of the biblical and historical record on Jesus' words and acts, and vote on whether the papers fit the Jesus that their historical approach has caused them to believe in.

Critics of the Seminar say that "voting on whether something is true or false" may seem silly, but it is one way of producing (or some might say, creating) a consensus across a spectrum of religion experts. And it is in accord with the Enlightenment approach to human governance, which relies on the will of the majority to determine policy on social programs and goals.

Higher Critics

For example, an early theory proposed and widely accepted in academic and liberal religious circles was that the Old Testament books traditionally attributed to Moses (Genesis, Exodus, Leviticus, Numbers, and Deuteronomy) were actually the work of a variety of authors adapting much older oral traditions. Among that movement's higher critics were the following four scholars.

Daniel Schleiermacher

Daniel Ernst Schleiermacher (German, 1768–1834), called the father of modern or liberal theology, taught that Christianity should be viewed as an entirely new religion, not an extension or enlargement of Judaism. He believed that Hellenizing (Greek philosophical) influences on the New Testament books obscured the real Gospel Christ represented.

fallacy

Though "criticism" may suggest conceit or arrogance (to the extent that the critic is judging what is critiqued), "higher criticism" was not applied to modernist biblical text research out of arrogance, but to differentiate it from "lower criticism." Lower criticism examined the minutiae of the texts, getting close to find tiny clues; higher criticism examines the whole picture.

Adolph Harnack

Adolph Harnack (born in Livonia, now Estonia, taught mostly in Germany, 1851–1930), one of the most influential liberal professors of religion, taught that in the Reformation, Protestantism had begun to get rid of the "husks" of Christianity as handed down by Rome to get to the kernel of its true message, and should continue the process of winnowing out more. He believed most of the accretions to "true Christianity" could be traced to the fourth century, when Christianity became an officially tolerated religion of the Empire, and shortly afterward, when it became the favored one, it was syncretized with classical Greek philosophy. Most importantly, he taught that the New Testament (produced, he thought, much later than the church claims) was overlaid with these Greek lines of thought that had to be stripped away to reveal the true or historical Jesus.

Albert Schweitzer

Albert Schweitzer (German, 1875–1965) held that Jesus was an eccentric Jewish Messiah figure and argued in the dissertation for his medical doctorate that Jesus probably would not have been considered mad in the time in which he lived because of the apocalyptic fervor of that generation, but might have been insane by modern psychiatric criteria. The most famous of the higher critics, by virtue of winning the Nobel Peace Prize in 1952 (for promoting the brotherhood of nations), he was a missionary physician in what was then French Equatorial Africa, and famous for a "reverence for life" that included avoidance of accidentally killing insects while walking through the mission compound.

Rudolf Bultmann

Rudolf Karl Bultmann (German, 1884–1976), though a student of Karl Barth (Swiss, 1886–1968), rejected Barth's call to accept the full text of Scripture "including the myth" portions of it. Bultmann called Martin Heidegger's existential philosophy a "profane" version of the biblical view of man, and he is considered the most influential modern demythologizing (or scientific) theologian of his generation.

Modern Approach

Though this approach to study of the Scriptures is relatively recent, one Roman Catholic source from almost a century ago found an early foreshadowing of it in the biblical studies produced by Theodore of Mopsuestia, 350–428, an orthodox bishop of Syrian birth whose "exegetical tendencies [demonstrated] an almost exclusively grammatical-historical and realistic explanation of the text." Though Theodore did not venture unorthodox conclusions, his method presaged that of the post-Enlightenment humanist theologians who wanted to make Bible teaching more compatible with modern science.

Though Roman Catholic, Eastern Orthodox, and evangelical Protestant communions generally reject or discount higher critical hypotheses and premises, they are widely considered to have had decimating impact on Christian numbers throughout Europe (even in Catholic strongholds) and to have greatly weakened most American Protestant denominations, though those seem to have been supplanted by new evangelical replacements that thrive as mainline denominations wither. Chapter 17 will take up this phenomenon in more detail.

The Edict of Milan

Many contemporary liberals in Christian higher education and denominations consider the fourth century the time when the early Jesus movement went wrong, and there has been a strong current of thought among even conservative Protestants (as suggested by Harnack, as mentioned earlier in this chapter) that considers that period one of defection from the original substance of Christianity into a new hierarchical institution.

But it was not until the fourth century that the church began to emerge from generation after generation of persecution and martyrdom from all quarters, and was able to worship above ground in buildings that could openly display Christian signs and symbols.

Praying for Guidance

Eusebius, the church historian, says that Constantine felt his military strength insufficient to ensure victory, so he decided to turn to God, but seeing the "downfall of those who turned to idols," he pondered what God to pray to for help, and concluded that "his father's God" had been faithful when others failed.

When he prayed this God to reveal his identity to him, Eusebius says, "a most marvelous sign appeared to him from heaven, the account of which it might have been hard to believe had it been related by any other person, but the victorious emperor himself long afterwards declared it to the writer of this history. . . . He said that about noon, when the day was already beginning to decline, he saw with his own eyes the trophy of a cross of light in the heavens, above the sun, and bearing the inscription, Conquer by this. At this sight he himself was struck with amazement, and his whole army also. . . witnessed the miracle," (Eusebius' *Life of Constantine*).

The victory that followed this vision in 312 led Constantine to liberate the Christians of the empire in 313 by issuing the Edict of Milan jointly with his co-emperor of the Eastern Tetrarchy, Licinius. In 311, Emperor Galerius had issued an indulgence to the Christians of the empire, stating that if they would pray for him and the empire he would ensure their safety in their homes.

Ensuring Religious Freedom

But the Edict of Milan went considerably farther, the main provisions of which were "to remove all conditions whatsoever, which were . . . formerly given to you officially, concerning the Christians and now any one of these who wishes to observe Christian religion may do so freely and openly." The Edict of Milan also promised to return to anyone property confiscated by the government because they were Christians "without payment or any claim of recompense and without any kind of fraud or deception." Promising the same protections to other religions represented in the empire for the sake of peace, the Edict of Milan also promised the return of "those places in which they were accustomed to assemble, but also other property, namely the churches, belonging to them as a corporation and not as individuals."

Though many later historical references to Constantine question the genuineness of his conversion based, in part, on his deferring baptism until the end of his life, both the Roman Catholic and Eastern Orthodox, following the witness of his contemporary bishop, Eusebius, consider him a genuine believer, and the Orthodox, especially, revere him as a saint. His saint's day is commemorated, along with that of his mother, Helena, who converted after her son and traveled the empire establishing churches and researching sites of biblical significance.

fallacy

Though it has been a widespread opinion that Constantine made Christianity the official religion of the Roman empire, this is not the case. The Edict of Milan made Christianity a legal religion, no longer subject to persecution. It was under Theodosius I (A.D. 379–395) that Christianity was elevated to the preferred religion and paganism was dismantled.

The Edict of Milan has been a model for religious toleration by governments from its issuance by Constantine and Licinius, especially in the republican nations descended from the Roman Empire in most of Europe and the Americas.

Adjusting to Success

Success always extracts its price. Even discounting the claims of some Protestants (which the most influential sixteenth-century Reformers, Luther and Calvin, did not make) that the church had lost its way by the end of the fourth century, many scholars agree that some of its success in becoming the empire's favored religion cost it some of its previous innocence and holy zeal. For example, one bishop is said to have considered Emperor Constantine an "angelic being," who would rule in some capacity alongside or under Jesus in the Kingdom of Heaven.

But that was not an opinion the emperor himself claimed or that most Christians shared. Constantine made reforms that demonstrated the seriousness of his newfound profession of faith in Jesus. For example, for the first time in Roman law the abduction of girls was criminalized; divorce was made more difficult; Sunday was elevated to equality with pagan feasts; and Christian Passover (Easter in English-speaking countries) was declared a holiday. Constantine also encouraged owners of slaves to emancipate them.

Martyrdom Missed

But the loss that was most widely felt throughout the church of the empire, surprisingly to anyone with modern priorities and values, was the loss of martyrdom. By 313, the call to sacrifice one's own life or that of a loved one to the Jesus movement had occurred for nearly three centuries. The "opportunity" to be a victim came to be seen as its own reward, and many instances are recorded of "collateral martyrs" coming forward, when someone they loved was about to be sacrificed, and boldly proclaiming, "I stand with Jesus, too!"

Those devout believers who most regretted the loss of such opportunities became founders of the monastic movement. Following the footsteps and example of John the Baptist, the prophets of the previous covenant, and of Jesus himself, they sought the desert and lives of ascetic struggle. The ascetic life was a substitute form of martyrdom, of sacrificing normal life for the life centered, in every moment, in Christ. It was not ever considered an escape from life, but rather the removal of the distractions of the world that keep believers from staying in constant communion with the Lord.

Monasticism Begins

Post-New Testament monasticism began in the very first generation after the Edict of Milan, in the Egyptian desert by Anthony the Great (Antony in Greek), c. 252–357. His biographer, St. Athanasius, indicates early monasticism was then much different than the way most Western people may encounter it at beautiful, prosperous-looking, campus–like monastery and convent settings. The early monasteries were in poor and bare quarters, often caves in the desert hills, and Spartan huts.

Within a century, accounts were circulated of pilgrims going to visit monks in Egypt and finding communities, sometimes numbering thousands, who had rejected secular life. But despite the comparative austerity of primitive monasticism, Anthony was typical of all Orthodox and Catholic monks from the beginning until now, in renouncing property and a sex life (not to say all succeed, of course). And although Anthony started out alone, and therefore had no vow of obedience to other ascetics, within a short time he had been joined by other faithful who were required to choose obedience to their spiritual father and the rules that his experience in the life produced.

Monasticism is from the Greek *monos*, meaning alone. Though most monastics from early times have worked at tasks from agriculture to copying manuscripts to creating items for sale to the public, their main task is continual prayer, with those employed learning how to pray even while doing other tasks. From the time of Anthony they have also ministered to the faithful by giving spiritual counsel and instruction to pilgrims and the brothers and sisters in their communities less advanced in their journeys.

Early Heresies, Councils, and Defections

A profound price of the church's success was that security from persecution gave greater leeway for controversies to develop that led into factions that developed and that caused the propagation of heresies. But a benefit of having an emperor who professed to believe in Christianity was that the church was able to call an ecumenical (churchwide) council to debate the controversies and propound an orthodox position.

Gnosticism
Gnosticism was already extant when the church began, in the time of the Book of Acts. In general, Gnosticism believes in "secret

knowledge," which is akin to and sometimes overlaps occultism. It is dualistic, meaning it believes in virtually equal good and evil divinities, and that the good divinity rules the spirit, and the evil, the material realm. Orthodox Christianity professes, conversely, that in becoming a man in the form of Jesus Christ, God took on material form, and that in this, all of his creation was blessed and to be appreciated, not rejected. Some claim that despite Gnosticism's early origin, its best-known representation is in Dan Brown's contemporary novel, *The Da Vinci Code.*

factum

Many attribute the early church's development of baptismal creeds (one of which may be an early form of the Apostles' Creed) that summarize basic differences of Christian teaching versus Gnostic teachings, as a factor in the decline of early-church Gnosticism.

Considering all the persecution of Christians in the church's first three centuries, the numbers of Gnostics were diminished by the fourth century, though there have been small groups of them throughout modern history. New Age philosophy, which had a resurgence in the late 1960s and 1970s, is widely considered a revival of Gnosticism, as was the emergence of theosophy (religious philosophy based on mystical insight into the divine), and other attempts to introduce Asian dualism (yin and yang) in western forms earlier in the nineteenth and twentieth centuries.

Though much of Gnostic writing is prescientific, some of its source material has been used in some of the "scientific" or humanist approaches to Christianity advocated by form criticism (analyzing the literary forms of biblical passages) and evolutionary theology.

Montanism

Montanus presented himself as a prophet from Phrygia, a province of Asia Minor (now Turkey) in the mid to late second century. He and his female disciples, prophetesses Prisca (Priscilla in English) and Maximillia, predicted an apocalypse in their time and claimed superiority over the church because they claimed to have received revelations directly from God. The Montanists taught that a convert who fell away from baptismal vows or beliefs could not be restored, though the church taught that repentance was always efficacious for any who lost the light and later returned to it.

Though the bishops of the church at the time counseled their followers to flee from persecution, Montanus and his followers advocated seeking out persecution. Part of the success of the sect was its tendency to exaggerate teachings that many others in the church also held, and eventually to dogmatize about their exaggerations. Orthodox believers in Asia Minor met in councils, and, after examining the Montanist teachings, condemned them and excommunicated their proponents. The sect died out, except in the immediate area of its origin, when its self-styled prophets died.

Manichaeism

Founded by Persian seer Mani in the third century, Manichaeism blended elements of all known religions at the time, especially Gnosticism, Christianity, and Zoroastrianism, under a strongly dualist umbrella. Mani is actually a title (something like "light king"), not a name, the name of the founder having been lost through the general use of his title. Mani claimed to have received a revelation from an angel of God at age twelve, and to have been told to wait another twelve years before launching his public ministry. This he did with this preamble: "As once Buddha came to India, Zoroaster to Persia, and Jesus to the lands of the West, so came in the present time this prophecy through me, the Mani, to the land of Babylonia."

The sect is believed to have practiced forms of baptism and Eucharist. A Catholic source says that it's clear that Mani intended a convergence between his teachings and those of Christianity, which may have been the chief religion in Mesopotamia at the time he lived.

discussion question

What was the Paraclete?
Mani claimed to be the "Paraclete" or "Comforter" Jesus had fore-told. Orthodox Christianity has held, since the time recorded in Luke's Book of Acts, that the Paraclete was the Holy Spirit revealed and received at Pentecost (see Acts 2).

Mani is said to have rejected all of the Old Testament and adapted parts of the New Testament to suit his doctrines. In his dualism he regarded Jesus of Nazareth a fiction, and the true Jesus to be a personification of light. Like Gnosticism, Manichaeism taught that salvation comes through intellectual knowledge, and that ignorance is sin.

The sect spread rapidly beyond Babylon (or Mesopotamia) to India and other territories east of Persia, and throughout the Roman Empire, despite the persecution of its followers. In the Christian world, its strongest following was in Egypt, though it also had strong followings in Italy and seems to have penetrated to southern France, to the west of Rome, and to Bulgaria in the east.

Augustine (A.D. 354–430), the seminal theologian of the early church era among Roman Catholics and Protestants, and the bishop of Hippo on the North African coast (now Algeria), wrote against the Manicheans and described the extent of their heretical influence.

Donatism

After the persecutions of Emperor Diocletian described earlier, Donatus, a bishop of Carthage in North Africa (now Tunisia), refused to reinstate those who had renounced their baptisms to avoid martyrdom. He and other bishops he influenced said the sacraments of such "apostates" were invalid. He refused priests and bishops permission to serve sacraments in their sees, and also forbade their parishioners to receive sacraments from such when traveling.

A council in Arles, France, called by Emperor Constantine in 314 (just a year after his Edict of Milan) condemned the Donatists' refusal to forgive the repentant former apostates.

The Donatists refused to accept the council's decision and seceded from the rest of the church. Most of the churches in North Africa sided with the Donatists until Augustine's writing against the heresy won the majority back.

Arianism

The most important heresy and controversy in the early church was Arianism, as it forced the church to define the Trinity and hold its first Ecumenical Council. Arius (256–336), a priest in Alexandria, Egypt, taught that Christ, though divine, was not coeternal with God the Father, and was therefore inferior to him. His teaching was originally offered as an alternative to a less widespread heresy, Sabellianism or modalism, which held that the three persons of the Trinity were merely different modes of God's appearing or interacting, or roles he was using with his creation.

Arianism became popular in the church, and for some time it seemed to have won more support than the Trinitarians (who believed that the Father, Son, and Holy Ghost of the Trinity were equal parts of one Godhead), whose cause was most eloquently argued by Athanasius, also an Alexandrian, ordained a priest a little after Arius. Emperor Constantine called the first Ecumenical Council of the church in Nicea, just outside Constantinople, in 325 to settle the controversy. Athanasius accompanied Alexander, the bishop of Alexandria, a Trinitarian and the council's president, to the Council, and Athanasius emerged as the most persuasive speaker for the Trinitarian side.

The Council adopted Athanasius' position, and issued the original form of the Nicene Creed to define it. Though the Council had spoken, Arius' defenders continued campaigning against the Trinitarian position and persuaded Constantine to grant amnesty to the Arians who had been exiled after the Council and, instead, to exile Athanasius. By A.D. 360, another debate had broken out over the divinity of the Holy Spirit. After Constantine's death in 337, his successors were less interested in Christianity than he had been, until the succession of Theodosius I the Great in 378. He convened the second Ecumenical Council in Constantinople in 381 to finally settle the Arian/Trinitarian debates and to ratify the first Ecumenical Council.

Pelagianism

Pelagius, a monk who lived in Rome in the fifth century, taught that Adam's sin was not transferred to all human beings, and that salvation through works (in other words, keeping of the Old Testament Law) was possible without the work of Christ. Little is known about Pelagius, but Augustine said he lived a long time in Rome before he was excommunicated and exiled. Several regional church councils condemned his teachings, and the Ecumenical Council of Epheus ratified those condemnations in 431.

factum

Semipelagianism (a later movement in churches not condemned in church councils) teaches that human beings can seek God by their own efforts without prevenient (preparatory or leading) grace from God.

Nestorianism

Nestor, appointed patriarch of Constantinople by Theodosius II in 428, opposed the use of the term *Theotokos* to describe Mary, the Mother of Jesus. *Theotokos* is Greek, meaning "God-bearer," and is usually rendered as "Mother of God" in English. Nestor's point was that while God was the Father of Jesus' divinity, Mary was the mother of only his humanity. This idea, however, separates Jesus into two distinct persons, which orthodox Christianity rejects. The Council of Ephesus was called in 431 to settle the controversy. The Council ruled that the Nicene Creed presupposes Mary's motherhood of both the divine and human natures (not persons) of Jesus by affirming that no separation is possible between his godhead and his manhood.

Division of the Roman Empire

Emperor Diocletian, who ruled from A.D. 284 to 305, divided the administration of Rome into four areas ruled by four caesars. Though the scheme was never completely successful because of rivalries among the caesars, it led to the division of the empire into two major and eventually permanent divisions. When Constantine gained control of the eastern major region (as well as the western one, which he originally ruled), he moved his capital from Rome to his own new city in the east, Byzantium, renamed Constantinople, which was on the strait between the Black Sea and the Sea of Marmara that demarks the border between Europe and Asia. Constantinople was, at that time, in the territory of ancient Greece, and is now in Turkey.

fallacy

Though many social commentators have claimed that civilizations seldom survive three or four centuries (the approximate lifespan of ancient Greece and of the western Roman Empire), historians sympathetic to the eastern Roman Empire contend that it actually improved after four centuries and continued intact for fully a thousand years. The eastern Roman Empire and its churches had no "dark ages."

Under Theodosius I, who ascended Constantine's throne after him, the division became officially permanent. But while the west, administered from Rome, got weaker and was overrun by Germanic tribes, the eastern empire, which always called itself "the Roman empire" but which those in Rome have called "the Byzantine Empire," thrived and continued to be generally stable for a millennium after Constantine.

Greek became the language of the eastern empire, with Latin continuing as the official tongue in the west. Eventually, this division led to a division of the Catholic Church, between western (Latin) under the supreme magisterium of the bishop of Rome, and eastern (Greek) Christendom that continued under a pluralism of bishops of equal power throughout the far-flung empire.

The Great Schism

The secession of the North African churches over their Donatism was a minor and relatively short-lived schism in the catholic and apostolic churches. A more serious and thus-far permanent schism, however, was the defection of the Coptic Orthodox and the Armenian Apostolic Church (referred to as the "Oriental Orthodox" churches) after the Ecumenical Council of Chalcedon, which condemned monophysitism.

factum

Monophysitism refers to belief in only one nature in Jesus, which both Armenian and Coptic churches don't hold. Committees of the Oriental and Eastern Orthodox churches have reached agreement that the schism between them is based on semantic rather than substantive issues, though they have failed to re-enter into communion.

Considered by the churches more tragic, because of the hundreds of millions of believers it involves, is the Great Schism between the Latin churches (Roman Catholic) under the bishop of Rome, and the Greek churches (Eastern Orthodox), whose ecumenical patriarch (archbishop) is in Constantinople (now officially Istanbul). Eastern Orthodoxy includes the Greek and Russian Orthodox, and many other autonomous and national churches like the Romanian, Ukrainian, Serbian, Antiochian, Bulgarian, and Carpatho-Russian Orthodox.

The Great Schism culminated with the serving of excommunication letters between the pope of Rome and the ecumenical patriarch in 1054, and has been exacerbated by doctrinal disputes such as the *filioque* (Roman Catholic doctrine that states the Holy Ghost proceeds from the Son as well as from the Father) and papal authority. Most historians say that it had been in the making for centuries, from the time the Roman Empire was divided, and most educated people on both sides no longer spoke both official languages.

Since the Schism, the Latin Crusaders' sacking of Constantinople in 1204 and certain innovations in Catholic dogma have exacerbated the conflict. In the other direction, Pope John Paul II apologized for the atrocity of the Crusaders, and both sides have rescinded their excommunications of the other. The main doctrinal issues between the communions now are papal authority, the filioque, the immaculate conception of Mary, purgatory, and indulgences.

The Reformation

The third significant schism was the breaking away of the evangelical and reformed churches under Luther and Calvin in the sixteenth century. There is a case for saying the Reformation brought long-overdue corrections and renewal, both in the churches that originated from it and, by reacting to it (as in the Council of Trent, 1545–1563, the major event in what is called the Counter-Reformation), in the Roman Catholic communion. A more complete account of the roots of the Reformation is found in Chapter 13.

The leaders of the Reformation—Luther, Calvin, Zwingli, Cranmer, and others—set out to reform the one Catholic Church they knew, not to create new churches, or what came to be called denominations. But they set in motion a process that led to that end, and continues to produce new denominations to fit every taste in doctrine, liturgy, polity, and ecclesiology.

Chapter 12

Salvation

More than 175 passages in the New Testament refer to salvation, being saved, and to Jesus as the Savior. Even the Old Testament may be called a testament of salvation, because its dominant themes are the deliverance (salvation) of Israel and specific Israelites from various captivities and the anticipation of the Messiah. But what is meant in the New Testament by salvation and, specifically, the salvation that Jesus came to bring and that the churches offer?

What Must I Do to Be Saved?

"'What must I do to be saved?' the jailer of Phillipi asked his inmates Paul the Apostle and Silas (Acts 16:30). "'Believe on the Lord Jesus Christ,'" Paul and Silas answered, "'and you and your whole household will be saved.' And they spoke to him and to all in his house the word of the Lord, and the same hour of the night the jailer washed the wounds of Paul's and Silas' scourging. And immediately he and all his household were baptized."

Paul's Definition of Salvation

Paul's take on what salvation means is deliverance from sin, both from the consequences, or the "wages of sin," which is death (Romans 6:23), and from the power or attraction of sin over the person saved. Salvation from sin was the most holy act in the Jewish calendar, when people asked forgiveness of God at Yom Kippur, the Day of Atonement. As Charles Haddon Spurgeon, probably the most highly esteemed Baptist preacher in history, said, salvation includes "the delivery of our soul from all those propensities to evil which now so strongly predominate in us."

Not an Evangelical Franchise

"Being saved" is well known to be a priority in the evangelical churches like Spurgeon's Baptists, the Wesleyans (evangelical Methodists, Holiness, and Pentecostal denominations), and many other denominations and nondenominational churches, but many Protestants are unaware of the high priority the need for salvation also has in Catholic, Orthodox, traditional Anglo-Catholic (Church of England), and Lutheran teaching, prayers, Scripture readings, and liturgies. Catholics are taught to pray the prayer of contrition every day. It says:

> O my God, I am heartily sorry for having offended Thee, and I detest all my sins, because I dread the loss of heaven and the pains of hell; but most of all because they offend Thee, my God, Who are all good and deserving of all my love. I firmly resolve, with the help of Thy grace, to confess my sins, to do penance, and to amend my life. Amen.

The Orthodox ask salvation from their sins in the Trisagion (thrice holy) prayers that are part of both the morning and evening prayers all faithful make, and which also are part of every Orthodox worship service (as excerpted here):

Glory to you O Lord, glory to you. O heavenly King, O Comforter, the Spirit of Truth, who are in all places and fill all things, Treasury of good things and the Giver of life, come and abide in us, cleanse us from every stain, and save our souls, O Good One.

There are differences in the interpretations by various Christian communions of how salvation is effected, but the goal of salvation, and salvation's being a consequence of faith through grace are generally agreed on.

Teachings on salvation are complicated by questions like these:

- Is salvation a once-and-for-all "event," or a gradual transformation?
- What conditions, if any, are attached to being saved or receiving salvation?
- Can salvation be lost?
- What must those "saved" do after receiving salvation to keep it?
- Are "the saved" incapable of sinning again?
- Can a person be "saved," lost again, and saved again? (And, perhaps, again and again?)
- Can a person be baptized more than once?

Such questions and the way they are answered have launched numerous denominations and factions within Christendom, ever since the Donatist heresy arose (see Chapter 11).

Believing: *Sola Fide*

"Only believe, only believe," says an old evangelistic hymn by Paul Rader. Then the hymn paraphrases the angel's words to Mary prior to Jesus' conception, "with God nothing shall be impossible." The hymn's words reflect the five principles, or the "five solas" of the Protestant Reformation: Sola Scriptura, Solus Christus, Sola Gratia, Sola Fide, and Soli Deo Gloria; which translate to: Only Scripture, Only Christ, Only Grace, Only Faith, and Glory Only to God.

Sola Fide, only faith, is a core teaching that all Protestants traditionally affirm. The reformers, stung by corruption in the church (especially in the sale of indulgences), used this teaching to highlight that the only thing efficacious for salvation is faith. Works of the law, whether of the Old Testament or the rules of the church, are not enough.

factum

Indulgences are release from sin in return for donations to the Catholic Church. In Martin Luther's time (1483–1546), the Catholic Church sold indulgences to raise funds for the building of St. Peter's Basilica in Rome. Indulgences are not permissions to sin, though many have thought they are. Though no longer technically sold, indulgences are still given, especially to large donors to Catholic institutions.

The proponents of Sola Fide didn't want to discount works of the law (being moral, for example), or imply that obedience to Christ (a form of keeping the law) wasn't necessary, but the law was not the means of salvation. Again, faith through grace from God (the "free gift," to use a favorite redundancy of evangelists) is the sole efficacious way of salvation.

Fundamentals Only

Many preachers and teachers have, however, taught that everything beyond "only faith" can actually get in the way of salvation.

At this point they part company with most Catholics, Orthodox, and more traditional Protestants, including most contemporary evangelicals.

Many call this emphasis on belief "fundamentalism," which means, in this case, "fundamentals only." Jesus certainly taught much more than "only believe," as did the apostles and the church from its beginning, though believing is the necessary first step toward getting on the way to salvation.

Once Saved, Always Saved

Many Protestants, like Luther, Calvin, and Zwingli especially, have taught that salvation is a once-and-for-all event (some calling it "once saved, always saved" or "the security of the believers"). However, even most of the people who believe salvation is a one-time event have allowed that a person can be misled to think he or she has been saved, only to fall back into sin again later (or seem to fall back, if the person was never saved in the first place) and, in some cases, be saved again, this time for real.

Catholics, Orthodox, and Wesleyans (followers of the teachings of the great Protestant revivalist John Wesley), emphasizing Jesus' repeated words, "he who endures to the end shall be saved," generally teach that calling oneself saved is presumptuous. Orthodox writers like to put it, "I have been saved; I am being saved, and, God willing, I will be saved," referring to the need to "endure," or, as Calvin famously rendered that word, "persevere."

Sacraments

The Christian sacraments are the (traditionally seven) rites instituted by Jesus and mentioned in the New Testament that confer sanctifying grace on the faithful. The seven sacraments of Catholicism are baptism, confirmation, the Eucharist, penance and restoration, anointing of the sick, holy orders (ordination to the ministry), and matrimony. The Eastern Orthodox Church has the same seven, though some of them are defined slightly differently, and the Eastern Church also teaches that anything exhibiting the presence of God (described in the Trisagion Prayer as being "in all places and filling all things") can be considered sacramental, or holy.

Though fundamentalist Protestants generally reject the notion of sacraments, one of the most famous fundamentalists, Dr. Bob Jones, is often quoted as having preached, "all ground is holy ground," which raises the question whether fundamentalist objections to "sacraments" are mainly semantic, since most Baptists and many other "Bible" church members refer to communion and baptism not as "sacraments" but as "ordinances."

Overlaps and Differences

What Catholics call confirmation, the Orthodox call chrismation, and what Catholics refer to as penance and restoration is referred to in Orthodoxy as repentance. Protestants, understandably, with their hundreds (some say their tens of thousands) of denominations, have many divergent views on sacraments. Virtually all practice baptism, and communion or the Eucharist (which means "thanksgiving"), also called "the Lord's Supper."

symbolism

Symbols are said to mean something different in Eastern and Western perception. In the Eastern Churches, symbols are not figurative but are actually essential to the thing symbolized. So, for example, Orthodox believers consider Christ the true symbol of God, while actually being God himself. Western believers think of symbols of Christ as "tokens" or "suggestive" ornaments, like the *Ichthus* (fish) symbol.

In a recent book of dialogues between Orthodox and Reformed (Calvinist) theologians, the Reformed writer agreed that the two communions could find agreement on the Eucharist and baptism. Calvin (the founding father of the Reformed and Presbyterian Churches) spoke of the sacraments of communion and baptism as "means of grace." Lutherans, likewise, are in virtual agreement with Catholics and Orthodox about the two main sacraments. Neither Lutherans nor the Orthodox use the Catholic term "transubstantiation" for the miraculous change of the bread and wine into the body and blood of Christ, but neither do either of them consider the term a stumbling block.

Sacraments Not Enough

Though earlier teachings may have been widely interpreted as holding that Catholics, the Orthodox, or both believe the sacraments are efficacious for salvation by themselves, the teachings of both communions now clearly state that without underlying faith on the part of the recipients, the sacraments do nothing in terms of achieving salvation. On the other hand, in virtually all of the sacramental liturgies, the salvific (or saving) work of Jesus Christ is so plainly presented that anyone hearing and sincerely believing the words could find saving faith through them.

The use of the word *ordinance* rather than *sacrament* by some evangelicals is sometimes explained as stemming from their rejection of any "means" of grace. A look at some of their documents on the issue shows that they take communion because Jesus mandated it, not because it does them any good in terms of achieving salvation. Though they may call the communion a "symbol," they distance themselves from the use of that word as understood in more traditional churches.

Not Always Literalists

Though evangelicals usually claim to take the Scriptures literally, they sometimes reject a literal (and usually even a spiritual) interpretation of Jesus' words, as when he instituted communion at the Last Supper, he said, "this is my body, this is my blood." They likewise do not take literally "baptism for the remission of sins" in Mark 1:4 and Acts 2:38, or Acts 22:16, which describes baptism as "washing away your sins." The best explanation of communion they have is that it "memorializes" Jesus' shedding his blood and having his body broken for those who believe in him.

factum

In much of the evangelical tradition, baptism is performed primarily for a "testimony" to the world that the believer (either an adult or a youth having achieved the "age of accountability") has come to saving faith in Christ and therefore wants to follow him into this symbolic act (some shudder at calling it either a "rite" or a "ritual").

But across the Protestant spectrum, some consider baptism a sacrament, some see it as the very means of salvation (as in "baptismal regeneration"), and many see it as merely following orders. Many (Lutherans, Anglicans, Presbyterians, Methodists) practice infant baptism, as do Catholics and the Orthodox. All of the infant-baptizing Protestants administer the water by sprinkling or pouring, as Catholics do. The Orthodox, uniquely, immerse infants, and they also immerse any adults converting who have not previously been baptized or have been baptized in a non-Trinitarian church (one that does not adhere to the doctrine of the Trinity).

Works of Righteousness

Paul writes to Titus, "Not by works of righteousness that we have done, but according to his mercy he saved us by the washing of regeneration and by the renewing of the Holy Spirit" (Titus 3:5). Many consider this text a summary of Paul's theology: not by works, but by grace, are we saved. Here "works" is defined as keeping the laws of the Old Testament, and sometimes it is interpreted in preaching as also referring to good works like social programs, alms-giving, and standing up for justice.

One can hardly read Paul without concluding that salvation comes not by works, but, conversely, that works can even get in the way of what is needed for salvation by giving false hope to those doing and depending on their works. Paul's Gospel is bad news to those who think their good deeds will get them into heaven. "All our righteousness is as filthy rags," Isaiah the prophet says, as though anticipating Paul (Isaiah 64:6).

Faith Without Works Is Dead

Nevertheless, James writes, "faith without works is dead" (James 2:17 and 20). Indeed, James adds, "Yes, a man may say, 'you have faith and I have works; show me your faith without your works and I will show you my faith by my works'" (2:18) and even, "a man is justified by works, and not by faith only." Having already written in the margin of his Bible the word *alone* next to Paul's "a man is justified by faith without the deeds of the law," (Romans 3:28, compare Romans 5:1 and Galatians 3:24) Martin Luther was sorely vexed by James's epistle and labeled it "an epistle of straw" or "a right strawy epistle," depending on how you translate his German.

James explains that Abraham demonstrated his faith by taking Isaac to the mountain to sacrifice him to God as God had ordered, his work thus proving his faith. All of James's "works" fall under obedience to God and his Christ. The apostolic church has traditionally advocated works or, as discussed in Chapter 10, "violence," or force, to "take" the Kingdom of God. This work—*ascesis*—is prayer, bolstered by fasting and more prayer, known as keeping vigil or praying all through the night. Fasting is also accompanied by alms-giving or giving help to the poor, but the alms-giving without the faith demonstrated in prayer with fasting is not advocated as a good work.

Sanctification or Divinization

Catholics, traditional Protestants, and the Orthodox alike profess that salvation is primarily a relationship with God through Christ. Though there is much tongue-wagging about "a personal relationship with Jesus," a formula most often uttered by American evangelicals, no genuine Christian prayer life exists without connecting in prayer with God through the God-man, Jesus Christ, the only mediator between Creator and created, Eternal and temporal, the Sinless and the sinful.

discussion question

What is *intercession*?
Though Catholics and the Orthodox refer to saints as "interceding for us," they mean nothing more by that intercession than an evangelical means when calling the prayer circle to ask it to "intercede with God on our behalf."

Divine Nature

Athanasius, the saint described in Chapter 11 as leading the opposition to the heresy of Arianism, wrote that God "gave himself to us through his Spirit. By the participation of the Spirit, we become communicants in the divine nature. . . . For this reason, those in whom the Spirit dwells are divinized." Athanasius is referring to the Apostle Peter's second epistle: "By his divine power [he] has given to us all things needed for life and godliness, through the knowledge of him who has called us to glory and virtue, by which are given to us very great and precious promises that by these you may be participants in the divine nature, having escaped the corrupting lusts of the world" (see 2 Peter 1:3, 4).

Divinization, as Athanasius called it, is more commonly known as *theosis*. Theosis is the goal of salvation in Orthodoxy, and is also taught but not widely known in Catholicism. It means that the human nature is intended to be united with the divine nature in heaven, through what Protestants call sanctification and the Orthodox call theoria, the process of becoming holy.

Theosis

The most famous summary of the doctrine, also from Athanasius, is, "The Son of God became man that we might become God." Orthodox theologians say that theosis takes believers in Christ beyond the perfection of Adam and Eve before the Fall and on to what Adam and Eve were intended to attain, had they obeyed God.

Several passages in the Old Testament refer to the judges of Israel as "gods": "You shall not revile the gods nor curse the ruler of your people" (Exodus 22:28); "God stands in the congregation of the mighty; he judges among the gods. . . . I have said, 'You are gods; and all of you are children of the most High. But you shall die like men, and fall like one of the princes,'" (Psalms 82:1, 6–7). Jesus refers to these passages when he says, "Is it not written in your law, I said, 'You are gods?'" (John 10:34).

Immortal Creatures

C. S. Lewis affirmed this aspect of salvation in *Mere Christianity* when he said any of us can become "immortal creatures" whom God calls "gods." In all cases, this "divinization" is distinct from pantheism and far eastern religions, which believe that eventually we become one with the totality of the universe, or "god." Nor is it similar to "progressive divinization" as taught in Mormonism, in which human beings become part of the godhead. But as "immortal creatures," we will be Lords over worlds Christ has gone ahead to the Kingdom of Heaven to prepare for us.

The Great Awakenings

The Reformation may be seen as a Christian adaptation to the Renaissance and the introduction of Renaissance humanism into the ekklesia, to use a term religion writers occasionally employ to refer to "the church" in its essence, without images of an organized superstructure.

The Methodist Movement

The Enlightenment is about the dawn of the modern scientific age, but its radical effect on common Europeans and especially the American colonists, and on western Christendom, was its experiments in popular self-government. The new ideas in human democracy caught fire, and a new fervor broke out in American intellectual, pastor, and theologian Jonathan Edwards, in England's John and Charles Wesley, who started the movement called Methodism, and in their colleague John Whitfield. Methodism brought revivals in England, Wales, and, through the travels of the Wesleys and Whitfield to America, to the colonies that were moving toward a revolution.

Methodism was an even bigger success in America, and the Great Awakening also awoke a small dormant movement called the Baptists, who were influenced a little by Europe's and Pennsylvania's Anabaptists (from whom they took their approach to baptism), and much more by the Congregational and Presbyterian Calvinists of New England and New Jersey (from whom they adopted most of their theology and social theory).

Baptists Multiply

The Baptists soon eclipsed even the Methodists. They quickly seemed to be the form of Protestantism best suited by the fledgling American people, and they have remained so ever since, by this generation outnumbering all of the other American Protestant denominations combined. Except for Princeton's Jonathan Edwards, the Great Awakening seemed to affect the grassroots population both widely and deeply, but the intelligentsia very little. After the creation of the Baptists and Methodists (both of which communions grew by millions of members), the movement's main innovation was the Sunday school.

Starting in the 1730s, the Great Awakening was a force through the American Revolution, and continued being one into the nineteenth century. And no sooner had its strength begun to wane than a Second Great Awakening began in the 1820s.

The Second Great Awakening

Though the first Great Awakening seemed sociologically oriented to the frontier and the widespread rural population of the late colonial and Revolutionary periods, the second was most influential in New England (where it was a reaction to deism and Unitarianism), and in Western New York, which was the home of the Chautauqua Campgrounds that spawned a nationwide revival camp meeting movement. The Second Great Awakening also heavily influenced religious life in Appalachia, where a new burgeoning Protestant movement began that produced the Christian Churches and Disciples of Christ, which became one of the country's largest denominations.

factum

The Latter Day Saints, or Mormons, started in the same period as the Second Great Awakening. Like the founders of the Disciples and Churches of Christ, their founders thought they provided an alternative to the proliferation of denominations, and didn't want to be thought of as spawning new ones. The Mormons do not accept orthodox Christian creeds.

The Third Great Awakening

A third Great Awakening, starting in the 1880s, seemed oriented to the burgeoning cities of the United States, especially Chicago. It brought another wave of fervor across the continent, though it was strongest among women and helped launch the suffrage and prohibition movements. This revival period was the time of evangelist Billy Sunday and political leader William Jennings Bryan.

The Salvation Army, brought to the United States from England, and the YMCA, also an import from England, were taking hold in the cities with the support of Dwight L. Moody (1837–1899), Billy Sunday (1862–1935), and other evangelicals. Moody bridged the gap between the Second and Third Great Awakenings and made a lasting impact in New England and especially Chicago, where the Moody Bible Institute, Moody Press, and Moody Broadcasting continue to flourish.

Born Again

Born again as a term for salvation seems to have entered the Christian lexicon through the Wesleyan revivals in the United States, and the term underwent permutations with each wave of revival. For example, Wesley called it the "new birth." A 1911 encyclopedia of Catholicism defines baptism as "the sacrament by which we are born again of water and the Holy Ghost, that is, by which we receive in a new and spiritual life, the dignity of adoption as sons of God and heirs of God's kingdom."

discussion question

Who was Billy Sunday?
Billy Sunday was famous as a baseball player, and was a heavy drinker when he attended a revival meeting at Chicago's Pacific Garden Mission. After attending several times, he was "born again" during the Third Awakening. His previous affinity for alcohol may have contributed to his becoming a major force behind Prohibition.

Probably the greatest recognition for the "born again" name for salvation occurred in the 1970s, when a revival called the Jesus Movement or Jesus People Movement swept American campuses and other youth-culture enclaves, and when Jimmy Carter, while running successfully for President, declared that he was a born again Christian. In 1976, Charles W. Colson, former chief counsel in the Nixon White House and a convert after being indicted on charges related to Watergate, wrote a book entitled *Born Again*. The next year Billy Graham published *How to Be Born Again*.

Chapter 13

Christian Culture

In Revelation, John describes a vision of a city of gold, "And the city had no need of the sun or of the moon to shine in it, for the glory of God lit it and the Lamb is the light of it." Then John continues: "The nations of those who are saved shall walk in the light of the Lamb and the kings of the earth will bring their glory and honor to it." John is trying to show that believing in and following Jesus changes every aspect of life.

Biblical Culture

The Old Testament illustrates that Israel is—and has been since Abraham received the covenant establishing it—a culture, a social matrix of transmitted values, behaviors, beliefs, and institutions. In certain times and under certain conditions, Israel has also been a religion and a nation, but even when it was only one or neither of those, and through all the dispersions of the Jewish people, Israel has always been a culture.

Over the millennia, some of the Jewish people became atheists, agnostics, or secular humanists, but Jewish culture survived and continues to endure. Though life in Jesus is much more than culture and religion, the church has tried to instill a similar sense of culture and the place religion plays in it.

Further consideration of the Old Testament leads readers to conclude that Jewish culture was important to God. He purposely established it, and intended its continuation for his purposes of having a testimony among the nations of the world, and, pre-eminently, as a vehicle or medium through which to give the world his Son, its Savior. His covenants were everlasting, and their lasting depended on their being handed down through a stable social milieu, a culture.

Culture Matters

As Jesus said, God, who created Adam from the dust, could have raised up descendants of Abraham from the stones (Matthew 3:9, Luke 3:8); he could have sent his son into any society and historical setting, but he did not. He sent him to these people, this time, this place. Culture mattered, as the recitation of Joseph's genealogy in Luke's and Matthew's Gospels, along with Matthew's constant citation of Old Testament prophecies to Israel, underscores. This culture was not just accidental, but the result of a mandate God gave to Israel's ancestors, as recorded in Genesis 1:26–28.

Some find fault with the fourth century developments in the Roman Empire—Constantine's conversion and his participation in the church, and his attempt to accommodate Jesus' teachings to secular government. Culture is messy, and many people think religion should not be messy, so they try to divorce religion from culture and keep religion internal. Or, as the radical Anabaptists (the Amish) do, they keep religion within the extended family and their likeminded neighbors, and allow only as much interaction with "the world" as is necessary for survival.

discussion question

Who are the Anabaptists?
Anabaptists (the Greek name means "rebaptizers") is the generic name for the descendents of the "radical Reformation" in sixteenth century Holland and Germany. Their most visible branch is the Amish, who eschew modern conveniences, but other Pennsylvania Dutch (actually "Deutsch," meaning German) are part of this pacifist movement, including the Mennonites, the Church of the Brethren, and the (German-descended) Brethren Churches.

But such separatists are not the only Christians who eschew participation in the larger culture. Many others reject the dominion role described in Genesis 1:26–28 ("and let them have dominion . . . over all the earth") and which is confirmed by example through Israel throughout the Old Testament and in the testimony of the Fathers of the Church in its first three centuries.

The Christian Empire
The Roman Empire continued in the east for more than a millennium after Constantine, mindful of its Christian mandate. Sometimes that "Christian mind" was stronger, at other times weaker, but it was never absent. In 1453, its last bastion of the Roman Empire fell to the Muslim Ottomans after centuries of being threatened and whittled down from its original domain of Asia Minor, the Middle East, and Northern Africa to a territorial remnant around Constantinople.

This culturally Christian empire had extended its influence into the Balkans and Russia through missionary outreach, and the Russian empire that eventually emerged proudly proclaimed itself the Christian successor of Constantine's Rome. But Edward Gibbon (1737–1794), author of *The History of the Decline and Fall of the Roman Empire*, taking clues from the church in Rome and European xenophobia about Byzantium, dismissed the Eastern Empire as a thousand years of decline, a notion that still influences European attitudes toward followers of Jesus taking leadership in human cultures.

Church Traditions

Jewish culture and its products were always tied to the religion, transmitted through the Law and the covenants that the ethnic nation had from and with God. The Temple and synagogues, feasts, fasts, dietary restrictions and proscriptions, attachment to the "land of promise," and attitudes toward travel and pilgrimage all were part of the religion.

Likewise, Catholic countries exhibit cultural distinctiveness, reflecting national histories, myths, and achievements. Protestant countries tend to reflect fewer accoutrements of religion, as the Reformation stripped away most of the saints and their feast days and the attendant myths, leaving different kinds of art and literature.

Orthodox Art

Orthodox countries also reflect variations in their values and emphases compared with Latin-formed cultures. For example, art in the Catholic west tends toward lushness, realism, passion, and sensuality, whereas Orthodox artists try to reflect the Orthodox emphasis on dispassion, holiness, ascesis, and spiritual truths. Western critics often call Orthodox art "primitive," to which the Orthodox reply that there's a message behind their methods in art. It's not that they haven't noticed the third dimension and how to paint using perspective, for example; they have generally chosen not to.

Catholic Magisteria

Perhaps the biggest influence church traditions have on national and regional cultures, however, stems more from assumptions and intangible values of the respective churches than their outward policies and practices. For example, the magisterial role of the pope and bishops of the Catholic Church tends to give it a more authoritarian demeanor than the Orthodox and Protestant Churches, who have nothing quite like it.

Though *magisterial* means only "teaching," in Catholicism the interpretation of Scriptures is the sole province of the magisterium (the authority of the Catholic Church to teach religious truth). The magisterium's interpretation is capable of being considered infallible, a claim that the Orthodox would reserve only for ecumenical councils, and even then a condition of finality is the acceptance of Council findings by the laity of the church at large.

Christian Art and Science

A worldview based on Jesus and his teachings, and the mandate to adapt the religion to the cultural environment as necessary, have influenced the arts and scientific research and discovery since the early church. One of the divergences early Christians took from their Jewish predecessors was opening their culture for representational depictions in art, whereas Jewish orthodoxy said all images violated the commandment to avoid graven images.

But during the building of the Tabernacle that served as a mobile precursor to the Temple, not long after giving Moses the Commandments, God mandated the creation of images of cherubim to grace the altar. Exodus 25:18 says these images were to face the mercy seat and describes how they should appear.

Graven Images

Though Orthodoxy has generally eschewed (but not absolutely prohibited) statues, still under the influence of the Second Commandment, Eusebius (referred to previously) reported that the first known statue of Jesus was put up in Caesarea-Philippi by a woman Jesus had healed of a hemorrhage.

factum

Church historian Eusebius noted the existence of images of Peter and Paul, though he personally declined to provide an image of Jesus to the wife of a caesar who requested one, citing biblical restrictions. Some early churches forbade images, but historians say they spread quickly nevertheless.

Statues, paintings, and mosaics were common in pagan Rome, and early converts may have made their artwork before they knew that Jewish law prohibited them and that some Christians frowned on them. But eventually the church declared that images of Jesus and saints were permitted because, in Jesus' incarnation as God, he made himself visible to man for the first time.

Icons

By the seventh Ecumenical Council in the eighth century, icons had become widespread, but so had opposition to them. The Council determined that icons were proper aids to worship, but that any veneration given before them was to the saint depicted, not the painting itself.

A tract by St. John of Damascus, "On Holy Images," best stated this position. He said that not all images are idols, and not all veneration is worship; for example, the veneration soldiers on the battlefield give when kissing photographs of their wives and children is not religious devotion.

Architecture

The church's first major contribution to artistic expression was in architecture, especially the architecture of church buildings. Influenced by the Jewish tradition of having an elaborate Temple in Jerusalem, and imposing synagogues in major cities inhabited by Jewish people in Roman times, once Christians were free to start raising their own temples, they wanted them to represent their devotion to God, as well as to wear well in daily use.

Early churches imitated the Imperial basilicas (large public buildings) of the Roman Empire, and many of the first ones built after the end of the persecutions were made for the church by Constantine and his mother, Helena.

discussion question

What is Hagia Sophia?
The Great Church, as it was originally called, was built in Constantinople by Constantine, and was so named because it was larger than the other churches of the time. Rebuilt by Justinian in A.D. 537, it still remains one of the largest and oldest domed buildings in the world. It was eventually renamed Hagia Sophia, or the Holy Wisdom (of Christ).

At its peak, 80 priests, 150 deacons, 40 deaconesses, 60 subdeacons, 160 readers, 25 chanters, and 75 doorkeepers served the Great Church in Constantinople. In 1204, Catholic Crusaders pillaged the church and also sacked the city.

St. Peter's Basilica

Emperor Constantine ordered construction of the original St. Peter's Basilica in Rome, completed in A.D. 349, on the site where Peter had been buried in A.D. 64. During the removal of the papacy to France (1305–1378), the basilica fell into disrepair, and was replaced by a restored and larger church mandated by Popes Nicholas V and Julius II. The architect of the restored church, Donato Bramante, was succeeded in 1547 by Michelangelo, who died two years before its completion in 1626.

In the same period, most of the rulers, abbots (heads of monasteries), and bishops of Europe supported the construction of elaborate cathedrals, each city trying to outdo the next. Many of these, called Gothic in architectural style, are still in use, and are generally regarded as great treasures of human culture in the western world. St. Patrick's in Manhattan, Grace Cathedral in San Francisco, and the National Cathedral in Washington are examples of cathedrals built in the United States in the Gothic style.

symbolism

Ottoman Turkish Sultan Mehmet the Conqueror took Constantinople in 1453, and converted Hagia Sophia into an imperial mosque. Later, the Muslim Turks turned it into a museum, as it is to the current time, the best-preserved relic and symbol of the Byzantine Roman Empire.

Papal Art Patrons

Popes of Rome were among the world's main art patrons from antiquity until the eighteenth century, so the Vatican houses many of Europe's most valuable artworks, including Michelangelo's frescoes on the ceiling of the Sistine Chapel, and his *Last Judgment* on a chapel wall. Also found in the Sistine Chapel are works by Renaissance artists Botticelli, Domenico Ghirlandaio, Pinturicchio, and Luca Signorelli. Among other prized Vatican art treasures is a jewel-encrusted cross that was commissioned in the sixth century by Byzantine Emperor Justin II as a gift for the pope.

The Crusades

The 500 years after the fall of Rome to the Germanic Vandals is often thought of as Europe's Dark Ages. The period from about A.D. 476 to 1000, the Dark Ages originally referred to the lack of Latin literature produced in the period. Later, the term Dark Ages was expanded to cover a dearth of cultural advances in general. The

Middle Ages refers to the period between the Dark Ages and the Renaissance (400 to 500 years later); some Renaissance writers called the Renaissance the modern age.

The most historically memorable though highly debated phenomenon of the Middle Ages was the crusades, military campaigns carried on in the name of Jesus and under the banner of his cross, under papal sanction, from the eleventh through thirteenth centuries. The first of these was launched in 1095 by Pope Urban, inspired by a letter from Emperor Alexius Comnenus in Constantinople to Robert, Count of Flanders, asking for aid to stop the persecution of pilgrims to the Holy Land by Muslims who were conquering more and more of the empire.

Crusaders Take Jerusalem

Count Robert forwarded the letter to the pope, who used it to raise an army to travel to the Holy Land and take Jerusalem and the Holy Land back from the Muslims. An army of both knights and peasants traveled over land and sea to reach Jerusalem, took it in 1099, and established a Kingdom of Jerusalem ostensibly under patronage of Jesus Christ, their professed High King.

The crusades arose from pietistic fervor that swept Europe at this time coupled with a desire of thousands of people to make radical changes in their poor and drab lives. The First Crusade was also boosted by its proximity to the change of millennia, and events in the heavens, including the appearance of a comet and a meteor shower.

A dozen or more crusades followed in this period, depending on how they are counted (some are considered subcrusades of larger or earlier ones), but nine are identified by number. As a whole, the crusades can be called the most clearly defined holy war in Christian history, in the sense that the crusaders—mainly uneducated peasants—considered themselves defenders of the sovereignty of Jesus Christ against a newer competing religious movement.

Papal Superiority

A subtext of the holy war was gaining papal superiority over the Orthodox churches in the east, which was temporarily achieved by the sacking of Constantinople in 1204 during the Fourth Crusade. Byzantine ruler Michael VIII Palaeologus recaptured Constantinople in 1261.

Only the First Crusade succeeded at achieving its goal, gaining control of Jerusalem. The general view of history, including that of the modern Catholic Church, is that the crusades were a misapplication of religious zeal, trying to win infidels in a way that was against the teachings of Jesus.

Rise of the Universities

Europe's first universities grew out of motivation to apply the teachings of Jesus and the Bible's cultural mandate to all of life. The first university began in the Italian city of Bologna in 1119. The University of Paris also began before 1200, though a specific year is not available, and Oxford University also has no clear date of origin, but claims it grew rapidly beginning in 1167, when King Henry II banned English students from going to the University of Paris.

Two other Italian universities date from the same period: Siena began in 1203, and Vincenza, 1204. Cambridge dates its beginning from 1209. The universities (the word is Latin for "corporation") were seen as providing higher educational opportunities to sons of the expanding merchant class. Though still related to the churches and providing a Christian worldview, the universities provided the first higher education for secular vocations, the only educational institutions in most of Europe before then being monasteries. Though monasteries fostered and extended literacy, their main charter was not imparting specialized knowledge.

Secular university studies required something else that was not readily available in the world at that time: nonreligious books. Texts were handwritten by experts, who left them in stationers' stores, where the student, or someone he hired, could go and copy them by hand.

Enhancing the Christian life and worldview was also the main impetus for the beginning of a revolution in publishing. Though some books (especially Bibles) were circulated in Europe prior to the invention of the printing press by using a single block of hand-carved characters for each page, movable type and the printing press for using it were invented by Johann Gutenberg in the 1450s. His first book created after introducing the printing press was the Bible.

factum

Thomas Cahill, in *How the Irish Saved Civilization*, claims that Ireland, after St. Patrick, became the first European bastion for monasticism. After the Dark Ages began, the Irish monks copied the literature of the time and exported books and sent monks of intellectual strength to the continent, and probably as far as Russia, to help keep learning alive in an otherwise dark era.

The Renaissance

The Renaissance, a period of expanding knowledge in the arts and sciences, is considered to be a bridge from the Middle Ages to the modern era. Beginning in Italy in the fourteenth century, it spread to northern Europe in the late fifteenth century. The word means "rebirth" in its Italian form (*rinascenza*) and in its French and English form.

The first person many historians identify as embodying the Renaissance spirit is poet Dante Alighieri (Florence, 1265–1321), famous for *The Divine Comedy*, a volume containing three books including his best-known work, *The Inferno*, an allegorical tour of hell and a Christian classic.

Dark Ages

Petrarch (full name Francesco Petrarca; 1304–1374), educated in the law but more interested in literature and writing, is considered, with Dante, a major early figure in the Renaissance and the father of the term "Dark Ages" to describe the period after the fall of

Rome. He was named the first poet laureate of Rome since antiquity, and also worked as a diplomat.

During the Renaissance, new breakthroughs also occurred in architecture and, most notably, in sculpture and painting. Some believe that much of the innovation was spurred by the patronage of the De Medicis of Florence, whose money inspired new heights of creativity. Probably the most famous Florentine painter, among many, is Leonardo da Vinci, whose *Last Supper* and *Mona Lisa* are known everywhere. Besides his paintings, he was also an accomplished architect, anatomist, and inventor.

English Renaissance

In England, the Elizabethan-era Renaissance produced William Shakespeare, John Milton, Christopher Marlowe, and Edmund Spenser, all writers and playwrights. Albert Durer, Pieter Bruegels, and van Eycks are also Renaissance painters who worked in the northern European Renaissance.

In science, the Renaissance was led by Kepler, Galileo, Nicolaus Copernicus, Sir Francis Bacon, and Isaac Newton.

Cracks in the West's Christian Culture

Though often studied as separate phenomena, many historians consider the Protestant Reformation an extension of the Renaissance spirit into religion. The most common date for the beginning of the Reformation is October 31, 1517, when Martin Luther posted a challenge to debate on the door of All Saints' Church in Wittenberg, Germany, in the form of ninety-five theses or propositions.

Luther

Martin Luther (1483–1546) was a pious Augustinian monk who became dissatisfied with corruption in the Catholic Church, especially the sale of indulgences to raise funds for the building of St. Peter's Basilica. His father wanted him to study law, but a brush with death turned him to the monastery, where his superior sent him back to academic life to prepare for the priesthood. He was such a quick study that four years later, with a doctorate of theology, he joined the faculty of the University of Wittenberg as a professor of theology.

Becoming immersed in study of the Bible, Luther quickly came to question Catholic interpretations of certain biblical teachings, including repentance/penance, righteousness, justification by faith, and grace. His challenge to debate the sale of indulgences ("The Ninety-five Theses") was quickly printed using the newly introduced printing press, and circulated throughout Germany within two weeks of their posting.

Invitation to Rome

Counter-challenged by the pope to come to Rome, Luther, fearing treachery, resisted and, further examining his claims, replied by challenging the pope's authority and the papal office as it existed at the time. As the gap between his views and the pope's demands widened, his writings were being disseminated throughout Europe, and throngs of students were traveling to Wittenberg to hear him directly.

On June 15, 1520, the pope warned Luther that he risked excommunication if he didn't recant 41 points in his writings. The following year, the emperor of the Holy Roman Empire banned Luther's writings and declared him an outlaw and a heretic before the Diet (legislature) of (the city of) Worms.

factum

On his return trip from Worms, Luther was abducted and taken to Wartburg Castle in Eisenach, but it was a friendly kidnapping carried out by his protector, Frederick the Wise. He was kept in the castle in voluntary exile for a year, and during that time received and responded to correspondence from people stirred by his reform doctrines.

Demands for Reforms Spread

Meanwhile, the Reformation had begun, with throngs of people demanding church reforms, including an end to masses conducted for private individuals, an end to the magisterial role of church hierarchs, and the removal of images from churches. The rest, as they say, is history, as about half of the population of Germany followed Luther into the newly organized Evangelical Church.

Calvin

John Calvin (in French, Jean Chauvin, 1509–1564), eight years old when Luther posted his ninety-five theses, studied law and humanities at the University of Paris. He was summoned to Geneva by Swiss reformer William Farel and there, except for a three-year preaching stint in Strasburg, he lived for the rest of his life. Not as outgoing as Luther, Calvin's main influence was through his writings, especially his *Institutes of the Christian Religion*, which he first wrote at age twenty-six and revised and reissued three times over the next twenty-five years.

Calvinism

Calvinism spread widely and became the dominant variety of Christian theology in Scotland (as the Presbyterian Church), the Netherlands (the Reformed Church), parts of Germany (Reformed), France (Huguenots), Hungary (Reformed), and Poland. The early settlers (in other words, the Puritans and Pilgrims) of the American colonies that eventually became the United States were mostly Calvinists. The Puritans and Pilgrims later became known as Congregationalists, Dutch Reformed emigrants settled in New York and New Jersey, and Scots-Irish Presbyterians came to New Jersey, Pennsylvania, and south through Appalachia. Additional seminal figures in the Reformation were:

- **Thomas Cranmer**, Archbishop of the English Catholic Church when it transformed itself into the Church of England under Henry VIII. He consulted with both Luther and Calvin and leaned more strongly toward Calvin's theology.

- **John Knox**, the fiery reformer of Scotland who visited Calvin in Switzerland and adapted Calvin's theology to the Scottish temperament. The Reformation took Scotland like a firestorm, with Presbyterianism adopted by the Parliament as the established church of Scotland.

- **Ulrich Zwingli**, reformer of the church in Switzerland, beginning in Zurich. Half of Switzerland's ten cantons followed him and Luther into the Reformation; the other half remained Catholic. The cantons went to battle over their disagreement, and Zwingli was killed in battle.

- **Menno Simons**, a Dutch Catholic priest who became a critic of the church, and eventually led a group of dissenters, known as Anabaptists, to leave. Having become convinced infant baptism was unacceptable, they became rebaptized as adults, which is the source of the name. Simons also advocated pacifism and withdrawal from the world, including politics. Mennonites, Amish, and German Brethren see him as one of their source teachers.

The Age of Exploration

Probably the aspect of the Renaissance that affected more lives in Europe than any other, except the Reformation, was the increase in worldwide exploration, especially across the Atlantic Ocean. Christopher Columbus' "discovery" of the Americas in 1492 led to an era of increased trade and economic growth, and the development of new missions to take Jesus to "unreached peoples." The potato, introduced from Peru where it was a dietary staple, is credited as making it possible for the average European family to feed more members better than they could before. That led to a population explosion in some countries, including England and Wales.

Taking the Gospel of Jesus Christ to new peoples was a major impetus in settling the New World. According to *Christian History* magazine, Columbus himself was "a very devout Catholic who observed all the fasts of the church and prayed regularly. His very name Christopher . . . means Christ-bearer." He named the first land he claimed San Salvador, (Holy Savior), and dedicated it with a prayer "that thy holy Names may be proclaimed in this second part of the earth."

Chapter 14

Modernity

Historians have different opinions of life in medieval Europe; some think it was unbearably difficult, and others think that despite the poverty of most people, there was generally a high level of satisfaction with life during the whole medieval period. Regardless of which assessment is more accurate, once the Renaissance and liberated thinking appeared, there was no going back.

The Rise of Skepticism

Skepticism is as human a condition as curiosity or longing. The New Testament's most famous example of it is the Apostle Thomas' doubt when confronted with the testimony of his fellow disciples that Jesus had risen from the grave and visited them. When the other disciples told him "We have seen the Lord," Thomas replied, "Unless I see in his hands the print of the nails and put my finger into them, and put my hand into his side, I will not believe it."

Zachariah Struck Dumb

John the Baptist's father, Zachariah, when visited by an angel telling him his prayer for a child had been answered, and that Elizabeth, his wife, would give birth to John, "who shall turn many of Israel to their God," was incredulous. "How can I believe such a thing?" Zachariah exclaimed. "I am an old man and my wife well up in years."

The angel answered, "I am Gabriel who stand in the presence of God, and I have been sent to give you these glad tidings. For not believing, you shall be struck dumb and not able to speak until the day these things come to pass" (see Luke 1:18–20). The Gospel says Zachariah was unable to speak until John was born and it was time for him to name the infant.

Abraham Laughed

In the same way, even Abraham, the "Father of the Faithful," had a skeptical side. "God said to Abraham, 'As for Sarai your wife, do no longer call her Sarai, but her name shall be Sarah. And I will bless her and give you a son also by her. Yes, I will bless her, and she shall be a mother of nations; kings of people shall be descended from her.'

"Abraham fell upon his face, laughing, and thinking in his heart, 'Shall a child be born to one who is a hundred years old, and shall Sarah, who is ninety years old, bear?' And Abraham said to God, 'O that Ishmael [Abraham's son by his concubine] might live for you!' But God replied, 'Sarah your wife shall indeed bear you a son, and you shall name him Isaac, and I will establish with him and with his seed after him an everlasting covenant'" (Genesis 17:15–19).

fallacy

Some think God is an unyielding taskmaster, but in these instances he recognizes human skepticism as part of fallen nature, and throughout his dealings with his people, he encourages their questions and transparent reservations, and is willing to negotiate. But also in the cases reviewed in this section, there is a prior commitment to faith and a prior relationship with God.

Accepting Miracles

All three of these doubters wanted to believe but seemed afraid to accept that such wonders could happen. When God approached with gifts of miracles, he wanted belief and gratitude. The attitude of a father who brought a speechless child to Jesus for healing seems to be one God wants all to have. "Jesus said to him, 'If you can believe, all things are possible to him who believes.' And the father of the child, not hesitating, cried with tears, 'Lord, I believe; help my unbelief'" (Mark 9:23–24). And Jesus healed the child.

The Enlightenment Begins

The Enlightenment was the first serious challenge of the Lordship of Jesus over western culture. Historians often approach it as having been a response, primarily, against the Spanish Inquisition, a reign of terror in the name of Jesus that turned many against the church and from identifying with Jesus as Lord.

Spanish Inquisition

In its root meaning, "inquisition" means nothing more than an inquiry into teachings that contradict dogma within the Catholic

Church, or an inquiry in territories where Catholicism was the established church. But in its popular usage, an inquisition denotes an era of persecution of non-Catholic people, mainly in Spain, Peru, and Mexico, from 1497 until 1836, when it was officially ended, though the last execution of a heretic in Spain occurred ten years earlier.

Spanish King Ferdinand (who, with Queen Isabella, sponsored Columbus' explorations) petitioned the Vatican to authorize an Inquisition, which Pope Sixtus IV opposed, but was persuaded through political maneuvering to permit. Experts disagree about how many people were put to death for dissenting from Catholic doctrine. Historians range in their estimates from several thousand to well over 100,000.

There is also wide disagreement about the role torture played in the punishments and confessions, with some claiming it was severe and widespread, while defenders of the church say few instances of torture, and those "not lasting longer than 15 minutes," can be validated from the historical records. The Inquisition remains the most damaging charge ever laid against Catholicism and, by extension, against Christians in general. Although there is nothing comparable to the Inquisition in Orthodoxy or Protestantism, it is sometimes compared with the Salem witch trials in the seventeenth century.

Witch Trials

Outside Catholicism, the only thing comparable to the Inquisitions in post-medieval Christendom is the Salem (Massachusetts) witch trials in 1692. The Salem trials contrast with the Inquisition in that they were carried out by a town and its church, which, being Congregational, was not contractually connected to any other church, communion, or denomination. The persecution lasted nearly a year, with twenty-five executions by burning, and the jailing of several scores of other suspects.

At the end of the Salem persecutions, highly respected Boston Congregational pastor Increase Mather published a plea that there be no more such trials, saying, "It were better that Ten Suspected Witches should escape, than that the Innocent Person should be Condemned." The statement became a widely quoted slogan that some historians believe inspired the United States constitutional provision that the accused are presumed innocent until proven guilty.

Prominent Enlightenment Thinkers

The Enlightenment, considered as a frame of mind tending toward "modernism" and secular humanism, extends from the Renaissance through the seventeenth century. Some of its main players are sketched here, in chronological order by date of birth.

Rene Descartes (French, 1596–1650)

Considered by some the father of modern philosophy and of modern mathematics, Descartes was the founder of analytic geometry and Cartesian philosophy. He is credited with giving the natural sciences their first philosophical framework. Though the Vatican put his works on the "Index of Prohibited Books," he claims in *Meditations* to have proven the existence of a benevolent God. *Cogito ergo sum*, I think therefore I am, is his succinct summary of his philosophy.

Blaise Pascal (France, 1623–1662)

A mathematical genius, Pascal was a child prodigy, and, though he sometimes lived a worldly life, he died an orthodox believer in Jesus Christ. He is most famous as the father of probability theory, which is essential to actuarial research and economics. He also wrote a brilliant critique of casuistry (the use of deceptive reasoning), calling it a Jesuit system for justifying moral laxity. Though the Pope condemned the book, he later ordered an end to laxness in church standards. At the time of his death at age thirty-nine, Pascal was working on a theological apologetic, published posthumously, as *Pensees*, which Will Durant, in *The Story of Civilization*, calls "the most eloquent book in French prose."

John Locke (England, 1632–1704)

The philosopher who introduced the Lockean social contract, from which the American colonies' Declaration of Independence got its phrase "consent of the governed," he is widely regarded by historians as the philosopher most influential to American thinking through at least the nineteenth century. Brought up a Puritan, he studied and advocated religious toleration, and later joined the Church of England and supported latitudinarianism, a theological openness to many points of view, which later became known as "broad church" policy and led to the Anglican tolerance of later times. Though considered a major influence on modern political liberalism, which some people feel doesn't promote religion, Locke taught that because governments have a vested interest in their citizens keeping their promises, and because there is no moral constraint to be honest other than religious scruples, governments may promote religion.

Sir Isaac Newton (England, 1643–1727)

A major figure of the English Renaissance, and considered by many the most ingenious thinker in history, Newton is best known for his discovery of gravity and as the inventor of calculus. A bridge from the Renaissance to the Enlightenment, he is often cited for his Christian orthodoxy, with quotations like: "I have a fundamental belief in the Bible as the Word of God, written by those who were inspired. I study the Bible daily." Like some of the founding fathers of the United States, however, some maintain that he had "deist leanings" despite the seeming orthodoxy of some writings. He wrote an essay about the Trinity that was sent to John Locke but has never been published. He is said to have scientifically calculated the crucifixion of Jesus as occurring on April 3, 33.

factum

During the French Revolution, churches were confiscated, and their priests were required to make a vow of loyalty to the state. In the Napoleonic Republican era that followed the Revolution, the Vatican condemned Napoleon, and in response he invaded Rome.

Voltaire (French, pen name of François-Marie Arouet, 1694–1778)

A poet, playwright, author, social commentator, and defender of civil liberties and freedom of religion before either were available in France, Voltaire's most famous work is *Candide,* which ridicules orthodox views of God in the wake of an earthquake that leveled Lisbon and was followed by a tsunami and fire. His major contribution to the Enlightenment may have been his outspoken agnosticism, which in old age hardened into atheism, by encouraging many more timid skeptics to declare themselves. One of his most famous quotations is: "One hundred years from my day there will not be a Bible in the earth except one that is looked upon by an antiquarian curiosity seeker."

Jean-Jacques Rousseau (French-Swiss, 1712–1778)

A writer, political theorist, musician, and philosopher, Rousseau's writings influenced the development of socialism and nationalism, and of the French Revolution. Having grown up in Geneva reading *Plutarch's Lives* and Calvinist theology, after entering into a liaison with a French lover, he converted to Catholicism. He later fathered five children by a second lover and put the children in a foundling home at birth, saying they would fare better growing up in an orphanage than in his home. His most famous philosophical kernel is that human nature is corrupted by society, and his major tome is *The Social Contract,* which claims, among other things, that true disciples of Jesus would make poor citizens, an opinion that won him condemnation in both his Catholic and Calvinist home cities, Paris and Geneva, respectively.

Thomas Paine (English, American, 1737–1808)

As the author of *The Age of Reason*, Paine, of the American founding fathers, is the most representative of the Enlightenment mindset. On meeting Benjamin Franklin in London at age thirty-five, Franklin suggested he move to the colonies, which invitation Paine accepted, moving to Philadelphia in 1774, just two years before the creation of the Declaration of Independence and the launch of the

American Revolutionary War. Considered an archetypical liberal, Paine supported universal public education, social security, a graduated income tax, and a guaranteed minimum wage, all generations before they came about. His tract *Common Sense*, supporting independence of the colonies from England, was widely read and influenced much of the free population of the colonies at the time, including George Washington. As a Deist, Paine weighs-in against organized religion in *The Age of Reason*: "I do not believe in the creed professed by the Jewish church, by the Roman church, by the Greek church, by the Turkish church, by the Protestant church, nor by any church that I know of. My own mind is my own church. All national institutions of churches, whether Jewish, Christian, or Turkish, appear to me no other than human inventions set up to terrify and enslave mankind, and monopolize power and profit."

Secular Humanism

Paine's declaration, "My own mind is my own church," a profession of the rationalism, or the reason he refers to in his title *The Age of Reason*, has also been called a confession of secular humanist faith. Most Christian critics believe that secular humanism, though the term is not found that early, derives from the predominant Enlightenment worldview. Though Paine begins his treatise with a statement of faith in "one God," his only admitted way to perceive that God is his own reason. In other words, his god is of his own creation.

Thomas Paine went to France after the American Revolution to encourage the anti-monarchy forces there (and it was while he was in Paris that he wrote *The Age of Reason*), and he found a receptive audience for his views. Generally, the French Enlightenment thinkers considered the church an impediment to the Revolution's goals of "liberty, equality, and fraternity."

Napoleon worked out a concord with the Vatican that brought the churches under the state, a radical reversal of the medieval practice in which states were under the church. In 1905, France passed a separation of church and state law that has been interpreted as making public schools religion-free zones.

symbolism

A BBC analysis of French secularism was occasioned by contro- versy over Muslim girls wanting to wear headscarves to school, against state rules, as symbols of their religion. Christian philoso- phers critical of France's turn to secularism often cite the guillotine as the main symbol of their Revolution and their invasion, under Napoleon, of most of Europe in the next generation.

The Protestant Ascendancy

Most of the early colonists in what became the original thirteen American states were professors of faith in Jesus as Calvinists. Many Lutherans, Quakers, and Anabaptists from Germany, Holland, and England also were among the colonies' earliest immigrants, espe- cially to Pennsylvania. Even in the latest national census, persons of German descent were found to still be the most populous ethnic group in Pennsylvania, with Scots-Irish (mostly Protestant) a close second.

The original immigrants to New England—Pilgrims and Puritans—were fleeing England for greater religious freedom in the New World, as were the Quakers and Anabaptists who colonized Pennsylvania. The Dutch Reformed who first settled New York and overflowed in large numbers into New Jersey were primarily entre- preneurs rather than religious refugees. The Presbyterians who dominated New Jersey, Pennsylvania, and Delaware were mainly northern Irish seeking better opportunities for advancement in life, as Presbyterianism was the religion favored by their British rulers in Ireland at the time.

Members of the Church of England dominated the southern colonies such as Virginia, the Carolinas, and Georgia, with noticeable numbers of Huguenot refugees from France in South Carolina, and Moravian refugees (descended from the ministry of reformer Jan Hus in Moravia, in what is now the Czech Republic) in Salem (now Winston-Salem) in North Carolina. An earlier sizable colony of Moravians had also been established earlier in Bethlehem and Nazareth, Pennsylvania.

factum

All of the American colonies except Maryland—which was founded through a land grant to an Irish Catholic aristocrat, Cecil Calvert, Second Lord Baltimore—had established churches. But as the colonies grew and began competing for new settlers, they downplayed their religious preferences, and by the time of the American Revolution, the established church was no longer a significant issue.

Most of the early settlers of America, refugees from countries where the Catholic Church dominated, strongly feared Catholic immigration or, at the least, Catholic domination of their towns. Many towns and localities barred Catholic churches by either tacit or explicit measures through the nineteenth century, and some such towns were still known as Protestant towns well into the twentieth century.

Anti-Catholic Sentiments

There are reports of a Catholic church being burned down by disgruntled Protestants in New York in 1831, and of Protestant-Catholic riots in Philadelphia claiming thirteen lives in 1844. A political party campaigning as the American Party in 1854, which elected governors in Massachusetts and Delaware, and got Millard Fillmore on the presidential ticket, asked prospective party members to pledge to "elect to all offices of Honor, Profit, or Trust, no one but native born citizens of America, of this Country to the exclusion of all Foreigners, and to all Roman Catholics, whether they be of native or Foreign Birth, regardless of all party predilections whatever."

Another gauge of anti-Catholic sentiments is the historical record of the American Protective Association, sometimes wrongly called the American Protestant Association (APA). Founded in 1887 in Clinton, Iowa, the APA is said to have drawn membership largely from the Masons, who at that time did not admit Catholics (though it's debated whether the Vatican permitted Catholics to join quasi-religious Masonic organizations).

An APA Oath

An oath required of APA candidates for membership said, in part: "I do most solemnly promise and swear that I will always, to the utmost of my ability, labor, plead and wage a continuous warfare against ignorance and fanaticism; that I will use my utmost power to strike the shackles and chains of blind obedience to the Roman Catholic church from the hampered and bound consciences of a priest-ridden and church-oppressed people; that I will never allow any one, a member of the Roman Catholic church, to become a member of this order . . . to promote the interest of all Protestants everywhere in the world that I may be; that I will not employ a Roman Catholic in any capacity if I can procure the services of a Protestant." Though most American Protestants may have been ignorant of the APA and its oath, such attitudes were still widely found during the campaign for the presidency of John F. Kennedy in 1960. That campaign, in fact, may have been a turning point in the decline of such attitudes. As the first nation on earth to have a pluralistic but Protestant-dominated population enjoying freedom of religion, it's understandable that despite the changes of the modern age, American Protestants would only reluctantly welcome change.

Protestant Power

At the time of the American Revolution, the population was 98 percent Protestant. And in 1900, Protestants of English, Scots, Irish,

German, and Dutch background comprised 55 percent of the population, with national immigration laws favoring immigration from similar ethnic backgrounds well into the twentieth century.

symbolism

To the current era, the United States is considered a country controlled by Protestants, with that religious group dominant in every branch of federal government and most state governments as well. Even in 2005, the media considered it newsworthy that the U.S. Supreme Count had its first Catholic and non-Protestant majority among the nine justices.

Under the gentle husbandry of the American Protestant mainstream, Protestantism has also grown exponentially in the Third World in the past generation. According to recent statistics, there are 1.1 billion Roman Catholics and over 800 million Protestants, Independents, and Anglicans worldwide, which is approximately four times the 218 million Eastern Orthodox worldwide. Considering that up to now, in this consideration of Jesus' world impact, the Orthodox have received second-place attention after Catholics, this signals a significant turning point in the history of the Jesus movement.

Chapter 15

The "Christian" Century

I t's hard to imagine that the twentieth century may be seen as the "Christian" century, the first or best representative of the church giving of itself for the world. The church did not win over the world through its appealing words and strategies of evangelism so that the world gave up its strife and self-serving and -aggrandizing attitudes. The century of Hitler, Stalin, Mao, Pol Pot, Slobodan Milosevic, and Saddam Hussein wasn't quite the breakthrough for the Kingdom Come many hoped for.

Higher Criticism

The Christian world may have had reasons for optimism as the nineteenth century faded into the twentieth. Great Britain was the empire on which the sun never set, and its monarch, Queen Victoria, was the most influential one since Henry VIII made England Protestant (and she was far better loved). Also, Queen Victoria was, by multiple testimonies, a devout believer in Jesus who prayed for her world and how to best serve it.

One of her granddaughters, Alexandra, arguably even more pious and sincere in her devotion to Jesus, was married to the ruler of the second-largest empire at the time, Russia, which still thought of itself as Holy Russia. Even if Alexandra's German cousin Kaiser Wilhelm II (also a grandchild of Queen Victoria) may have sometimes seemed a bit of a loose cannon, what were the odds of his upsetting the whole world?

Breakthroughs

In the world professing to belong to Jesus, and the churches, there was enthusiasm about the breakthroughs of the nineteenth century, especially in biblical scholarship, an academic domain that higher criticism had already turned upside down in Germany and the rest of European academe. Around 1900, biblical scholarship was beginning to influence the pulpit speech of Protestant America, the sleeping giant, still isolated from European intrigues and happily ignorant of just about anything Asian.

factum

By 1910, one researcher claims, up to 25 percent of American clergy looked positively on the higher criticism that claimed to disprove the miracles claimed in Scripture by using scientific assumptions and techniques of literary scholarship.

Nineteenth-century higher criticism revolved around the Graf-Wellhausen documentary hypothesis propounded by German biblical scholars Julius Wellhausen (1844–1918) and Karl Heinrich Graf (1815–1869). The hypothesis is that the Pentateuch, the first five books of the Bible, were not written by one author, Moses, as held in tradition, but by a collection of unknown sources whom Graf and Wellhausen named J, E, D, and P.

Christianity Without Jesus

Robert Anderson, author of *The Bible and Criticism*, wrote that higher criticism "directly challenges the authority of the Lord Jesus Christ as a teacher; for one of the few undisputed facts in this controversy is that our Lord accredited the books of Moses as having divine authority." He was referring to John 5:46, which has Jesus saying, "Had you believed Moses, you would have believed me, for he wrote of me." If the author of the first five books of the Bible wasn't Moses, but four authors, Jesus' authority is undermined.

As another critic of higher criticism put it, if John 5:46 and many other references to Moses in Jesus' teaching are not factual, either he was himself misled or he was misleading his hearers, but "in either case the Blessed One is dethroned." Wherever higher criticism has been influential, faith and churches have atrophied.

Missions in Crisis

Missionary outreach is considered by all branches of Christendom to be a response to Jesus' commission in Matthew 28:19, "Go and teach all nations, and baptize them." The history of planned missionary outreach to faraway lands by the church begins with St. Paul's accepting the call described in Acts 16:9–10: "And a vision appeared to Paul in the night. There stood a man from Macedonia who asked, 'Come over into Macedonia and help us.' And after he had seen the vision, immediately we endeavored to go to Macedonia, convinced that the Lord had called us to preach the gospel to them."

discussion question

Did early missions succeed?
Throughout the first generation of the church, missionary travels like Paul's and Thomas' were common and far-reaching. Partially because of them, the church was being built in Europe, the Levant (roughly "the Holy Land," and to all points east, into India), and Africa.

Some historians believe that the first intentional missionary after the early church period was Patrick (A.D. 387?–493). Having been kidnapped as a youth on the west coast of Britain or Wales, he was a slave in Ireland for seven years. After escaping, he spent twelve years as a monk living in France where, like Paul, he saw a vision "of the children from Focluth, by the Western sea, who cried to him: 'O holy youth, come back to Erin, and walk among us once more.'"

Apostle to Ireland

Appointed bishop of Ireland, where a church barely existed at the time, his mission was so successful that virtually the entire island nation converted from paganism to Christianity in his lifetime. He is considered the apostle to Ireland (the title used since the original apostles were only for missionaries who converted whole peoples), and is the first of Ireland's patron saints, along with St. Columba and St. Bridgid.

The next most notable missionaries in church history were Cyril and Methodius, brothers and priests who were called when living at a monastery on the Bosphorous to minister to the Slavs. The language of the Slavs had no written form at that time, so they created an alphabet for it based on the Greek alphabet.

Colonizing efforts of Roman Catholic countries like Spain and Portugal in Central and South America included missionaries who taught Christianity to the indigenous peoples. Such missionary work is dramatically depicted in the 1986 feature film *The Mission*. Many

Americans are aware of the missionizing work of Junipero Serra, the Franciscan priest who had twenty-one missions constructed, each a day's journey apart from the next one, along the path called El Camino Real in California, stretching hundreds of miles.

factum

All four of California's largest cities, San Diego, Los Angeles, San Jose, and San Francisco, as well as many of its smaller ones, have grown up around Junipero Serra's missions and take their names from them.

Mission to Alaska

The most famous Russian Orthodox mission is that of Innocent of Alaska (Fr. John Veniaminov, 1797–1879), who brought the gospel from Irkutsk, Russia, to what was then Russia's territory in North America, Alaska. Like many other missionaries, he learned the local dialects (six of them), translated portions of the Bible into those languages, and created the first written version of the languages to do so. The Alaskan churches eventually sent out their own missionaries, reaching as far south as what is now Fort Ross, north of San Francisco, in California.

In the modern era, one of the most important developments was the organizing of the Mission Society by Anglican, Presbyterian, and independent church clergy and laity in London in 1794, "to spread the knowledge of Christ among heathen and other unenlightened nations." Its first outreach was Tahiti in the South Seas in 1796, and it expanded to North America and South Africa. Renamed the London Mission Society in 1818, it later sent missionaries to Russia, Greece, Malta, and the Jewish population in London. Other nineteenth-century lands it served include China, Southeast Asia, India, the Pacific, Madagascar, Central and Southern Africa, Australia, and the islands of the Caribbean.

American Board for Foreign Missions

A similar endeavor began in the United States with the American Board of Commissioners for Foreign Missions (ABCFM), organized in 1810 as a nondenominational, voluntary association not controlled by any denominational body. The ABCFM was responsible for most American Protestant overseas missionary efforts through the Civil War period. It considered its first priority, however, the settling and Christianizing of the expanding continental United States.

factum

Estimates are that by 1900, some 5,000 American missionaries were taking "their version of the gospel of Protestantism and American civilization" to far reaches of the planet. By this time, denominational mission boards, rather than the previous interdenominational board, were sending out most of the missionaries. A century later, the number of American foreign missionaries is about 40,000.

From the late 1870s on, there was some debate over whether—or how much—preaching of "civilization," as defined by American Protestants, was part of the missionary calling, and whether civilizing or Americanizing indigenous peoples along with missionizing them, was part of the missions charter. The dominant view is that missionaries should Americanize indigenous people, in part because raising funds to support missions becomes easier when it is seen as being both patriotic (or serving national interests) and a way to save souls. The issues of whether certain countries persecute American missionaries abroad, as well as whether foreign countries welcome missionaries, have long influenced the foreign-policy stances of some members of the United States Congress.

American Protestant Vision

Foreign missionary ventures from early times produced an American Protestant alternative to the hagiographical books and legends from the church in the centuries of Roman persecution. Books about foreign lands and the sacrifices made by missionaries, and books often about their lives in general, were widely read and served to broaden the perspectives about the world of many Americans. Even today, icons of foreign missionaries, in the form of color glossy photos, grace the foyers or vestibules of thousands of American evangelical churches.

By 1900, about 60 percent of the foreign missionaries going from the United States to foreign fields were women, many of them unmarried field workers, and the others wives of male missionaries who generally worked alongside their husbands.

symbolism

Foreign missions were considered symbolically romantic in a classical sense, going beyond the normal calling of all Christians to live for Jesus, and the missions gave women a chance to devote their lives to ministry in an era when almost no denominations ordained women to pastoral ministries.

The World Missionary Conference in Edinburgh, Scotland, in 1910 drew 1,200 participants from denominations and mission agencies around the world. Chaired by an American Methodist lay leader, John Mott, it laid the groundwork for the ecumenical movement and the formation of the World Council of Churches in 1948.

The Ecumenical Movement

In the early church, ecumenical councils were called, usually by the emperor, to sort though disparate views about issues like the

Trinity; whether Jesus Christ was two persons or had two natures, and how they were defined and related to each other; and so on.

The following is a list of the councils that had representatives from both the Western (Latin) church and the Eastern (Greek) church, their locations, and their findings:

- **Nicea, 325.** Called by Emperor Constantine, with 318 bishops attending, to settle the Arian teaching, which denied the eternal consubstantial existence of the Son with the Father (see Chapter 11). The result was the first ecumenical creed, an incomplete version of the Nicene Creed, and the first creedal definition of the Trinity.
- **Constantinople, 381.** Called by Emperor Theodosius the Great, with 150 bishops attending, to further define the Holy Spirit. Produced the final version of the Nicene Creed.
- **Ephesus, Asia Minor, 431.** Called by Emperor Theodosius II, grandson of Theodosius the Great, with 200 bishops attending, to settle the Nestorian claim that Mary gave birth to a divine man but not the eternal Logos (Word of God). It defined Christ as the Incarnate Word of God, and Mary as Theotokos (God-bearer).
- **Chalcedon, Asia Minor, 451.** Called by Emperor Marcian, with 630 bishops attending, to settle the monophysite controversy (the belief that Christ has a single nature that is both human and divine). It defined Christ as Perfect God and Perfect Man in One Person.
- **Constantinople II, 553.** Called by Emperor Justinian the Great, with 165 bishops attending, to settle Nestorian and Eutychian (the belief that Christ is solely divine and does not have a human nature) heresies (see Chapter 11). Further defined the two natures of Christ and condemned certain Nestorian writings.
- **Constantinople III, 680.** Called by Emperor Constantine IV, with 170 bishops attending, to settle the monothelite

controversy. Affirmed that though Jesus had two natures, he had only one (divine) will.

- **Quinisext Council (Trullo), Constantinople, 692.** Held in the Imperial Palace under the Trullo Dome, it ratified acts of the previous two councils, with no new agenda.
- **Nicea, Asia Minor, 787.** Held under Empress Irene, with 367 bishops attending, to settle the iconoclastic controversy (to determine whether icons should be displayed). Ruled that the holy icons should be exhibited.

Twentieth-century Ecumenism

The ecumenical movement of the twentieth century, rather than debating heresies, considers heresy an outdated concept of no use to an evolving church. Instead, it studies ways to overcome doctrinal differences in the church bodies that participate in it. Though originally intended to create one communion out of many (or, critics claimed, one world church), it has met with little success in that direction. Mainline Protestants now organize and administer the ecumenical movement.

Since the movement began in 1948, the mainline Congregational Church has merged with the Hungarian Reformed Church in America and the Evangelical and Reformed Church to become the United Church of Christ, the Methodist Church has merged with the Evangelical United Brethren Church to become the United Methodist Church, the United Presbyterian Church has merged with the Presbyterian Church (US) to become the Presbyterian Church (USA), and three mainline Lutheran churches have merged to become the Evangelical Lutheran Church of America, ELCA.

The main agencies for the ecumenical movement are the World Council of Churches, and the National Council of Churches of the USA. Based in Geneva, Switzerland, the WCC numbers 340 denominations, including most of the Orthodox Churches, which say they are there only to be witnesses to believers in Christ from other communions. They do not participate in ecumenical communion services or plan to merge into any evolving church.

discussion question

Has the contemporary ecumenical movement been successful?
Though ten denominations have merged to become four since the movement began, many more small Protestant denominations (including new breakaways from the Methodist and Presbyterian bodies that merged) have been started, and the independent church movement has exploded.

Catholicism and the World Council of Churches

The Vatican sends observer-participants to WCC conferences, but the Catholic Church has not officially become a member denomination. The Pontifical Council for Promoting Christian Unity at the Vatican sends twelve members to the Faith and Order Commission of the World Council as full members.

The National Council of Churches in the USA is composed of thirty-five member denominations and Orthodox jurisdictions, and is the United States affiliate to the World Council of Churches. Its major projects have included publishing the revised standard version and the new revised standard version of the Bible, and an annual *Yearbook of American and Canadian Churches* that attempts to give comprehensive statistical data on churches regardless of their affiliation with the Council.

Twentieth-century Fundamentalism

Since the hostage crises in Iran during the Carter Administration (1977–1981), the major American news media have used the term fundamentalist as if it were synonymous with Islamic terrorists and conservative Christians, especially those conservative Christians active in political campaigns. Even before its reassignment to Muslims, fundamentalist had gone from its original use as a self-applied label used by orthodox Protestants in the mainstream, especially Presbyterian faculty members at Princeton Theological Seminary in the 1920s, to an epithet for TV evangelists, snake handlers, and tent-show faith healers.

The leading light of the earlier group was J. Gresham Machen, who had been on the Princeton faculty for twenty-three years. When Princeton Theological Seminary reorganized along more liberal lines, he left it to form Westminster Presbyterian Seminary in Philadelphia in 1929.

When the denomination's mission board refused to stop support for liberal missionaries, he established an independent mission board to support only missionaries that orthodox Presbyterians would feel comfortable supporting. The denomination ordered members of the independent board to resign from it or be stripped of their ordination. He and other members refused to resign and, facing being defrocked, started a new denomination, the Orthodox Presbyterian Church.

After graduating from Johns Hopkins University and Princeton Theological Seminary himself, Machen had studied in Germany for a year with one of the leading proponents of the higher critical approach to biblical studies, Wilhelm Hermann, at Marburg. In correspondence, he relates that this was a great crisis of faith, because although Hermann disbelieved most of what orthodox Christians consider essential, his faith seemed so radiant that Machen found it magnetic, almost entrancing. By contrast, he said that one of his professors at seminary, B. B. Warfield, revered for his orthodox theology, was "a very heartless, selfish, domineering sort of man."

The Fundamentals

A decade before Machen became the leader of the early Protestant fundamentalists, an anthology of ninety articles about the essential doctrines of Christian orthodoxy appeared in a twelve-volume set of paperback books titled *The Fundamentals*. Intended for use by pastors and church leaders to understand the issues that were very controversial in many churches by that time, some three million copies of the booklets were circulated throughout the United States. Some of the titles and authors are:

The History of the Higher Criticism, by Canon Dyson Hague, M.A.
The Mosaic Authorship of the Pentateuch, by Prof. Geo. Frederick Wright, D.D., LL.D.
Fallacies of the Higher Criticism, by Prof. Franklin Johnson, D.D., LL.D.
Old Testament Criticism and New Testament Christianity, by Prof. W.H. Griffith Thomas
Science and Christian Faith, by Rev. Prof. James Orr, D.D.
My Personal Experience with the Higher Criticism, by Prof. J.J. Reeve

These monographs were republished in a four-volume set in 1993, and they are now available online (see Appendix A: Web Resources, and Appendix B: Bibliography). The main focus of the writings these monograms critiqued was the findings of biblical criticism.

New Evangelicalism

The movement that is now positioned in the American media as the leading force in American religion, evangelicalism, fronted for a half century by evangelist Billy Graham, *Christianity Today* magazine, and longer by Baylor University, Wheaton College, Calvin College, and scores of other similar colleges and seminaries, descends directly from the fundamentalists of the beginning of the Christian century. Seeing the writing on the wall (see Daniel 5) that "fundamentalist" was going to be a hard designation to live with, they intentionally recast themselves as the "new evangelicals" and eventually, just evangelicals. The subject of evangelicals will be taken up further in Chapter 17.

Vatican II

Another major development of the twentieth century is Vatican II, the Second Vatican Ecumenical Council, opened in 1962 by Pope

John XXIII and closed in 1965 by Pope Paul VI. The Council may be misnamed as "ecumenical," in the sense that only Roman Catholics had voting privileges in it. But it certainly was ecumenical in the sense that the reforms it instituted made the Catholic Church much more accessible by all other orthodox Christians and conservative members of other religions, especially the other monotheistic ones, Judaism and Islam. "Accessible" here means comprehensible, easier to find common ground with, and open.

Liberal Catholic Hopes

Liberal Catholics are generally perceived in Christian periodicals and Web sites as having had higher hopes for the reforms to come from the Council than actually appeared (especially women priests and an end to the celibacy requirement for priests). Conservative Catholics and confessing Protestants are generally pleased, especially in the way Vatican II has been interpreted in the administrations of Pope John Paul II and Pope Benedict XVI.

symbolism

Catholic use of hymns by Martin Luther and Charles Wesley is now common in masses—even Billy Graham's theme, "How Great Thou Art"—as well as praise songs of the type seen in most evangelical and mainline churches trying to appeal to young worshippers. The use of these songs may be the most pointed symbolical proof of the Roman church's hopes for reconciliation or reunion with Protestants.

Protestants who may have visited Catholic services in pre-Vatican II days but not since are often amazed at how different they have become. Though the magisterium felt that folk masses went too far in the early years after the Council, restraints they put in effect in the intervening years have made Catholic masses almost as visitor friendly as typical evangelical services.

Biblical Support

Almost as radical as the decisions of the Council, probably because it is the most hands-on medium of the Council's reforms that the average person can get access to, is the revised Catholic Catechism, published in 1992 by Pope John Paul II. A catechism is a compendium of the teachings of a religion, with answers to just about any question a person might raise, from church teachings on birth control and homosexuality, to the seven deadly sins and seven virtues.

From a church that, its own scholars admit, hardly ever cited scripture in its literature before Vatican II, the new Catechism makes profuse use of proof texts. And a feature that the Eastern Orthodox appreciate is the liberal use throughout the catechism of citations of church fathers and the ecumenical councils of the early church.

Pope John Paul II and Mother Teresa

Possibly more important to the Catholicism of the twentieth century and to the relations of the Catholic Church to Christians of other communions are the persons of the late Pope John Paul II and Mother Teresa. Before their sojourns were over, the joke was, the main thing, maybe the only thing, Protestants, Orthodox, and Catholics had in common was appreciation for the author and lay theologian C. S. Lewis. But John Paul and Mother Teresa are a level even higher, embodying holiness besides great wisdom and insight into the human spirit. Billy Graham calls the late Pope "unquestionably the most influential voice for morality and peace in the world during the last 100 years," a sentiment shared by the last Soviet leader, Mikhail Gorbachev, who called him, "the highest moral authority on earth."

factum

President George W. Bush remarked of Pope John Paul II, "One journalist, after hearing the new Pope's first blessing in St. Peter's Square wired back to his editors: 'This is not a pope from Poland, this is a pope from Galilee.'"

Likewise, Mother Teresa was so inspiring that a lifelong agnostic journalist and church dissenter, Malcolm Muggeridge, who chose to write a biography of her (*Something Beautiful for God*) and was able to get personal time with her, became a Catholic and spent his latter years writing Christian apologetics. Often her own words reveal her better than those of her admirers. For example, "I once picked up a woman from a garbage dump and she was burning with fever; she was in her last days and her only lament was: 'My son did this to me.' I begged her: You must forgive your son. In a moment of madness, when he was not himself, he did a thing he regrets. Be a mother to him, forgive him. It took me a long time to make her say: 'I forgive my son.' Just before she died in my arms, she was able to say that with a real forgiveness. She was not concerned that she was dying. The breaking of the heart was that her son did not want her. This is something you and I can understand."

Chapter 16

Meanwhile, in the East

Most Americans' impression of Eastern Orthodoxy likely comes from gold-leafed onion-domed churches, clergy traveling in cassocks and wearing untrimmed beards, and metropolitans in what seem to be Russian versions of the top hat. To many Americans, such images may invoke the most foreign and distant subculture imaginable. Even the Orthodox observance of Christmas doesn't coincide with the American celebration, many think. And what, they might wonder, does this religion have to do with Jesus and Christianity?

Byzantium: The Orthodox Empire

Paul writes in 1 Corinthians 1:12–13 that he has heard about dissention in the Corinthian Church, that some were following one teaching, one faction were disciples of another teacher, some were Paul's disciples, and some were claiming to be only Jesus' followers. "Is Christ divided," Paul inquires. Likewise, critics of the churches have been known to ask over the millennium since the split between the Latin West and the Greek East, "Is Jesus divided? Is his body split?" And with the Reformation they now ask, "Has he been splintered into not two, but now scores and hundreds of factions and pretenders to the claim of being his true body?"

Is the Catholic body his real expression? Did the Reformation recover what Jesus meant—and what he left of his body—to the world two millennia after his earthly life and sacrifice? Or has the Orthodox representation of Jesus followed the course most faithfully? Is diversity in unity the real key to Jesus? Is the church, the body of Christ, somehow mystically present in all these and more efforts to find and serve him? Such questions can only whet our appetites in this survey, but in raising them we can hope for new insights on these issues.

Byzantium has been discussed in other contexts several times earlier, but now takes center stage in an examination of its particular expression of the Jesus movement. Byzantium, from the name of the village that was built up into the city of Constantinople in the fourth century, is being used here to refer to both the Roman empire in the configuration it took almost a thousand miles east of Rome, and for the ethos of Eastern Orthodoxy, the variation of Christianity that had Greek rather than Latin as its mother tongue.

Historian Eusebius (see Chapter 7) reports that after seeing the vision of a cross in the sky before a crucial battle near Verona, northern Italy, in A.D. 312, Emperor Constantine described it to his colleagues and ordered its likeness rendered in precious metals and gems and raised, accompanied with a banner adorned by the first two letters of the Greek form of "Christ," X and P, (chi, written as X, for "ch," and rho, written as P, for what in the western alphabet is "r"), as well as portraits of himself and his children. Called a labarum, he had it duplicated repeatedly and appointed that it precede his armies into battle.

symbolism

The symbol that Constantine ordered to lead his armies is still used in Orthodox and Roman Catholic religious processions. Called a labarum, it is also often called the chi-rho or a Christogram. Some believe Constantine's labarum was the first time a cross was used to symbolize Christianity.

Constantine the Great

Constantine's vision came in two parts, the appearance of a cross in front of the sun as he marched with his troops in daylight, and in a dream where he was told to conquer under that symbol. Eusebius also records that after his vision sank in, Constantine asked his counselors to explain the religion of the Christians to him.

fallacy

Some sectarian teachers have accused Constantine of corrupting Christianity, merging church and state, or both, thus interrupting the progress of the true faith. Most historians say this claim is unsupported. And most Bible scholars (Catholic, Orthodox, and Protestant) say such actions would have contradicted Jesus' words, "the gates of hell shall not prevail" against the church.

Another historian, Lactanius, an earlier Christian convert and writer of apologetics for his new religion, having been persecuted under Constantine's predecessor Diocletian, was taken under Constantine's wing. He became a tutor of the emperor's son, and probably was one of Constantine's teachers of Christianity. It is thought, however, that Lactanius was not well taught in Christian beliefs, as his apologetic works show little knowledge of the Bible. Later in life, it is reliably reported, the emperor preferred the company of bishops of the church, and the emperor's active role in addressing the Arian heresy controversy indicates that he was fascinated by discussions of Christian theology or doctrines.

Classical Rome, like Greece, its model, used paganism as what modern sociologists and political scientists call civil religion, the glue that holds the society together. It's possible that the pagan gods of either Greece or Rome were not taken very seriously by the people or the leaders, all considering them mythological, but there is much evidence that the leaders wanted the gods respected and to be called upon to bless their enterprises.

factum

Lord John Julius Norwich ranks Constantine fourth in world influence after Jesus, Buddha, and Mohammed. Constantine's most important decisions include making Christianity a tolerated religion of Rome, and establishing his capital at Byzantium, renamed Constantinople.

The creation of pagan gods accords with the recognition, universal among human cultures, of a spiritual dimension native to mankind: If we want god(s), then such realities must precede our very existence. Plato and Aristotle taught variations on this motif, suggesting that even before pagan people heard of Christ, they were being prepared to look for their savior.

Civil Religion

There is some indication that Constantine consciously chose Christianity as his empire's new civil religion in part because it was growing rapidly despite the extreme measures his predecessors employed to stop it, and in part because when he understood it, regardless of the depth of his faith, it made more sense, and seemed more effective at promoting public welfare, than pagan mythology.

So Constantine was the first world ruler who had to deal with the separation and the interplay between the dominant religion and state or national life, and he was the first to endorse Christianity as his state's leading civil religion. That he may have chosen Christianity out of political motives, as some have written, is not in itself evidence of nefarious motives. Nor does it discount his sincerity, the authenticity of his vision, or his eventual choosing baptism into the church near the end of his life. When something is the right thing to do, it's usually the best choice for a variety of reasons and motivations.

fallacy

Though many think Constantine intended to move to Byzantium, there's no definite reason why he moved his capital from Rome. The eastern region of the empire was the last portion he controlled, so he likely wanted more direct presence there to consolidate his political power. Historians believe he didn't mean to make "New Rome" the only capital; it became that by default.

Constantine's "Control"

Some claim that the fact that Constantine sponsored the Council of Nicea proves that he ran the church, but the fact that controversies like the Arian heresy raged back and forth for decades discounts such claims. The church had no dictator. Bishops at the time were equal and independent, deferential but not required to answer to a synod or the bishop of Rome, and they were scattered from Britain to the Holy Land and Africa.

Though many heresies are recorded as being held from time to time by early bishops, none of the bishops are on record as claiming to have been pressured to conform their teachings to ones Constantine may have wanted to promote. The fact that Constantine was on the side of the heretic Arius for most of the bishops' lives, and that the church still prevailed against Arius, is overwhelming evidence that Constantine did not dictate to the church, as often claimed.

Orthodoxy's Different Take on Salvation

All traditional Christian communions teach that salvation is being in a relationship with the personal God through Jesus, and that salvation is made possible by faith through God's grace. But there are varied interpretations on the teaching of the Apostle Paul that God has highly exalted Jesus and "given him a name which is above every name, that at the name of Jesus every knee should bow, of things in heaven, and things in earth, and things under the earth, and that every tongue should confess that Jesus Christ is Lord, to the glory of God the Father. Wherefore . . . work out your own salvation with fear and trembling" (Philippians 2:9–12).

Why does Paul, the champion of salvation by grace (the gift of God), and whose writings are often used to counter any suggestion of "working" to earn or get grace, exhort his readers in Philippi to "work out your own salvation"? Some might propose that he means this only in the sense of "live out your lives as saved people," but the counter to that idea is that Paul does not waste words or embellish, and is always careful to teach the straight truth, mindful of the dangers of being ambiguous. When he says "work out your own salvation" he means it all.

Keep the Faith

The Orthodox take is that he is referring to the fact that, being under house arrest in Rome, he might not be visiting the Philippians again. They might have found it relatively easy to keep on keeping on when an actual apostle was among them, but the Orthodox feel he is saying, "You're on your own. I'm not around to pick you up and brush you off when you fall. Take care of the gift you've received without my help. You've been saved by faith; now save yourselves by not failing to guard it." In other words, though Jesus is the only savior in the sense of having eternal life that no one else has or can give, Paul might save some just by being around to protect them, to pick up on their lapses in enthusiasm, their starting to backslide. But they can also save themselves in his absence if they will heed his words. They have to work at it. Again, when writing to Timothy, his young bishop over the flock in Ephesus, he tells him to "Study to show yourself approved to God, a workman who need not be ashamed, rightly dividing the word of truth" (2 Timothy 2:15). Even bishops have to work at it.

discussion question

What does the "work" consist of?
The context provided answers the question. "Every knee—the knee of every thing in heaven, and of every thing in earth, and of every thing under the earth" should be subjected to the Lord Jesus. Conversation, thoughts, vocations, avocations, friends, life-style, use of money, use of leisure time . . . every thing must be made worthy of God's approval.

Being saved is not just a bath in the baptistery; it's constantly working on not getting dirty again. The Orthodox emphasis on this idea, which is not as readily found in the western churches, is what was cited in Chapter 12 as divinization or theosis, which means saving more and more of the person until all of the person is in Christ and therefore is maximally partaking of the divine nature.

Salvation Past, Present, and Future

So for the Orthodox, salvation is past (been there), present (doing it), and future (going farther). Some part of the person has already been changed by grace and sealed in baptism, some is still being remodeled by faith, and some will be revealed as still needing work as grace abounds or becomes more visible in the saved person's life.

A second difference in the understanding of salvation is the purpose of the atonement. Though the Orthodox do not take issue with the traditional biblical references used by western theologians in support of their doctrine of penal substitutionary atonement derived from Augustine of Hippo (such passages as Isaiah 53:6–10; Romans 1:18; 3:22–5; 5:8–9; 2 Corinthians 5:21; Galatians 3:13; Hebrews 9:11–28; 1 Peter 3:18; and 1 John 4:10), Orthodox fathers have never emphasized the penal aspect, which sometimes gets presented as God the Father angrily punishing his Son on the cross to get vengeance for human sin (some have even called it "divine parental child abuse"). God's love and Jesus' love, not the vengeful wrath of any person of the Trinity, sent Jesus to the cross for humanity's sins, in the Orthodox emphasis.

Salvation from Death

A third difference in the understanding of salvation between western and eastern Christendom, linked to the second difference, is the emphasis on what salvation is from. In western teaching it is often expressed as salvation from sin, but Orthodox teachers more generally emphasize the salvation from the effect (or wages) of sin, which is death. Salvation is centered more in the resurrection, and victory over death, than on the atonement of Jesus wrought on the Cross, which was the means to the victorious end. This is not to say Orthodoxy minimizes the work of Jesus on the cross or the atoning sacrifice of Jesus as Lamb of God (language that is part of every Eucharistic offering in the Orthodox church), but that the main emphasis is the paschal (Easter) morning rather than the Good Friday afternoon.

Orthodoxy does not charge St. Augustine of heresy in his different emphases; he is regarded a saint of the preschism church by Orthodoxy as well as by Catholicism. Orthodox opinion does think Augustine's atonement emphasis has been exaggerated in the works of Luther and Calvin and in some attempts to popularize these views, and considers these other perceptions a somewhat inferior understanding of the core meaning of salvation.

Between Constantine and Czar Nicholas II

How did the Jesus movement fare after Constantine the Great? After his death in 337, Constantine's sons governed the empire, with Constantine II in the west; Constantius II in Constantinople; and the youngest, Constans, in the central prefecture, composed of Italy, Africa, and Illyricum. Challenges to the brothers' rule from outside pretenders eventually left Constantius II (the namesake of Constantine's father) the sole ruler of the empire.

Constantius II was strongly Arian in his Christian preferences, resisting the first draft of the Nicene Creed, but also attempted to enforce reforms based on Christian doctrines, like outlawing magic and dismantling pagan temples. One account says that he called a church council in A.D. 360 (which is not recognized by the surviving church) to issue a revised, Arian, creed. And apparently, after visiting Rome and seeing the continued splendor of that city's pagan temples, he lost his enthusiasm for dismantling them. His reign from 337 until his death in 361 is one of the longest of any Roman emperor.

Constantius II was succeeded by Julian the Apostate, a cousin of Constantius as the son of a half brother of Constantine. One of his first acts after succeeding Constantius II was declaring his strong commitment to paganism, and he began disenfranchising the Christians and undoing their gains since Constantine's edict of toleration. He died just two years after Constantius II, in a battle with Persians on a canal between the Tigris and the Euphrates rivers.

factum

Jovian (Flavius Iovianus in Latin, c. 332–364) was a soldier and a Christian the army selected to succeed Julian, but he ruled less than a year, dying from an accidental asphyxiation. Valentinian, who the army also chose, ruled for eleven years in the west (from Milan and cities in Gaul), and after his succession appointed his brother Valens to rule the east from Constantinople.

Valentinian was succeeded by his son, Gratian, at nineteen years of age. He, in turn, appointed Theodosius I to rule the east on the death of his uncle Valens in A.D. 379. Under Gratian, who was counseled by Bishop Ambrose of Milan (the first bishop so popular that he could be seen as a threat to the government), pagan practices were curtailed and orthodox Christianity dominated the entire empire for the first time.

Rebel generals assassinated Gratian in 383, after which Theodosius I, ruling in Constantinople, emerged as the most powerful Caesar. He also turned out to be the last emperor of the entire empire, east and west, was the one to declare Christianity the state religion, and called the First Council of Constantinople in A.D. 381 to ratify the First Ecumenical Council, fine-tune the Nicene Creed, and finally settle the Arian controversies.

The Eastern Empire, though marked as the unified empire had been by ups and downs, expansions and contractions, continued for another millennium, until the fall of Constantinople under Constantine XI to Ottoman Sultan Mehmed II in 1453. While the pope of Rome became the figurehead successor of the western caesars (as the primary focal point for western European cultural integration and progress), the Eastern Orthodox Church, under its equal and independent bishops (though not officially separate from its western counterparts until 1054), continued to make spiritual progress.

discussion question

When did Rome fall?

Visigoths sacked Rome in A.D. 410 under Alaric, and the fall of the Western Roman Empire was underway. The empire ended officially when Odoacer, a German tribal chieftain, deposed Romulus Augustus in A.D. 476.

Second-Longest Surviving Empire

The Byzantine or, more properly, the Eastern Roman Empire, under Orthodox influence and tutelage, is one of the longest-lasting empires in world history. If it is considered as the successor of the Roman Empire (as most historians would), the Roman Empire lasted just twenty years fewer than the Chinese Empire founded in 221 B.C. by Qin Shi Huangdi, which lasted until 1279.

The leader of the Bulgarian Empire claimed the title czar (also spelled tsar and tzar), meaning caesar, when it had a victory over the "Byzantine" Empire in A.D. 913. Ivan IV of Russia also appropriated it for himself in 1547, and some Russian Orthodox promote the claim that Russia succeeded Byzantium as the next embodiment of the spirit of the Roman Empire. This claim may be an attempt to promote the patriarch of Moscow, the leader of the world's largest Orthodox church, as the rightful Orthodox hierarch deserving the place of highest honor among Orthodox bishops, but as long as the Russian Orthodox remain in communion with the ecumenical patriarch in Istanbul, they can't press that case very far. And there's little evidence to support Moscow's claim that, since the rise and fall of the Soviet Union, it has the largest membership in the Orthodox world.

Piety of Nicholas II

The biographies of the last czar of Russia, Nicholas II (who was executed with his family in Yekaterinburg by the Bolsheviks), leave little doubt that he was a successor in the tradition of religious Byzantine emperors. His biographers say he and his czarina Alexandra were pious Orthodox believers, and that he was motivated because of his convictions to abdicate his throne, believing it was the best thing for his people when the Communists overthrew his government.

Icons, Saints, and Monasticism

For Orthodox believers, the church's witness to Christ through the lives of its saints and martyrs, and the consistent teaching of its fathers and preaching of its pastors are of utmost importance. Saints and martyrs overlap in the church's teaching, as to be a true martyr for confessing Christ is to be a saint. Thousands were martyred in the early church, and probably millions more saints were made in the twentieth-century church during the reigns of Stalin, Hitler, and other dictators.

Saints are considered to be icons of Christ in Orthodoxy, an understanding that is related to the Orthodox teaching on theosis, or believers struggling with their passions to become partakers of the divine nature. Saints, perfected people, are windows to heaven and images of Jesus. And icons (wood and paint representations of saints) are windows to the saints, which in turn open on to the presence of the Lord.

fallacy

Though Orthodox worshippers appear to venerate or even worship icons, they are taught that the veneration is only to that which the icons represent, in other words the saints depicted, and that the saints in turn are depictions or representations of God in Jesus Christ.

Saints, though gone to glory, are not dead but living, as Jesus said regarding the meaning of the resurrection: "Have you not read what God said to you, 'I am the God of Abraham, the God of Isaac, and the God of Jacob?' God is not the God of the dead, but of the living" (Matthew 22:31–32).

Monasticism, as a school in which to train the passions or re-educate human nature to divine ends, is also seen in Orthodoxy as integral to making saints. Though most monks and nuns are not thought of as achieving the level of perfection that leads to talk of sainthood, most of those who do achieve that level of retraining, apart from those suffering physical martyrdom, are men and women who take up the monastic life.

discussion question

Who was St. Seraphim of Sarov?
St. Seraphim of Sarov (1759-1833) has been an inspiration to thousands who chose the pursuit of theosis. The purpose of life, he taught, was to acquire the Holy Spirit. "Acquire the Holy Spirit, and thousands around you will acquire salvation" was his answer to how to best become a witness for the Gospel.

There are still many Orthodox monasteries in Russia (most of the ones now in use have been rehabilitated after the fall of the Communists), Greece, Romania, and even a few in Great Britain and the United States. The oldest one that has been in existence from ancient times is St. Catherine's Monastery in the Sinai Peninsula between Egypt and the Holy Land, which was begun in the fifth century A.D. with support of Emperor Justinian. The most famous center of Orthodox monasticism is Mount Athos, a rugged peninsula that juts into the sea near Thessaloniki in northern Greece. It is the home of scores of large monastic communities, most of which are accessible only by boat from the sea and, once off the boat, by footpaths.

The Jesus Prayer

The Way of the Pilgrim is a story, now available in paperback book form, by an anonymous writer. In 1884, the abbot of St. Michael's Monastery at Kazan found the story in the possession of a monk at Mt. Athos. The tale is set in Russia before 1861. The story tells of a wandering man looking for a way to pray without ceasing, as the Apostle Paul teaches in 1 Thessalonians 5:17.

Eventually, the pilgrim finds a monk who counsels him that, according to the teaching in The Philakalia (The Love of Good Things, a four-volume work of teachings on how to pursue the spiritual life, by fathers of the church), the way to achieve this state of spiritual advance is by reciting the Jesus Prayer continually. The Jesus prayer is, "Lord Jesus Christ, Son of God, have mercy on me, a sinner."

factum

Advocates of the prayer recommend using variations for praying for others, such as, "Lord have mercy on dear Patricia, who is ill with the flu," or, "Raymond who is struggling with anger," without judgmentally calling anyone else a sinner.

In The Way of the Pilgrim, the young man is told to start by reciting the prayer 3,000 times a day, using a knotted prayer rope to keep count of his total. Eventually, he says he was counseled to move his total repetitions per day up to 20,000.

Eastern Christianity Missionizing the West

In Becoming Orthodox, Father Peter Gillquist tells the story of a nationwide fellowship of evangelicals, whose leaders had begun as staff members of Campus Crusade for Christ in the 1960s, setting out to find the most perfect expression of the church they could.

Though some of them were already ordained as Presbyterian or Baptist, or had backgrounds with charismatic and other traditionally conservative evangelical churches, the more they searched, the less satisfied they became. Eventually, they decided to form their own denomination, and trying as best they could to make it conform to all the New Testament had to say about the early church, they launched another Protestant church.

But eventually someone noticed that the church they'd come up with was similar to the Orthodox Church, which they hadn't even considered in their initial search, so foreign to them was the idea. And on that realization, they went back to the source documents and found some additional changes that made their church look even more like the Orthodox Church.

discussion question

Do the Orthodox set out to convert members of other communions?
Orthodoxy officially does not proselytize, and the Orthodox jurisdictions (the largest are the Orthodox Church of America, the Greek Orthodox Archdiocese of North America, and the Antiochian Orthodox Archdiocese) would not say they're out looking for converts from other communions. However, many books like Fr. Peter Gillquist's indirectly support that end.

Finally, they merged their fellowship of nearly 2,000 believers across the country into an established Orthodox jurisdiction in communion with the ecumenical patriarch in Constantinople. But theirs is only a small portion of a similar pattern of long-time Protestants, and some Catholics, converting to Orthodoxy in the United States, and, to some extent, in Great Britain. Over half of all the Orthodox priests in the United States now are converts from other faith communities, and the movement continues.

Chapter 17

Evangelicalism

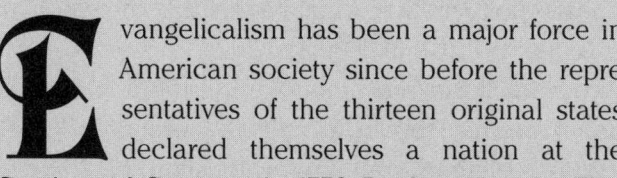vangelicalism has been a major force in American society since before the representatives of the thirteen original states declared themselves a nation at the Continental Congress in 1776. By that time, the First Great Awakening, or first nationwide religious revival, had passed its peak, but its effect was still being felt in the churches, mindsets, and lifestyles of many of the great number of rural Americans too isolated to be able to attend church regularly.

The New Force in Church Growth

It was only since the Democratic presidential campaign of Jimmy Carter in 1976 that evangelicalism has re-emerged from a relatively dormant phase back into general American consciousness as a dominant religious force in public life. And whereas the Great Awakening revival supported liberal reforms, and especially the political aspirations of Thomas Jefferson, himself not an orthodox Christian, by A.D. 2000 the American evangelical world had swung to the opposite political pole to make possible the election of conservative George W. Bush in 2000 and 2004.

How does the Jesus movement fare in the first decade of the third millennium A.D.? The world total of adherents to Christianity is approximately 2.1 billion; compared with Islam, 1.3 billion; secular-irreligious-atheist, 1.1 billion; Hinduism, 900 million; Chinese traditionalism (Taoism and others), 394 million; Buddhists, 376 million, and many others, all under 25 million (probably of most interest in current events, Judaism has 15 million adherents).

factum

Among the Christian groups, Catholicism is by far the largest, with 1.1 billion adherents, with an estimated 675 million Protestants in the world, ranging from the most traditional (Lutherans, Anglicans, and Calvinists) to some out of the range of the orthodox definition of Christian, like Mormons and Unitarians.

Among the Protestants, the fastest growing group of all is the Pentecostals, who account for an estimated 100 million Protestants worldwide, after having originated little more than a century ago. If Pentecostals are seen as a subset of evangelicals (where, most, but not all Pentecostals fall), it is clear that evangelicalism in general is the fastest-growing segment of Christendom.

Defining Christian groups isn't easy. Some statistical studies want to lump together Catholics and the most Catholic–like groups, by which they mean Anglicans and the Orthodox, though most adherents of Anglican and Orthodox confessions would probably resist this categorizing. Though many Anglicans have taken to resisting being classified as Protestant, English law requires that the monarch be a Protestant, by which it is generally understood to mean "an Anglican," that being the established church of England. So in that sense Anglicanism is definitely Protestant, and its defining thirty-nine articles are definitely part of the Protestant Reformation.

Anglicanism's American branch, the Episcopal Church, was until recent years known officially as the Protestant Episcopal Church. Many Orthodox feel that their differences with Catholicism put them closer to (though by no means in) the Protestant camp, rather than the Catholic one. Orthodoxy's long membership in the World Council of Churches, an agency established and run by Protestants, accords with this opinion.

fallacy

"Speaking in tongues" doesn't appear in church history from the second through nineteenth centuries. In 1901, Agnes Ozman talked in tongues at Bethel Bible College in Topeka. Considered a sign of the Holy Spirit, it spread to the Holiness movement. In 1906, people began speaking in tongues during the Azusa Street Revival in Los Angeles. Many consider that revival the beginning of Pentecostalism.

Likewise, the vast majority of Pentecostals, who are generally defined as believing in a need for "being filled by the Holy Spirit" and in signs of that filling, like gifts of healing and speaking in tongues, are products of American evangelicalism and its exportation to places like Brazil and other far-flung mission areas. But some

Pentecostals are not Trinitarian. And some denominations, mostly aligned with theologically liberal mainline Protestantism, most notably the Evangelical Lutheran Church of America, are not in the evangelical column, as that word is popularly used.

Big Names: Graham, Robertson, Dobson

In America, the most visible evangelical denominations are Baptist, especially the Southern Baptists, which is by far the largest Protestant denomination, with nearly 19 million adherents. The only other American religious group to exceed 10 million members is the United Methodists, which is much larger than any other relatively liberal church, with 11 million believers. More or less tied for third place among American religious communities are Jewish people and Evangelical (liberal) Lutherans, with over five million adherents each.

discussion question

What are the post-Reformation Protestant groups?
Baptists and Methodists come from the First Great Awakening, led by John Wesley (the Anglican who founded Methodism), and John Whitfield, the Calvinist whose preaching boosted American Presbyterian, Reformed, and Congregational denominations and ignited the then-fledgling Baptists. Most Pentecostals are off-shoots of Methodist Holiness movements.

While English evangelists Wesley and Whitefield, and American Presbyterian intellectual Jonathan Edwards were the spiritual icons of American Revolution-era evangelicalism, the subsequent awakenings as well as the current evangelical movement are seen primarily as revolving around spiritual leaders like Billy Graham, Pat Robertson, Jerry Falwell, James Dobson, and others. All but Dobson are Southern

Baptist, and all of them are influential in many other churches and institutions as well.

Billy Graham (b. 1918)

Billy Graham has been the most widely recognized religious leader in the United States since at least 1950, and has been one of the Gallup Poll's "ten most admired men" in the world forty-seven times since 1955, including forty consecutive citations, more than any other world figure, making him the most admired individual by Americans overall for the past four decades.

He was ordained in 1939 in the Southern Baptist Church and received his degree from Wheaton College in Illinois in 1943. He pastored a Baptist church in Illinois for several years before joining the staff of Youth for Christ as an evangelist, later founding the Billy Graham Evangelistic Association in Minneapolis.

factum

Billy Graham's 1949 evangelistic crusade in a tent in downtown Los Angeles was extended because of overflow attendance from the originally planned three weeks to eight weeks, gaining him national media attention. He went on to conduct similarly extended crusades in London and in New York and has been the world evangelist without peer ever since.

Though he began his ministry with messages often characterized as having strong politically conservative implications, criticism of Graham's ministry has come mostly from conservative voices, usually self-identified as fundamentalists to Graham's right, like the late Carl McIntire and, earlier in his ministry, Jerry Falwell. Their main complaint has been regarding the inclusiveness of his crusades, which he has consistently insisted be supported by citywide clergy and church associations, regardless of the orthodoxy of the ministers or their churches.

Graham doesn't respond to such critics, but those who interpret his actions favorably seem satisfied that in the long run his policy has enabled the Gospel to be preached to thousands who wouldn't have been in his audience if he were less inclusive, and that the net effect of his ministry has been strengthening the conservative and evangelical churches, while the liberal ones represented on the dais have consistently experienced membership declines.

A more general criticism has been that most of the commitments to Christ in his crusades don't seem to stick, and, despite his success at reaching probably more people in live appearances than any other preacher in history, no widespread revival comparable to the Great Awakening has taken place during his decades of active ministry (history may eventually dispute this claim).

Through his publishing, radio and television ministries, and his being instrumental in the founding of *Christianity Today* (arguably the only socially significant periodical in the United States with a clearly identifiable religious position), Graham undoubtedly gets major credit for the rise of evangelicalism to its current prominence.

Pat Robertson (b. 1930)

The son of a longtime United States congressman and senator from Virginia, after graduating magna cum laude with his Bachelor of Arts degree from Washington and Lee in 1950, Marion Gordon "Pat" Robertson served as the assistant adjutant of the First Marine Division in combat in Korea. He was promoted to first lieutenant in 1952 upon returning to the United States. Robertson received a J.D. from Yale University Law School in 1955 and a Master of Divinity from New York Theological Seminary in 1959.

Robertson hosts a television program called *The 700 Club*. Approximately half of this program is devoted to reporting and interpreting current events from Robertson's and his other hosts' perspectives.

Though detractors call Robertson a "televangelist," he prefers to be considered a "religious broadcaster, educator, religious leader, businessman, author, and philanthropist" as founder and chairman of CBN Inc., founder of International Family Entertainment, Inc., and because of his involvement with Regent University, Operation Blessing International Relief and Development Corporation, American Center for Law and Justice, The Flying Hospital, Inc., and several other enterprises. He was ordained a Southern Baptist minister in 1961 but surrendered his credential to run for president in 1986. He is also a figure in the charismatic movement by virtue of the word of knowledge healings and other miracles that are a regular feature of *The 700 Club*.

discussion question

How did Pat Robertson become the most visible Christian on television?
In 1960, Robertson raised funds to buy a bankrupt television station in Virginia, launching the Christian Broadcasting Network. Today, CBN produces programs in seventy languages seen in 200 nations. The network's best known program, *The 700 Club*, which Robertson hosts, is one of the longest-running religious television shows, and reaches an average of one million American viewers daily.

The International Family Entertainment company he founded developed the cable Family Channel and branched out into entertainment program production before he sold it to Fox Kids for $1.9 billion. The Family Channel was subsequently acquired by Disney's American Broadcasting Company. Now it is billed as ABC Family Network and is still contractually bound to carry *The 700 Club* as part of the terms of sale.

The American Center for Law and Justice that Robertson launched as an alternative to the American Civil Liberties Union has been in the forefront of legal actions defending Christian expression in the public square, especially public schools. In his

1986 campaign for the Republican nomination for president of the United States, he polled second in the early Iowa caucuses of that campaign, which was eventually won by George H. W. Bush, who was given Robertson's support in the party's national convention and subsequently won the office.

After Robertson's presidential campaign, he founded the Christian Coalition to continue supporting conservative political goals. It was a strong force in George W. H. Bush's second, failing campaign, but Robertson left the Coalition in 2001, turning leadership over to Ralph Reed who, in turn, left it in the hands of Roberta Combs.

Though often criticized in the mainstream press for remarks suggesting that the terrorist attacks on the World Trade Center and the Pentagon were God's retribution for American decadence, and later calling for the assassination of Venezuela's anti-American President Hugo Chavez, his constant exposure to a sizable audience and his generally erudite apologetics for his views tend to keep him one of the most influential American evangelicals.

Jerry Falwell (b. 1933)

A Lynchburg, Virginia, pastor and founder of the now-defunct Moral Majority (1979–1989), Jerry Lamon Falwell was one of the country's first pastors of what is called a megachurch. In Falwell's case, Thomas Road Baptist Church in Lynchburg has grown from a starting core of thirty-five adults in a temporary location in 1956 to a congregation of 24,000 in a city of 65,000. For some decades, the most visible proponent of self-described fundamentalist evangelicalism in the United States, and a member of the Bible Baptist Fellowship International, he changed his membership to the more moderate Southern Baptist Convention.

Voted one of the ten most admired men in America in a *Good Housekeeping* poll, Falwell was named one of the twenty-five most influential people in America in *U.S. News & World Report* in 1983, and has been featured on the covers of both *Time* and *Newsweek*. His Moral Majority claims to have been the first conservative organization labeled as the Christian right by the media, and to have started the campaign to elect Ronald Reagan president in 1980.

James Dobson (b. 1936)

An associate clinical professor of pediatrics at the University of Southern California School of Medicine for fourteen years, James Dobson also spent seventeen years in the division of child development and medical genetics while on the staff of the Children's Hospital of Los Angeles before launching his Christian psychology radio program, *Focus on the Family.*

factum

Dobson holds a Ph.D. in child development from the University of Southern California, and his first book, *Dare to Discipline* (1970), sold over three million copies among Christian families. His radio program now airs on 3,000 radio stations in the United States, and thousands more in other countries, and is heard by more than 200 million listeners daily.

His book on child discipline, *Dare to Discipline,* got widespread media attention for its approval of moderate spanking of children under age eight. The ministry, begun as a twenty-five-minute weekly discussion radio program in 1977 from Arcadia, California, has been relocated to Colorado Springs, Colorado, and employs some 1,300 staff members. Its public policy arm, the Family Research Council, is considered a major influence on government policies, extending to the White House.

Peale and Schuler

In the last half century, the only other members of the American Protestant clergy to become household names to any extent approaching the ones previously mentioned have been the late Norman Vincent Peale of New York City, and Robert Schuler of Garden Grove, California. Both were ordained in the Reformed Church in America, possibly the closest thing to a moderate denomination in the United States, if that is taken to mean midway between theologically liberal and conservative. Though both have described their denomination as similar to Methodism, in theology it is closer to the Presbyterian churches, with a Calvinist background. But socially, or socio-politically, it is very close to the United Methodists, who have many individual conservative evangelicals (like American Family Association founder and head Donald Wildmon) but is controlled by a liberal denominational establishment. Peale and Schuler carefully sidestepped making statements that could be called over the line from orthodoxy, but the emphases of their preaching and books have been more psychological, relational, and inclusive than evangelistic, and are more for believers than aimed at converting non-Christians.

Other Names: D. James Kennedy, Schaeffer, Pearcey

D. James Kennedy (b. 1930)

D. James Kennedy is pastor of the 10,000-member Coral Ridge Presbyterian Church in Fort Lauderdale, Florida, and claims to be "the most listened-to Presbyterian minister in America." His originally forty-five-member congregation was the fastest-growing church in the nation for fifteen years, which was the impetus for his writing *Evangelism Explosion*, which has been used as a cookbook for other congregations wanting to see similar growth results. His weekly televised services, called the *Coral Ridge Hour*, and his daily half-hour radio program, *Truths that Transform*, reach a national audience. His Coral Ridge Ministries includes the Center for Reclaiming America, which provides conferences, literature, and networking opportunities to Christians concerned about the nation's spiritual health.

Francis Schaeffer (1912—1984)

Francis Schaeffer was an evangelical Presbyterian minister who settled with his family in a remote chalet in Switzerland that he named *L'Abri* (French for "shelter") and waited for the world to come to him so he could convert it. Surprisingly, eventually it started to do so, as backpacking young tourists and truth-seekers found L'Abri and soon afterward found their worlds turned upside down this knickers-wearing and goateed American Calvinist transplant. *Time* magazine dubbed Schaeffer "an apostle to the intellectuals," and InterVarsity Christian Fellowship writer Gordon Govier wrote on the observance of the fiftieth anniversary of L'Abri that Schaeffer "may have done more to shape the culture of American evangelicals at the end of the 20th century than any one" other than C. S. Lewis and Billy Graham. This echoed similar sentiments by former University of Notre Dame professor Michael Hamilton in a 1997 piece on Schaeffer in *Christianity Today*.

factum

James Sire, retired editor of Inter-Varsity Press, which published most of Schaeffer's books, likens him to "Jeremiah, a weeping prophet whose message was that Christians need to be more involved in the public sphere."

Though Schaeffer's direct outreach was much smaller than the other evangelical icons discussed thus far—his books like *The God Who Is There*, *Escape from Reason*, *He Is There and He Is Not Silent*, and others had considerably smaller circulations than others cited—his critique of every philosophical trend from the Enlightenment to the current generation; and his knowledge of artists of all eras since the Renaissance and popular culture represented in music and movies reached the intellectuals and future intellectuals who came to visit. Often they ended up staying longer than they expected and coming back for more, and being changed for the rest of their lives. And they, now in places like college and university faculties, the media, politics, entertainment, and the arts are making the kind of impact he said Christians were meant to make in the culture of their times.

Nancy Pearcey

Nancy Pearcey is an example of one of those young seekers who found L'Abri and got converted back to Jesus and new meaning in her life. Raised in a Lutheran family and a devout child, like many she came to wonder if her faith was just there because it was all she'd been taught, and quietly and somewhat sadly, by the time she was in college, she'd left it behind. She says Schaeffer explained and demonstrated what the faith actually was—who Jesus really was—and slowly she started the metaphorical trek back home.

Now she is the author of *Total Truth: Liberating Christianity from Its Cultural Captivity*, a tour-de-force survey of the Christian worldview and its viability in opposition to secularism and post-modernism, which demonstrates that she has been blessed by Francis Schaeffer's influence. Appropriately, she is the Francis A. Schaeffer scholar at the Asheville, N.C.-based World Journalism Institute. Among other topics, her book covers the history of evangelical Christianity in America from colonial times, the chronicle of how American politics became secularized, modern Islam and the New Age movement, and the war between materialism and a Christian worldview.

Campus Crusade for Christ and InterVarsity Christian Fellowship

Probably no other single organization, including any denomination, has impacted the evangelical world more widely and deeply since its founding in 1951 by Bill and Vonette Bright at the University of California at Los Angeles than Campus Crusade for Christ. A veritable army of young evangelists who support themselves by raising pledges of sustaining contributions through friends, family, and churches, it is found at work in most campuses and many other locations, like high schools and military bases, around the world.

Some fellow evangelicals criticize the ministry for superficiality, as its "Four Spiritual Laws" booklet, used to begin most evangelistic conversations on campuses, omits some basic Christian teachings. Defenders maintain any shortcomings in the entrée mechanism are offset by intensive discipleship and fellowship, often spanning years of campus life.

factum

Campus Crusade is the largest evangelical organization in the United States, according to *USA Today* and others. Even governmental offices are targeted for outreach by Crusade staff members, through so-called Christian embassies in Washington and near the United Nations. Its film, *Jesus*, has been shown around the world more widely than any other film ever produced, Crusade spokespersons claim.

Though many see the modern secular university campuses as an unlikely environment for Christians and their faith, ministries like Campus Crusade, InterVarsity Christian Fellowship, Navigators, and other church-based and independent campus ministries help evangelical young adults get through the challenges of college life. These groups usually co-operate and try to be mutually supportive of major programs, though sometimes territorial disputes are claimed.

Part of the International Fellowship of Evangelical Students, InterVarsity, oriented more to serving already-persuaded Christian students than evangelizing, had 810 chapters at 560 campuses throughout the United States in the most recent year for which figures were available. Chapters are often organized around needs of specific student groups, like ethnic minorities (especially Asian Christian students), graduate students, and others. Tracing its roots to Cambridge University in 1877, the American branch has been incorporated since 1941, following InterVarsity's establishment in Canada by British campus missionary Howard Guinness. As of the latest reported figures, there are 1,000 InterVarsity staff members serving 35,000 American student members.

factum

InterVarsity Press supplies academically oriented books (like Schaeffer's, on trends in philosophy, the arts, and culture) to campus groups, adding 100 titles annually, with 800 currently in print. For years, campus chapters sold the books from tables in common areas, but since the 1970s, the books have been widely available through Christian booksellers and, more recently, secular bookstores.

Navigators dates its now-international ministry to 1933, when a southern California Sunday-school teacher, Dawson Trotman, enlisted his high school–aged class to join him in evangelizing sailors serving on nearby U.S. Navy facilities. Out of this work came the Navigators' ministry of spiritual multiplication. Today staff members minister to military installations around the world, on college campuses, and in many other locations. The Navigators have long led the after-decision follow-up ministry to Billy Graham evangelistic crusade converts. Incorporated in California in 1943, its headquarters is currently in Colorado Springs, Colorado.

The Christian College Movement

Though the original universities and other higher educational institutions were begun to serve their understanding of Jesus, many, like Oxford in England, Harvard in New England, and the University of Pennsylvania in Philadelphia (founded with financial support by Great Awakening evangelist John Whitefield) moved away from a Christian worldview once a secular humanist one was being widely accepted in academic circles. American evangelicals have attempted to counter this trend by establishing new Christ-centered (evangelical) colleges and universities.

According to the Council for Christian Colleges and Universities, only 102 American colleges are Christ centered. These member institutions are listed, along with associate members, in Appendix C: Evangelical Christian Institutions.

discussion question

How many American colleges are religious?
According to United States Department of Education figures, there are over 4,000 degree-granting higher educational institutions in the country, 1,600 of which are private nonprofit institutions, and 900 describe themselves as religiously affiliated.

Evangelical Media Initiatives

Pat Robertson's development of the Family Channel and the development of its related businesses were the furthest advances evangelicals ever made into that suspect world. Generations of preachers before Robertson considered the entertainment industry to be too worldly. But Robertson felt creating programming for his network was always a daunting challenge, since he wanted to avoid criticism and yet turn out commercially viable entertainment.

A former student at Wheaton (Illinois) College, who recalled the visit there in 1965 of Francis Schaeffer, told an interviewer that, at that time, some students were pushing school administrators to permit the showing on campus of movies like *Bambi*, a situation reversed over time because of Schaeffer's teaching. His lectures and books say that films and popular culture must be understood in order to better understand how Jesus' teachings apply to current culture.

Since Mel Gibson's phenomenally successful 2004 film, *The Passion of the Christ*, many serious Christians have expressed hope that what they had long perceived as the negative Hollywood attitude toward Christians may be past. *Christianity Today* reports that Christians in the entertainment industry are well entrenched and organized for mutual support and fellowship.

symbolism

For much of movie history, and still true in some evangelical circles, movies and evangelicals have had strained relations, the movies symbolizing the worst of worldliness, according to some preachers. The fact that whole churches went to see Gibson's *The Passion of the Christ* or rented it to show in their halls or sanctuaries is considered a historic turning point.

Many other efforts by Christians to offer viable Christian media, both aimed at the general public and the Christian subculture, have met with mixed reception, most not long sustained. One notable exceptions is *World* magazine, a Christian alternative to the mainstream news magazines, which is in its twentieth year of publication in a full-color format comparable to its much more famous counterparts. An outgrowth of the former *Presbyterian Journal* published by L. Nelson Bell (who also was a co-founder of *Christianity Today*), the founding editor and current CEO of *World* is Joel Belz.

World's editor-in-chief is University of Texas journalism professor Marvin Olasky, the author of *Compassionate Conservatism* and *The American Leadership Tradition*. Olasky has been credited with being the policy wonk behind the Clinton administration's welfare-reform legislation, and critics have blamed him for having had a hand in inspiring the Bush administration's faith-based initiatives programs. Published fifty times a year, *World* magazine claims to follow *Time*, *Newsweek*, and *U.S. News & World Report* as the fourth most widely read weekly newsmagazine in the United States.

Finally in 1965 Billy Graham founded *Christianity Today*, with theologian Carl F. H. Henry serving as its founding editor. Slotted as an evangelical alternative to the liberal and considerably older *Christian Century*, it has since left its competitor far behind, regularly reaching two million readers through its print and online editions.

Chapter 18

Jesus and the Culture Wars

During a public debate in 1999 among Republican candidates Steve Forbes, Alan Keyes, and George W. Bush for their party's nomination for president, they were asked which political philosopher or thinker had influenced them. Bush answered, "Christ, because he changed my heart." Some questioned whether the term "political philosopher or thinker" really applies to Jesus, but Bush's answer was well received by the public at large and was quickly taken up by the mainstream media pundits as another volley in the so-called culture wars.

The Apolitical Jesus

In the Sermon on the Mount, Jesus made it plain that he was no revolutionary, and that his was not a political movement (Matthew 5:17–20). In another case, he even advocated that the people of Judea pay their taxes, even though the taxes amounted to tribute the Judeans were forced to pay to their oppressors (see Luke 20:19–26). This "give to Caesar what is Caesar's" passage has been used for centuries to support the doctrine of separation of church and state, which was a founding principle of the American nation. American Protestants, especially, have been partial to this teaching of Jesus because, since the Great Awakening, when the new evangelical converts started to outnumber the old established-church members, it became more popular to be opposed to established churches that had previously been recognized as official state churches.

All of the original American states except Maryland (which was founded by Catholics) had its own established church, but after the Great Awakening, when new denominations came to dominate, the sentiment began to turn against having established churches.

fallacy

Some think that Pat Buchanan—erstwhile White House staff member, syndicated columnist, and conservative TV talking head—wrote the book on the culture wars, but actually he only gave a speech invoking the term at the 1992 Republican National Convention, a reference that ignited significant controversy. Many other books have taken up the culture-war theme.

No Established Church

"No established church" was what the separation of church and state meant for most of American history. The actual words of the First Amendment of the U.S. Constitution prohibit the "establishment of religion," meaning a tax-supported state church. Today most active American Protestants are now much more comfortable and trusting of their Catholic neighbors than they are of secularists, deists, and free-thinkers who claim to be in the tradition of Thomas Paine, Benjamin Franklin, and Thomas Jefferson. This was not the case in the era of the American War for Independence and the century and a half afterward.

Caesar's Due

As mentioned previously, when Jesus was asked if was okay to pay tribute to Caesar, he answered, "Render to Caesar what is Caesar's." Thousands might have been spared martyrdom if they said they were "just rendering to Caesar" and followed Roman law by sacrificing to the imperial deity's likeness. But if any early Christians used that defense, it hasn't been kept in the early church annals, as the memory of those who died is.

Following in the tradition of the martyrs who were burned alive rather than burn incense to Caesar, the fourth-century Christians whom Emperor Constantine consulted about his newfound faith apparently did not tell him he had no political responsibility before God; or that government is politics and faith is religion, and the two shall never mingle. Instead, they introduced him to the many teachings of Jesus, Paul, and the Old Testament concerning the imperative for righteousness and justice in all human pursuits, including law and government, and he immediately began reforming his government.

The discussion in Chapter 8 of Matthew 21:19–21, about the withering of the fig tree and Jesus' promising a faith that would move a mountain, involved interpreting the fig tree as Israel, the nation the church would leave behind; and the mountain as Rome, the empire the church would move from paganism to widespread belief in him. The political implications are apparent: Jesus has the power to change everything, and over time and with faithful obedience and sacrifice, faith moves mountains and can change systems of government from the bottom up.

Red State/Blue State, Left/Right, Sheep/Goats

In Matthew 25:31–33 Jesus foretells the great judgment. "When the Son of Man shall come in his glory, and all the holy angels with him, he shall sit on the throne of his glory and all nations shall be gathered before him. And he shall separate them one from another, as a shepherd divides his sheep from the goats, and he shall set the sheep on his right hand, but the goats on the left." His words no doubt struck a familiar chord with his Jewish audience, familiar with Psalm 33:12, "Blessed is the nation whose God is the Lord; and the people he has chosen for his own inheritance." And a very similar one on the way to win God's favor: "Righteousness exalts a nation, but sin brings reproach to any people" (Psalm 14:34).

Many conservative Christians use these verses from the Psalms to make a case for bringing more godliness to America or even making it, or declaring it, a Christian nation. But liberal critics see a specter of theocracy in such talk, and sociologists suspect that what the conservative Christians are doing is promoting their religion as America's civil religion.

Theocracy

"Theocracy," or a government subject to a religious authority, has become a label in many media treatments of Christian political action, especially when describing the political initiatives of the red-state conservatives. Writing in the *Village Voice* before the second George W. Bush election tallies were complete, James Ridgeway, under the headline, "Bush gets mandate for theocracy," wrote, "The dream of a secular, liberal democracy is lost: Christians are stronger than ever . . . ." It was a note sounded by many magazine feature writers and columnists in the subsequent months.

The president's invocation of Jesus as his favorite thinker and reports from journalists or White House insiders that he has a daily prayer life has been interpreted by some critics to imply that he thinks he has a pipeline to God or that he thinks he is getting his daily assignments through prayer exercises, and this gets him labeled a theocrat.

Though the American liberal political movement also has notable religious leaders among its well-known figures (for example, Jesse Jackson, Al Sharpton, Jim Wallis, Barry W. Lynn, Dr. Bob Edgar), their pronouncements are seldom described as injecting religion into politics, or promoting their own theocratic vision. Looking at the word in its roots, *theocracy* means government (*ocracy*) by God (*theos*) directly. First introduced as a term by Flavius Josephus in *Jewish Antiquities*, it described the way ancient Israel was governed under the Patriarchs (Moses in particular) and the judges (among the best known being Joshua, Gideon, and Samson, plus a dozen others between Moses and the first king, Saul). As Judges 8:23 puts it, "Gideon said to them, 'I will not rule over you, neither shall my son rule over you; the Lord shall rule over you.'"

discussion question

What ended the biblical theocracy?
There is much negotiating in the Old Testament between the people, petitioning God to give them a king so they could look good alongside the other kingdoms of their time, and God, warning that a king will do bad things like raise taxes, draft sons into the military, and lead the nation into idolatry.

Even after the establishment of the new Old Testament government as a monarchy, however, God continued to let his will be known directly to the king and the people through the prophets, whose sermons were God's word to them. For many generations after establishing the monarchy, Israel had good kings and bad kings. Good kings listened to the prophets and acted in accord with God's will revealed through them. Bad kings did "that which was right in their own sight."

Democracy or Anarchy?

As political theorists have observed, the theocracy under the patriarchs and judges was close to a true democracy or anarchy. If the judges told the people what to do and they voluntarily and ungrudgingly did it, it was democratic. If the judges told the people what God wanted and they refused, it was anarchic. Despite there being no physical coercion, rebellion against the judges seldom occurred. The Old Testament simile for this is expressed in 1 Kings 4:25: "every man under his vine and under his fig tree, from Dan to Beersheba." Sitting under his own "vine and fig tree" symbolizes the peace and security in Israel when they were faithful to God. Dan and Beersheba, the southernmost and northernmost cities in the land, is a simile for, "from border to border."

Current use of *theocracy*, as cited above, attempts to apply it to any political theory that supports a role for God or of godliness in any approach to governing. In November 2004, writer Stephen Pizzo said that the Democrats should avoid "values politics" rather than imitate the Republicans, because to do so would even more "Talibanize" the United States. Afghanistan under the Taliban and Iran under the Ayatollahs may be genuine theocracies, but using the democratic process to advocate for one philosophy of what constitutes public morality over another is politically poles away from such totalitarian systems. And though there is much work among Christian scholars to propose the best configuration of democracy in a Christian worldview, no Christian scholar or professor of political theory has been found who advocates turning modern democracies into theocracies.

Christian Theocracy Is an Oxymoron

Though many authoritarian figures in history have claimed to govern as Christians (Spanish dictator Francisco Franco, 1892–1975, to cite one recent example), Christian political theorists say the New Testament precludes theocracy as a viable form of government in pluralistic societies. The way the Gospel should be spread—by voluntary assent of the heart, rather than coercion of either the intellect or the body—favors pluralistic societies for Christians over monolithic or totalitarian ones. Jesus said the tares, weedy plants that grow in grain fields and a symbol of unbelievers, are to be lived with in toleration by the wheat, his metaphor for the believing children of God (Matthew 13:25–30 and 36–40).

Civil Religion

Defined as "the folk religion of a people," civil religion usually appears as a widespread acknowledgement of divine approval, guidance, or help in public life, usually by elected officials like the president, governors, mayors, and professional administrators, and especially in former times, in institutions like public schools and the military. Patriotism and civil religion are intermingled; ceremonies like military funerals, Memorial Day programs, and, formerly, high-school graduations use prayers, and even participation of clergy, but usually without sectarian or denominational distinctions.

factum

All United States presidents have invoked God as the nation's judge and provider, which usually has been perceived as civil religion or "saying what the people think they understand," even if they may be understanding it differently than the speaker does.

Some Christian scholars and authors caution against confusing civil religion or patriotism itself with Christianity, lest the government or its institutions become idols and God be nationalized as America's God, at the expense of any nations opposing America. Scholars also caution against equating the United States with Old Testament Israel or God's chosen people, or failing to understand biblical prophecies for Israel in historical and geographical context. Christian writers on this topic usually advocate looking for the personal and organizational application of biblical teachings, and making them part of a personal or organizational political perspective rather than trying to apply them to the nation. In the Constitution, the nation as a whole considers itself to be "governed by the people," not by God, and biblical revelation does not specify the role God has for the United States, as he had for the Israel of old.

Light and Darkness

A central teaching of Jesus that has been applied to Christian action in political situations is Matthew 5:15–16: "Neither do men light a candle, and put it under a bushel, but on a candlestick; and it giveth light unto all that are in the house. Let your light so shine before men, that they may see your good works, and glorify your Father which is in heaven." The passage was adapted by the Puritan colonists who came to Massachusetts in the early seventeenth century to describe how they perceived their goal and their mission as being "a city on a hill" to enlighten the other nations. Their minister, John Winthrop, used this passage in a sermon given while they were en route to the new world. Christians working on helping the still relatively new nation clarify and pursue its vision have reiterated this passage many times since.

God on All Our Sides

Ronald Reagan characteristically said, "We shouldn't worry so much about whether God is on our side as whether we're on his." Puritan preacher and Massachusetts Governor John Winthrop (of the "city on a hill" allusion made earlier) told his congregation (paraphrased): "if we deal falsely with our God in this undertaking, causing him to withdraw his present help from us, we shall become a story and a byword throughout the world; we shall open the mouths of enemies to speak evil of God's ways and all believers for God's sake; we shall bring shame on many worthy servants of God, and turn their prayers into curses on us, until we are consumed out of the good land that we are going to."

The Old Testament aligns God on the side of victims of unrighteousness, violence, and injustice. He sides with the oppressed, those who mourn, and those who seek him (see Leviticus 25, 1

Kings 21, Isaiah 5:8, Jeremiah 7: 5–7, Isaiah 58: 4–12, Micah 6: 7–8). Jesus affirmed that perpetrators of injustice will be judged harshly (Matthew 24 and Mark 13).

God is on the side of those who take a stand for righteousness, Psalm 14:34 says. He's on the side of justice, Jeremiah says in an Old Testament prophecy about the Messiah, "the day is coming, says the Lord, when I will raise to David a righteous Branch, and a King shall reign and prosper, and shall execute judgment and justice in the earth" (see Jeremiah 23:5).

The church in general says God is on the side of everyone on this planet, because everyone is his child, an object of the redemption Jesus obtained on the cross. God has invested in everyone in his world, and Christian politics is first about justice, a form of God's mercy to all people: "To do justice and judgment is more acceptable to the Lord than sacrifice" (see Proverbs 21:3).

Christian Politics

Lutheran scholar Dr. Gene Edward Veith, Jr., culture editor of *World* magazine and executive director of The Cranach Institute, a research and education arm of Concordia Theological Seminary in Fort Wayne, Indiana, has spoken and written about Martin Luther's seeing the world in terms of two kingdoms, comparable to the realm of darkness and the realm of light in Jesus' teaching. In Luther's view, Veith says, Christ is the Lord of both the secular kingdom and the spiritual kingdom.

In the secular kingdom, Christ reigns whether or not the subjects know they are his. To paraphrase Proverbs 21:1, the hearts of all human kings, all people in authority, are in the Lord's hand. But the main point Veith promotes is that the secular king can be an intentional servant of God just as legitimately as the ministers, missionaries, or evangelists who find their vocations in the spiritual kingdom.

Vocation, God's Calling

A vocation, in Veith's view, is doing one's calling in whatever can be of service to God. And inasmuch as the earth is the Lord's, and Jesus is king of (all) kings and Lord of all, any legitimate life's work is to be seen as a vocation given by the Lord.

This Lutheran foundational worldview is similar to one built on John Calvin's teachings about vocations, similarly legitimizing any work (other than those that are unlawful or immoral) for Christians wanting to serve the Lord through their talents. Since the latter years of the nineteenth century, scholars in the Netherlands and the United States have greatly expanded on Calvin's thoughts.

symbolism

Abraham Kuyper suggested the "kingdoms," which he called "spheres," be enlarged to six instead of two. He added a God or Creator sphere ruling over the temporal, or created, spheres of family, life work, recreation and education.

Abraham Kuyper (1837–1920), a Dutch Reformed pastor, scholar, journalist, educator, and political reformer, made the greatest addition to Calvin's foundation, which he laid out in a series of lectures on Calvinism he delivered at Princeton University in 1899. The main point of Kuyper's Princeton lectures, as McKendree R. Langley of Westminster Theological Seminary said in a centennial essay about these lectures, was "that the Christian faith is both for salvation and for the rest of life." And to show partly what he meant by "the rest of life," Kuyper established a university, The Free University of Amsterdam, which still thrives as a Reformed Christian alternative institution of higher education.

But Kuyper's main contribution was in the field of political theory. He is credited with having introduced democratic representative government to the Netherlands (which was a monarchy but had been won and lost several times as European superpowers ran over it in the eighteenth and nineteenth centuries). He created the country's first political party, and the first in the world to be based on Christian principles for doing politics and statecraft. Originally called the ARP, Anti-Revolutionary Party (a philosophical dig at the French exportation of their Revolution through much of the nineteenth century), it has more recently been merged with several other confessionally Christian parties to become the largest constituency in the Christian Democratic Appeal. From Kuyper's election as prime minister in 1905, the ARP remained in power most of the time, and the CDA, its successor, is at this writing the party in power. The ARP was the model for the other European Christian Democratic political movements, most of which have been based on Catholic teachings and constituencies.

Despite numerous secularist complaints and warnings that theocrats are taking over the United States government, the only Christian movement with a comprehensive approach to political reform for the United States was established on Kuyper's pluralist principles, which include equal treatment of all faiths, not on theocratic principles.

Public Justice

The Washington-based Center for Public Justice (CPJ) has been working for more than twenty-five years to bring principles of public justice to bear on American politics and government. Its most successful effort has been to help define the Charitable Choice provision of the 1996 welfare-reform law (signed by President Clinton), which requires equal treatment of faith-based and all other non-government social-service organizations that co-operate with government in delivering services. Stanley Carlson-Thies, the Center's director of social policy studies, also helped organize the White House office of faith-based and community initiatives in the first year of the George W. Bush administration.

The Center established that no helping program, whether conducted by government agencies like FEMA or nongovernmental ones like the Salvation Army, Catholic Charities, and Red Cross, works on a basis of values neutrality. The administrators of government programs can and do impose their own values on their programs and their administration, which competes with more openly defined helping programs.

fallacy

The Center for Public Justice says that although pluralism is widely misunderstood as based on compromise, principled pluralism is a biblically consistent alternative to multicultural politics. Where multiculturalism is based on ethnicity, nationality, and sexual orientation, pluralism is principle-based, with each minority defining itself by its worldview and goals, whether religious or secular.

War in the Flesh and in the Spirit

Besides light and darkness, there is also a clear exposition in the teachings of Jesus and the apostles on the relationship between the flesh and the spirit. However, this is not as simple a division between two kingdoms as it may seem.

Flesh and Spirit as Enemies

On the one hand, some teachings imply that the flesh is the enemy of the spirit, and often this is how the division is taught. Some examples suggest that kind of clear distinction. In Matthew 26:41 (also Mark 14:38), Jesus says, "The spirit indeed is willing, but the flesh is weak." In John 3:6, "that which is born of the flesh is flesh; and that which is born of the Spirit is spirit." John 6:63: "the spirit makes alive, the flesh profits nothing. The words that I speak to you are spirit, and they are life." The Apostle Paul also discusses the dichotomy between flesh and spirit. In Romans 8:1, he states: "There is no condemnation to those who are in Christ Jesus, who walk not after the flesh, but after the Spirit."

Spirit is Able to Cleanse the Flesh

But on the other hand, flesh participates in salvation and receives the spirit in itself. Luke 3:6 illustrates: "All flesh shall see the salvation of God." In Luke 24:39, Jesus says: "See my hands and my feet, that it is I myself. Handle me and see, for a spirit does not have flesh and bones, as you see me have." And in John 1:14 he confirms a positive aspect of the flesh: "the Word was made flesh, and dwelt among us, and we beheld his glory, the glory as of the only begotten of the Father, full of grace and truth."

Finally, the flesh of Jesus is able to purify the spirit of those who receive it. John 6:51–56 states: "'I am the living bread that came down from heaven: if any eats of this bread, he shall live forever, and the bread that I will give is my flesh, which I will give for the life of the world.' The Jews argued among themselves, asking, 'How can this man give us his flesh to eat?' To which Jesus replied, 'Truly I say, except you eat the flesh of the Son of man and drink his blood, you have no life in you. Whoever eats my flesh and drinks my blood has eternal life and I will raise him up at the last day. For my flesh is meat, indeed, and my blood is drink indeed. He who eats my flesh and drinks my blood dwells in me, and I in him.'" This is the institution of Holy Communion, the meal of thanksgiving or Eucharist.

Flesh and Spirit Reconciled

Paul seems to untie the knot in this riddle in Romans 8:3–5. "What the law could not do, in its weakness through the flesh, God, by sending his own Son in the likeness of sinful flesh, and for [the sake of] sin, condemned sin in the flesh in order that the righteousness of the law might be fulfilled in us who walk not after the flesh, but after the Spirit. For those who are born of the flesh are always mindful of the things of the flesh; but those who are born of the Spirit are mindful of the things of the Spirit."

discussion question

Is war inevitable?
There will always be wars between the lusts of the flesh, and those parties in the human community who find their glory in the flesh on one side; and the ineffable freedom of God's spirit renewing our flesh, and those parties that want the glory of the human race to be their risen King.

Verses 8–9 say: "So then, those who are in the flesh cannot please God. But you are not in the flesh but in the Spirit if the Spirit of God dwells in you. Now if any man does not have the Spirit of Christ, he is none of his." And finally, verse 12–13 state: "Therefore, brothers, we are not debtors to the flesh, to live after the flesh, for if you live after the flesh, you shall die: but if you through the Spirit mortify the deeds of the body, ye shall live."

Purification

The Christian mindset is not to be set against "flesh." Christianity is not a dualism like some strands of Gnosticism, which hold that matter is profane, bound, and binding, and the spirit is holy, free, and freeing. Christians believe Christ came to make the flesh holy. In taking his flesh into our own, we begin renewing our bodies into spiritual bodies. In the resurrection, our flesh is raised to new life: "Handle me and see, for a spirit does not have flesh and bones, as you see me have."

The Dividing Line

Spiritual warfare is inevitable for Christians, and one of the ways it makes itself evident is in what is currently called the culture wars. Each side tends to demonize the other and think that the other side epitomizes the evil tendencies in our time and in our socio-political life. But the great pitfall of engaging in such wars is that the focus may shift from the spiritual prize to the flesh-and-blood enemy, and the conflict may shift from fighting in the spirit to fighting in the flesh. "For we wrestle not against flesh and blood, but against principalities, against powers, against the rulers of the darkness of this world, against spiritual wickedness in high places," Paul writes in Ephesians 6:12.

The funny thing about the darkness and the light, the flesh and the spirit, is that all human beings have both of them. To paraphrase Alexander Solzhenitsyn, it would be nice to separate the good people from the bad. But it's not so easy because the line dividing good from evil cuts not through the sides of the culture wars, but through the heart of every human being.

Chapter 19

The Jesus of the Future

There is a general sense in human thinking that the end is nigh, our doom is sealed. To some extent every religion in human history has addressed such fears. "Run for the hills" echoes Jesus' words in Matthew 24, "When you see the abomination of desolation spoken of by Daniel the prophet . . . then let those who are in Judea flee into the mountains" (verses 15–16).

The Second Coming of Christ

Jesus' return was promised by two angels who appeared to his disciples at his ascension, as Luke relates in Acts 1:10–11: "While they looked steadily toward heaven as he ascended, two men dressed in white stood by them and said, 'You men of Galilee, why do you stand gazing up to heaven? This same Jesus, who is taken from you into heaven, shall come back in the same manner as you have seen him taken up.'"

Maranatha

Three New Testament texts refer to "Maranatha"; one in the Aramaic, and the other two in translation. In 1 Corinthians 16:22 the Apostle Paul says, "If any man does not love the Lord Jesus Christ, let him be Anathema Maranatha." In other words, "let him be accursed; the Lord comes." Or, more likely, he means the Lord is nearby, as in, "the Lord sees and judges; we do not have to worry about it." Many Bible scholars see Philippians 4:4–5 as having the same point, though the Aramaic form *Maran atha* does not appear there: "Rejoice in the Lord always; I repeat, rejoice. Let your moderation be known to all men. The Lord is at hand."

factum

Maran atha are two Aramaic words that mean "our Lord comes." Evangelicals, and especially Pentecostals, have anglicized it, and use the word as an indication of their expectation of and orientation toward the Second Coming or Second Advent of Jesus.

Jesus Returns

All Christians believe in the Second Coming (among those who hold the Nicene Creed, Apostles Creed, or both as definitive, which all but some liberal and post-Christians do). In the Apostles Creed that belief is expressed: "He ascended into heaven and sits at the right hand of God the Father Almighty, whence he shall come to judge the living and the dead."

In the Nicene Creed, the same belief is stated as follows: "he suffered and was buried; and the third day he rose again, according to the Scriptures; and ascended into heaven, and sits on the right hand of the Father; and he shall come again, with glory, to judge the living and the dead; whose kingdom shall have no end."

The epistle of James the Lord's brother has a similar teaching in chapter 5:8–9: "Be patient; establish your hearts, for the coming of the Lord draws nigh. Don't hold grudges against one another, brethren, lest you be condemned. Behold, the judge stands at the door." James' take on the Lord's nearness incorporates both the idea that the Lord is always present, watching, and also that his "coming back is drawing near," ambiguously connecting his omnipresence with his Second Advent.

Ambiguity Is Key

Most references to the Second Advent are widely believed to include this ambiguity. In fact, in Paul's epistles, this ambiguous sense of his presence and his return is thought of as the essence of the Christian's hope, which is a major theme in Paul's writing. The most pointed instance of this in Paul's writings is Titus 2:13–14: "Looking for the blessed hope and the glorious appearing of the great God and our Savior Jesus Christ, that being justified by his grace, we should be made heirs according to the hope of eternal life." Here, Paul specifically refers to our hope as the Second Coming, but also ties every other kind of hope we have arising from our faith in him to that event.

Patience Required

One of the most provocative passages about the Second Coming is Hebrews 10:36–39: "You must have patience so that, after you have done the will of God, you might receive what has been promised. For a little while yet, then he who shall come will come, and will not tarry. The just shall live by faith, but if any man draws back, my soul shall have no pleasure in him. But we are not the type who draw back to perdition; but the type who believe to the saving of the soul."

symbolism

Another way of referring to the Second Coming is as a metaphor for death or faith in the Lord. Evangelicals' use of the phrase "if the Lord tarries," has as its first meaning "if the Second Coming doesn't happen first," but people often mean by it "if the Lord doesn't take me first" or "if I live that long."

In other words, it won't be long until the Lord comes, so wait patiently. In fact, as seen in the previous passage, he's already at the door. The writer of Hebrews seems to think Jesus' coming is going to happen at any time in this first generation of the church, but as it did not occur, many Christians think the point that God wants to convey is that we should always live as though Jesus is at the door, but not be anxious about it. Death is, after all, a type of Second Coming also, as God sends his angels to escort home those of his faithful who have believed to the end.

Are These the Last Times?

Some believe that when Jesus refers to "the last times," he is referring only to the last times for the covenant of God with Israel, which these believers think ended with the First Jewish-Roman war and the destruction of Herod's Temple in Jerusalem in A.D. 70. Though this has some truth, others say the references to "last times" refer to the era of the church, and see that as extending from the time of the Book of Acts to the present, as suggested earlier in the point made about the intentional ambiguity of the meaning of the Second Coming.

When Will it Happen?

William Miller, a nineteenth-century Baptist farmer in New York state, studied the Bible according to prophetic tools he had developed, and with the help of Bishop James Ussher's dating of the biblical time periods, concluded that the Second Coming of Christ would take place in 1843. Upward of 100,000 people anticipated the fulfillment of the prophecy that year, many of them divesting themselves of their assets to prepare, but they were disappointed (or relieved).

In 1970, Hal Lindsey, one of the most widely read prophecy experts in American evangelical circles, wrote in *The Late Great Planet Earth* that, based on biblical prophecies about the restoration of the nation of Israel, within a generation of modern Israel's founding in 1948, all things prophesied in Matthew 24 should come to pass.

Critics say that, biblically, a generation is about forty years, so by 1988 all the prophesies Jesus made about the end times should have come to pass, according to Lindsey's timetable. But there is no evidence that the scenario presented in Matthew 24 was being played out between 1948 and 1988.

discussion question

What is eschatology?
Eschatology is the technical term in theology for the study of "last things" or the age to come, which in Greek is *eschaton*. Speaking of a church's or a teacher's eschatology refers to the view held concerning the end times or the culmination of the age, based on the interpretation of the biblical teachings on these questions.

Harold Camping, founder of the Family Radio network and its major on-air personality, predicted in 1994 that the apocalypse would occur in September that year, but that he could not predict the exact date because Matthew 24:36 says, "no man knows the day and hour, no, not the angels of heaven, but my Father only." Many in his radio audiences were disappointed, and some, it has been reported, were relieved when the apocalypse didn't occur.

Prophecy-based Cults

There have been many secular and cult groups built around prophecies. Some of these groups are infamous, like David Koresh's Branch Dividians, Jim Jones' People's Temple, and the "Heaven's Gaters" with their Hale-Bopp Comet prophesies. The prophecy experts cited previously profess to be traditional Christians, and are generally accepted as such within Christian circles.

Considering the way Old Testament prophecies about the Messiah are used by the writers of the New Testament (emphasizing the failure to discern the prophecies), it's not surprising that Christians in later times would look for signs that the Second Coming might happen soon. Many believe, even, that it would be an error to fail to look for such signs.

Christian Disagreements about "Ultimate Things"

In *The Church and the Last Things*, Dr. Martyn Lloyd-Jones, a South Wales native who became what some believe to be "possibly the greatest British preacher of the twentieth century," describes the difference between the preterist and the futurist views of biblical prophecies. Preterists believe the prophecies have now been fulfilled; futurists believe they are still to unfold in the future.

factum

Isaac Newton allegedly said, "About the time of the end ... men will ... turn their attention to prophecies, and insist upon their literal interpretation." And Blaise Pascal is quoted as saying, "Prophecies are to be unintelligible to the ungodly but intelligible to those who are properly instructed."

Controversy over the Millennium

One of the major points contested within theological schools is what the Bible teaches about the millennium, meaning "the thousand-year reign of Christ" that many find in Revelation 20. In the church at large, there are three major divisions of thinking regarding how prophecy about the millennium is to be interpreted.

Amillennialism

Also known as nunc millennialism, or no millennium, amillennialism holds that the thousand-year reign of Christ is figurative, not to be taken as referring to a literal thousand-year period. The reign of the church as the body of Christ is seen as the symbolical or spiritual millennium, which has already exceeded two literal millennia; this opinion also includes that the church is the earthly, spiritual expression of the Kingdom of God. Though some people believe in the relative inactivity of satanic forces in areas of the world where the church is influential, as opposed to those areas where paganism still prevails, amillennialists believe the church and the forces of evil will coexist throughout the reign of Christ as head of the church. With some variations, amillennialism is the traditional eschatology of the Catholic, Orthodox, Lutheran, Calvinist (Presbyterian, Reformed), Anglican, and Methodist Churches.

Premillennialism

Premillennialism teaches that the Second Coming of Christ will occur before the millennium, which will be a literal thousand-year reign on earth of the conquering Prince of Peace. In the United States and in the parts of the world where missionaries are primarily American evangelicals, premillennialism is by far the most widely held view among Baptists, Pentecostals, and most other evangelicals. Though advocates see a belief in premillennialism reaching back to early church history, it has had its greatest growth since the dispensational system introduced by John Nelson Darby (1800–1882).

discussion question

What is the Great Tribulation?
It is a seven-year period of persecution under the reign of the anti-christ. Pretribulationists believe that the rapture of the believing church occurs before the antichrist begins his reign of destruction, mid-tribulationists pinpoint it at three and a half years in, and post-tribulationists believe the rapture will come after the tribulation.

Postmillennialism

Postmillennialism teaches that the Second Coming will occur after the millennium, and therefore, like the amillennialists, they believe that the thousand-year reign of Christ is figurative, in and through the church, not literal, as from an earthly throne. The postmillennial emphasis is on purifying the church and, through the church, defeating and binding Satan in the world, and bringing about the peace of the Prince of Peace. In this way the postmillennialists hope to purify the world in order to make it ready to meet Christ as his bride. Postmillenialism is often characterized as triumphalism, pushing for the victory of the church in the present age. No major denominations are identified as postmillennial, but individuals like the late R. J. Rushdoony, Gary North, and Greg Bahnsen, and their movements (theonomy, reconstructionism) advocate it.

Dispensationalism

Dispensationalism, which is traced to a pietistic movement in England in the 1820s called Plymouth Brethren, interprets the whole Bible in terms of particular ways God interacts with his people under different covenants and time periods. So something true of one group of believers in one dispensation, meaning believers of a specific time period and under a specific set of covenants, may not apply to or be required of other believers in another dispensation. And there can be more than one dispensation at the same time, according to some dispensationalists. Followers of this approach think that God interacts simultaneously with the Jewish people under one dispensation, and with Christians under another.

factum

Many churches believe these opinions about the millennium are not required for salvation and so they are willing to tolerate any of these among their clergy. Positions that were described previously as being held by certain denominations and communions are indicative of the great majority in those communions, but are not necessarily the only view permitted.

Taken to its logical conclusion, the system ends up asserting that the teachings of Jesus in the Gospels are entirely for the Jewish people, and that only the teachings of Paul and part of the book of Acts are for the church. The *Scofield Study Bible* (1909) formalized dispensationalist teaching in some detail, and this system's major academic defense has come from Dallas Theological Seminary. For all Christians, at its simplest, the Old Covenant and the New Covenant (synonymous with the Old Testament and the New Testament) have at least two dispensations, but adding other modes of interaction between God and his people (beside the two basic ones—Old and New Testaments) becomes dispensationalism.

Chiliasm

Strongly committed amillennialists equate premillennialism with chiliasm (from the Greek, *chiliasmos*, meaning "a thousand years"), which the church condemned as a heresy at the second Ecumenical Council in 381. Critics of premillennialism say that the words in the Nicene Creed, "he shall come again, with glory, to judge the living and the dead; whose kingdom shall have no end" were specifically intended to oppose the teaching that Christ's reign would be for a specific thousand-year period, as chiliasm taught and contemporary premillennialists also teach.

discussion question

Why do some believe the millennium will be a time of decadence?
Early chiliasts believed that the thousand-year kingdom of Christ would be a time of gluttonous feasting and sexual excess, which others say contradicts Paul's declaration in Romans 14:17, "the kingdom of God is not food and drink."

Anabaptists in 1533 established the German city of Munster as the New Jerusalem, in fulfillment of the chiliast belief in the establishment of a physical kingdom of God on earth. According to Owen Chadwick in *The Reformation*, the "radical reformers" (mostly Anabaptists) banned all who refused to be baptized, and they proclaimed John of Leyden the king of New Zion. They interpreted Old Testament teachings as permitting polygamy, and some of their men took multiple wives.

The "kingdom" declared war on the rest of the world, calling for the annihilation of all the ungodly. Only after two years, when some saner minds in the city conspired against their leaders and opened the gates to outside troops, who had been sent to quell their revolution, was the insurrection put down.

The Kingdom of Munster revolution has remained infamous in church history as the saddest instance of Reformation fever gone wild. Luther was apparently chagrined that his declarations of independence from the Pope had been taken to such extremes. This disaster encouraged Luther and Calvin to speak and write against chiliasm and any efforts to establish a literal Kingdom of God in the temporal world. The Lutheran Augsburg Confession and the

Reformed Second Helvetic (Swiss) Confession specifically condemn chiliasm.

The Prophecy Trap

Dr. Martyn Lloyd-Jones in *The Church and the Last Things* cautions his readers against becoming "exclusivists," meaning they shouldn't be unwilling to consider views of the millennium and "ultimate things" other than the one they find most accord with. Dr. Lloyd-Jones feels exclusivism sometimes leads to an obsession about what will happen before the Second Coming.

Dedicated followers of Hal Lindsey and other dispensationalists generally have strong opinions about the modern State of Israel, based on their view of its role in the End Times. Some of them think the Jewish Temple must be restored in fulfillment of prophecy in order that the antichrist can rule the world from a throne there during the Great Tribulation. Lindsey has told audiences that he has been invited to present his eschatological views at the Pentagon and other governmental agencies, which he implies has helped mold United States policy toward Israel and her enemies.

factum

When interest in prophesy turns into obsession, it often leads to foolish moves like those made by the followers of William Miller, who sold homes and other assets to be unencumbered when the Lord returned, only to find themselves in embarrassing straits, if not dire ones, when he failed to appear at the prophesied time.

Christian financial planner Jim Parris has warned his audiences that "not investing because the Lord may be coming back soon" is a prophecy-based financial trap that may lead to years of regret, and investing or liquidating assets based on one's own interpretation of end-times events, or those of a favorite prophet, can be disastrous for yourself and those putting trust in you. Jesus himself, in his most prophetic sermon, warns, "There shall arise false Christs, and false prophets, who shall demonstrate great signs and wonders; so much so that, if it were possible, they shall deceive the very elect" (Matthew 24:24). Even some of God's chosen leaders have been deceived, as shown in the biblical record. Usually it was their own conceits that led them into error, relying on their own judgment rather than depending on God's guidance.

Jesus' Teaching on the End Times

Most of Jesus' teaching on the end of the age takes place on the Mount of Olives, and therefore scholars refer to it as the Olivet Discourse. Matthew's Gospel, chapter 24, begins with Jesus' describing the destruction of the Temple in A.D. 70, followed by his disciples asking for more input about the things that must come to pass before the end of the age.

symbolism

Prophetic passages in the Old Testament symbolize things taking place when the prophet speaks and preaches, but at the same time other phrases are dropped in that foreshadow the coming of the Messiah and the ultimate salvation of Israel.

Jesus' speech seems ambiguous, as though in the same sentence his focus may be on the disciples and the generation they still have to live out, but a few words later seems to be focusing a millennium or two into the future. It is not hard to see why Christians of every age since the first generation want to find in these words, which seem to scan down the centuries, ways to apply parts of them to themselves. At the very least, these words are intentionally, ambiguously, speaking to both the end of the age of Israel under the Old Covenant in A.D. 70 and the culmination of the age of the church some undefined time in the future.

Tribulations

At least some Catholics, Orthodox, and amillennialist Protestants take this discourse as speaking of both the end of the age of Israel and the culmination of the age of the church. Jesus is talking about the persecution of the church under Emperor Vespasian and Military Commander Titus in the first Jewish-Roman war, and of the persecutions of the Christians that would be just beginning when the abomination of desolation takes place in the Temple and it is destroyed.

Jesus' description of how Christians will die and will want to run for the hills closely captures the waves of persecutions that began when the Temple fell in the church's first generation, and continued for the next three centuries. He mentions repeatedly that those who withstand the tribulation, the great persecutions, meaning those who do not turn back on their baptisms to be spared, will be saved. The Orthodox churches have always said he does not give the people hope that they will escape the tribulation by being raptured.

Signs of the End

Yet amillennialists, too, find prophecies here pertaining to the Second Coming, still in the future. An anonymous Orthodox writer finds "signs of the second coming" in the Olivet Discourse, beginning with "The Gospel of the Kingdom shall be preached in all the world as a witness unto all nations; and then the end shall come" (Matthew 24:14). There are signs that this is being fulfilled in the twenty-first century as never before.

Another sign appears in Luke's Gospel, where Jesus asks, "when the Son of Man comes, will he find faith on the earth?" (Luke 18:8). Though the Gospel is being spread far and wide, its faith, especially in the churches established for many years in the West, seems to have waned, its depth eroded. Another sign of the end is the proliferation of false messiahs and false prophets trying to lure away the faithful, as Jesus says will precede the Second Coming: "many shall come in my name, saying, I am Christ; and shall deceive many" (Matthew 24:5), "for false Christs and false prophets shall arise and show great signs and wonders so much so that, if it were possible, they shall deceive the very elect" (Matthew 24:24).

Fulfillment of Prophecy

The Jewish people figure in this anonymous Orthodox writer's interpretation of what signs will precede the Second Coming, based on Paul's prediction in Romans 11:25–33:

> For I would not have you be ignorant, brethren, of this mystery, lest you be wise in your own conceits; that blindness in part has befallen Israel, until the fullness of the Gentiles be complete. And so all Israel shall be saved, as it is written, 'There shall come out of Zion the Deliverer, who shall turn away ungodliness from Jacob. For this is my covenant to them, when I shall take away their sins. As concerning the gospel, they are enemies for your sakes, but as touching the election, they are beloved for the fathers' sakes. For the gifts and calling of God are without repentance. For as you in times past have not believed God, yet have now obtained mercy through their unbelief, even so these have also now not believed, that through your mercy they also may obtain mercy. For God has concluded them all in unbelief, that he might have mercy on all. O the depth of the riches of the wisdom and knowledge of God! How unsearchable are his judgments, and his ways past finding out!

Dispensational premillennialists see the church as a small part of the larger plan of God for Israel. Under the amillennialism that sees the church as the inheritor of all the covenant promises of God to Israel, it is the church that becomes the fulfillment of what God promised to Abraham, that through his seed all the nations shall be blessed and his descendants would be uncountable.

The Apocalypse

The only book in the New Testament that is, as a whole, prophetic is The Book of Revelation, also known as the Apocalypse, which is Greek for revelation or disclosure. John wrote the Book of Revelation on the island of Patmos in Greece when, the biblical scholars of the Orthodox and Catholic churches generally say, he was nearly one hundred years of age and was living in exile after being spared in the latest round of persecutions. In *The Church and the Last Things*, Dr. Martyn Lloyd-Jones says that in the preterist view, all the prophecies in Revelation have now been fulfilled, while the futurists see most of them as still awaiting fulfillment.

Lloyd-Jones says that most Protestant Reformers looked at Revelation as a laying out (in advance) the stages of the church's history. His own view of it is what he called a "spiritual historicist" view, which sees Revelation as a spiritual map of where the church should be in its journey, and what it should do to avoid the pitfalls described in John's visions of various local churches. The early church interpretation of John's Apocalypse has been that the churches in his visions are actual congregations that the apostle had ministered to, and that he was writing to guide and comfort the people through the persecution they were enduring, and which he could foresee would not be ending soon (not for at least another two centuries, as it turned out).

factum

The important point of the Jesus of the future, for Christians who profess the Nicene or Apostles' Creed, is that, regardless of whether they are amillennial, premillennial, postmillennial, or dispensationalist, he is coming again, and his return is nearer every day.

Lloyd-Jones gives his readers premillennial, postmillennial, and spiritual readings of Revelation 20, a chapter very much under debate, as it presents the "chaining" of Satan for a thousand years, which has been interpreted as being the thousand years in which Jesus will reign on earth by the premillennialists, as an indeterminate period for the church to grow in the amillennial view, and for the church to gain dominion over the world in the postmillennial one. Catholic writer Mark A. McNeil writes about Revelation 20 as well. He reports that the church traditionally has interpreted the chaining by Jesus of Satan as occurring as part of the crucifixion and resurrection, at which time Jesus defeats Satan and binds him sufficiently so that the church can take up its work of being light and salt in the world and spreading the good news of the kingdom.

Chapter 20

Jesus as Lord and Savior

One of the favorite slogans of the "Jesus People" Revival of the 1960s and '70s was "if you won't have Jesus as your Lord, you don't have Jesus as your Savior." The Jesus freaks, as they affectionately called themselves, meant it is not enough to assent to an invitation to confess Jesus as Savior if you aren't willing to live for him. It was a restating of Jesus' own words, "If you love me, keep my commandments" (John 14:15).

In All Things the Pre-eminence

If you've become a believer in Jesus as your Savior, been baptized, and joined a church, you might be thinking: so now what? You attend church every week and gradually get involved in some chores around the church. Perhaps you hear an almost-identical sermon every week. It may be along the lines of, "are you sure you're really saved, and if there's any doubt, don't you think you should come up and get saved or recommitted to Jesus?" Or, "How much have you done for the church? What's your ministry? Couldn't you do more, like singing in the choir, leading a class or a clean-up crew, making the coffee, or bringing snacks for the fellowship hour? Have you talked to your friends and neighbors about the church? Are you doing enough for Jesus?"

Is that all there is? Admittedly, the homilies (or sermons, for the down-to-earth) are not the *sine qua non* of being a Christian, but they are the first line of initiation into what may seem like insider stuff. Isn't being a Christian supposed to bring some excitement, or at least some purpose into life? Is the only cost of discipleship what you put in the offering plate?

Some critics have said that people often experience church as either so seeker friendly and geared to making everyone feel at home that it's barely different than being in meetings at work or at the school parents' night. Or that the church takes the safe middle road of not rocking anyone's boat, making church seem like little more than a series of cerebral exercises in looking at safe, noncontroversial texts.

Christian Life Beyond Chores at Church

The Apostle Paul offers some radical propositions about what Christ should mean to believers, and what the Christian life is meant to be:

> [Jesus] is the image of the invisible God, the firstborn of every creature. For by him all things were created, that are in heaven, and that are on earth, things visible and invisible, whether they be thrones, or dominions, principalities, or powers; all things were created by him, and for him. And he is before all things, and by him all

*things consist. He is the head of the body, the church; the beginning, the firstborn from the dead, so that in all things he might have the pre-eminence. For it pleased the Father that in him all fullness should dwell, and, having made peace through the blood of his cross, by him to reconcile all things to himself, by him, I say, whether they be things in earth, or things in heaven (**Colossians 1:15–20**).*

Advocates of the Christian worldview like the late Francis Schaeffer, contemporary authors Nancy Pearcey and Gene Edward Veith, Jr., and minister D. James Kennedy have taken Paul's text as a homily worth taking to work on Monday morning. If "by him all things were created," and if the goal is that "in all things he might have the pre-eminence," they say your work is cut out for you. That work is figuring out, and applying, what it means for Jesus to have the pre-eminence in your particular vocation, and how the work you start again every Monday morning brings glory to him and points the people served by your work to his kingdom.

Everything Belongs to God

The separatist Puritans, better known as Pilgrims, who are given a nod of remembrance every American Thanksgiving Day, also took this sense of everything being Christ's seriously. Leland Ryken, author of *Worldly Saints: The Puritans As They Really Were*, says Puritans believed that "everything was God's." Nothing was experienced outside their commitment to God and their faith. For support they might cite "The earth is the Lord's, and the fullness thereof; the world, and they who dwell therein," as David the Psalmist wrote (Psalm 24:1), or "For the earth is the Lord's, and the fullness thereof," echoed by Paul the Apostle (1 Corinthians 20:26).

The influential Christian novel *In His Steps* is Charles M. Sheldon's story of a single congregation in a small American city taking a single sermon seriously. The takeaway thought for that homily was "What would Jesus do?" The 1886 novel doesn't present a full-fledged Christian worldview, but its message of making every decision in light of Jesus' teaching is powerful enough to change lives. And as Sheldon himself demonstrated though his example in civic projects, like pioneering kindergartens and being among the first to work for racial justice in his own city, it can change institutions and societies. Today the question "What would Jesus do?" (often abbreviated as WWJD) graces thousands of items, such as T-shirts, hats, bumper stickers, pens, magnets, and all kinds of jewelry, from silver necklaces to silicone bracelets.

The Christian Mind

In 1963, Oxford scholar (and former student and friend of C. S. Lewis) Harry Blamires wrote *The Christian Mind* in an attempt to encourage "integrated thinking" by Christians committed to taking a stand against the secularization of Western culture. It became an instant classic—a little book to treasure, reread often, and disseminate—among Christian thinkers moved by the profundity of its simple apologetic. Blamires has gone on to write *Recovering the Christian Mind* and *The Post-Christian Mind*, which challenge popular myths like private morality, calling the term an oxymoron, as any morality based on less than the universality of its principles is no morality.

factum

A keystone of Abraham Kuyper's writings and sermons was the advocacy of the creation of a Christian mind or the redemption of the intellect as the first line of defense against the eroding effects of the higher critical thinking of the eighteenth century Enlightenment.

Russian Orthodox educator and philosopher Paul Evdokimov (1900–1969) expressed the same understanding of New Testament declarations: "the educational concern of Christifying rational life, the saturation of every domain by the light of Christ, a saturation that is inherent to the Christian faith, derives organically from Christian anthropology." Christian anthropology, the Christian understanding of

what being human means, was described by Evdokimov's former colleague at St. Sergius Orthodox Institute in Paris, Alexander Schmemann,
as "the first, the basic definition of man [as] priest." Schmemann is not
referring to priesthood here as the clergy of the church but is referring
to a mandate from God to all human beings to mediate the blessings
of God to every aspect of the world. "You are a chosen generation,
a royal priesthood, a holy nation, a peculiar people; that you should
show forth the praises of him who has called you out of darkness into
his marvelous light," as the Apostle Peter says (1 Peter 2:9).

Academic Lordship

Christian philosophy is a growing discipline that is beginning to
influence the academic world. In *Total Truth*, Nancy Pearcey says
that, almost single-handedly, Notre Dame University philosopher
Alvin Plantinga has launched something of a revolution in academic
philosophy. Pearcey cites naturalist philosopher Quentin Smith
as "blaming" Plantinga for making Christian philosophy creditable
and a major movement in American secular university philosophy
departments, saying these new faculty members are having the
effect of desecularizing the discipline of philosophy. Smith noted
that, in other disciplines, Christian faculty members departmental-
ize their discipline and their private, religious, lives (being careful
not to come out as Christians, in other words), but in philosophy
the trend is in the other direction, with scholars openly discussing
Christian foundations for their work and ably defending them.

Trickle-Down Philosophy

If one of Francis Schaeffer's recurring themes holds true—
the claim of Quentin Smith that the Christian faculty members
in other departments of most secular universities are reticent to
come out—it may not remain true much longer. Schaeffer believes
that whatever happens in the field of philosophy trickles down
over a few years to become the trend into the arts next, and into
other academic disciplines a few years later, and a generation
or two after that becomes the trend in popular thinking. Today's

post-modernism could actually give way to a new-Christian movement, academically, artistically, and socially.

The Dominion

Paul Evdokimov's call, quoted earlier, for "Christifying rational life,
the saturation of every domain by the light of Christ" echoes the
many Old Testament prophesies and New Testament declarations
that "He shall reign forever and ever." Handel had passages like
Psalms 97:1 and Revelation 19:6, 11:15, and 19:16 in mind when he
wrote his Messiah oratorio. The dominion of Christ on earth is what
every Christian prays for every time she recites the Lord's prayer,
"thy kingdom come," or utters the simplest and most basic Christian
creedal declaration, "Jesus is Lord."

Dominionism (the belief that Christians are mandated to bring
the entire world under the rule of God) is sometimes confused
with Christian obsession with politics and wanting to wrest control over society or government through nefarious means, but for
many Christians, it entails learning to think consistently as disciples
of Christ as Lord. One of the church's favorite texts regarding Jesus'
dominion is Hebrews 1:2–3: "[God] has in these last days spoken to
us by his Son, whom he has appointed the heir of all things and by
whom also he made the worlds, being the brightness of his glory,
and the express image of his person, and upholding all things by
the word of his power, when he had by himself purged our sins, sat
down on the right hand of the Majesty on high."

Every Knee Shall Bow

Paul in his epistle to the Philippian church writes, "at the name of
Jesus every knee shall bow, of things in heaven, and things in earth,
and things under the earth," (Philippians 2:10) echoing Isaiah's prophecy (45:21–23), "there is no other God beside me, a just God and a
Savior, there is none beside me. Look unto me and be saved, all the
ends of the earth, for I am God and there is none else. I have sworn by

myself, the word is gone out of my mouth in righteousness, and shall not return, that to me every knee shall bow, every tongue shall swear." It seems that, if Jesus is what he claims to be, either he could force every knee to bow by simply saying the word, or he wants the bowing to be unforced and motivated by love in the hearts of those bowing.

The Temptation of Triumphalism

Triumphalism, as the word implies, means being sure you're right and that your truth shall prevail. But as the term is generally used in a negative and pejorative sense, it carries with it a connotation of conceit, pride, or cocksureness. Triumphalism is seen as woefully lacking in humility, and triumphalists fail to realize the universality of Jesus' principle that it is the meek who shall inherit the world. Such pride precedes a fall, and as pride is the mother of all other sins, it is to be avoided even in confessing the Lordship, dominion, and sovereignty of Jesus the Lord.

symbolism

"Confessing" faith is the most symbolic expression for expressing faith because to confess implies meekness of heart and attitude. Confessing acknowledges that even if the right shall eventually prevail, its defenders have often failed and been defeated by the wrong because of poor timing, poor planning, poor weapons, and most typically, poor attitudes.

A major factor requiring caution against triumphalism is the not-yet aspect of Jesus' redemptive work. The kingdom is "already here" in its formative stage; the church is its best but imperfect evidence. That imperfection is the rub; when the kingdom comes in its full-ness, but not before, the triumph will be *fait accompli*. "The king-dom of God has not arrived, nor have we Christians arrived," Isaac

C. Rottenberg says in a *Christian Century* article cautioning against triumphalism. If the kingdom had already fully arrived, we would be in error to pray "thy kingdom come."

The Last Enemy

Triumphalism forgets the last line of the Lord's Prayer: "yours is the kingdom, and the power, and the glory forever. Amen." The kingdom is Jesus'; the power is his, and his is the glory. The triumph is his, and for those he has saved to get triumphal means they have forgotten who is the servant and who is the Master; who is the sinner and who the Savior: "The disciple is not above his master, nor the servant above his lord" (Matthew 10:24). The Apostle Paul describes the greatest triumph in human history, part of which is still to come, in 1 Corinthians 15:21–28: "Then cometh the end, when he shall have delivered up the kingdom to God, even the Father; when he shall have put down all rule and all authority and power. For he must reign, till he hath put all enemies under his feet."

The Holy City

Revelation Chapters 21 and 22 relate the vision John the Beloved Apostle received on the Isle of Patmos, of Jesus enthroned in the New Jerusalem.

discussion question

How are we to understand "the new creation"?
The new creation in the New Jerusalem far exceeds the new creation that is the mandate all of his disciples are given to work at in this, their meaningful, integrated physical and spiritual lives in their priesthood callings. But rather than brush away the best efforts of his people, he transforms them into the new creation.

"And he that sat upon the throne said, Behold, I make all things new" (Revelation 21:5). From the lowliness of a stable in Bethlehem, Jesus is finally seen in Scripture enthroned over the New Jerusalem. And here we see Him finally, through John's masterful depiction. See Revelation 21:10–27; 22:1–4, the theme of which is, "I saw no temple therein: for the Lord God Almighty and the Lamb are the temple of it. And the city had no need of the sun, neither of the moon to shine in it: for the glory of God did lighten it, and the Lamb is the light thereof."

Appendix A
Web Resources

Online Bible, King James Version. Downloadable text of both Old and New Testaments; also various other languages are available. Though there are several online sources like this, this is one of the most varied in terms of languages and file types available. *bible.ccim.org/dcb.html*

History of the celebration of Christmas *www.christmas-time.com/cp-hist.html*

Astronomer Susan S. Carroll's star of Bethlehem Web site *sciastro.net/portia/articles/thestar.htm*

John Charles Webb Jr.'s star of Bethlehem, astronomy, and astrology Web site *www.aloha.net/~johnboy/sitemap.htg/sitemap.htm*

Christmas in public schools *www.catholicleague.org/research/religious_expression_christmas.htm*

Chronology of dates in Jesus' lifetime *http://en.wikipedia.org/wiki/Chronology_of_Jesus'_birth_and_death*

Traditional icon of the Virgin Mary *www.iconsexplained.com/iec/00011.htm*

The synoptic problem *www.mindspring.com/~scarlson/synopt/index.html*

The synoptic problem by Daniel B. Wallace, Th.M., Ph.D. *www.bible.org/page.asp?page_id=669*

Wikipedia concise summary of the Synoptic Problem *http://en.wikipedia.org/wiki/Synoptic_problem*

Calvin College Ethereal Library, Fox's *Book of Martyrs* *www.ccel.org/f/foxe/martyrs/fox101.htm*

The presentation in the Temple and the flight into Egypt discussed

⌐*christianwritings.net/ chapt-2.htm*

The Infancy Gospel of Thomas (an apocryphal Gnostic text) ⌐*www.gnosis.org/library/ inftoml.htm*

PBS page on Jewish life in first century Israel. ⌐*www.pbs.org/wgbh/ pages/frontline/shows/ religion/portrait/judaism.html*

Source for Gnostic texts ⌐*ww.gnosis.org*

Hidden Gospels article by Phillip Jenkins, Penn State University ⌐*www.bibleinterp.com/ articles/hiddengospel.htm*

Divine liturgy of St. John Chrysostomos (main Eastern Orthodox liturgy) ⌐*www.ocf.org/ OrthodoxPage/liturgy/ liturgy.html*

The Koran, one of many online sources ⌐*etext.virginia.edu/koran .html*

Complete words of Flavius Josephus ⌐*www.ccel.org/j/josephus/ JOSEPHUS.HTM*

St. John of Kronstadt ⌐*www.fatheralexander.org/ booklets/english/johnkr_ e.htm*

Information about St. Photini (Samaritan woman at the well) ⌐*home.it.net.au/~jgrapsas/ pages/photini.htm*

Joseph of Arimathea in England ⌐*asis.com/~stag/glastonb .html*

Bible maps ⌐*biblia.com/jesusm/maps .htm*

Catholic Encyclopedia of 1911 (public domain) ⌐*www.newadvent.org/ cathen/*

Encyclopedia of Christianity ⌐*www.ccel.org/php/wwec .php*

The Gospel of Nicodemus (aka The Acts of Pilate) ⌐*www.ccel.org/ fathers2/ANF-08/anf08- 76.htm#P6567_1985111*

Eusebius, church history ⌐*www.ccel.org/fathers2/ NPNF2-01/TOC.htm*

St. Ignatius, Bishop of Antioch
www.ccel.org/fathers2/ANF-01/anf01-22.htm

All about Jewish Passover
www.jewfaq.org/holidaya.htm

The Internet Medieval Sourcebook Web site at Fordham University
www.fordham.edu/halsall/basis/goldenlegend/

Statistics—Christian communions and denominations
en.wikipedia.org/wiki/List_of_Christian_denominations_by_number_of_members

World religions
en.wikipedia.org/wiki/Major_world_religions

Billy Graham and the Billy Graham Evangelistic Association
www.wheaton.edu/bgc/archives/bio.html

Pat Robertson and The 700 Club
www.cbn.com/

Christianity Today Online
www.christianitytoday.com/

Eastern Orthodox philosophical statements

www.hkbu.edu.hk/~ppp/HKPC/Orthodox_Wisdom_intro.htm

www.incommunion.org/articles/previous-issues/issue-36/becoming-the-jesus-prayer

Harper's article on the National Religious Broadcasters association
www.harpers.org/FeelingTheHate.html

Christian Century article, "Christian Fulfillment and Jewish-Christian Dialogue"
www.religion-online.org/showarticle.asp?title=842

Lloyd-Jones' book on eschatology reviewed
www.bible.org/page.asp?page_id=1652

Catholic view of the millennium, rapture
www.diogh.org/youngacm/left_behind.htm

Schweitzer and the quest for the historical Jesus
www.mcmaster.ca/mjtm/2-51.htm

www.westarinstitute.org/Jesus_Seminar/jesus_seminar.html

Billy Sunday's baseball statistics
🖱*www.baseball-reference
.com/s/sundabi01.shtml*

Billy Sunday's sermons, stories
🖱*articles.christiansunite
.com/preacher5-1.shtml*

The Book of Revelation of St. John
the Divine in both English
and Greek
🖱*www.ellopos.net/
elpenor/greek-texts/new-
testament/revelation/1.asp*

Icons and iconography
🖱*www.orthodoxinfo
.com/general*

The Roman emperors
🖱*www.roman-
emperors.org/*

Appendix B

Bibliography

Biblical Texts

The Scripture texts quoted in this book are drawn from:

The Holy Bible: Old and New Testaments
Self-pronouncing edition, conforming to the 1611 edition, commonly
known as the Authorized or King James Version. (Cleveland and
New York: The World Publishing Company).

Other Texts

Additional, supporting sources are as follows:

Boice, James Montgomery. *Foundations of the Faith: A Comprehensive
and Readable Theology.* (Downers Grove, IL: InterVarsity Press,
1986).

Bultmann, Rudolf. *Jesus and the Word.* (New York: Charles Scribner's
Sons, 1934).

Bultmann, Rudolf. *Jesus Christ and Mythology.* (New York: Charles
Scribner's Sons, 1958).

Bultmann, Rudolf. *Kerygma and Myth.* (London: S.P.C.K., 1953).

Bultmann, Rudolf. *Theology of the New Testament.* 2 volumes. (London:
SCM Press, Ltd., 1967).

Cairns, Earle E. *Christianity Through the Centuries: A History of the
Christian Church.* (Grand Rapids, MI: Zondervan, 1981 [1954]).

Chilton, Bruce. *Mary Magdalene: A Biography.* (New York: Doubleday,
2005).

Dobson, James. *Dare to Discipline.* (Wheaton, IL: Tyndale House,
1970).

Dobson, James. *New Dare to Discipline.* (Wheaton, IL: Tyndale House,
1992).

George, Margaret. *Mary, Called Magdalene*. (New York: Penguin, 2002).

Gillquist, Peter. *Becoming Orthodox*. (Ben Lomond, CA: Conciliar Press, 2002).

Hanegraaff, Hank, and Maier, Paul L. *The Da Vinci Code: Fact or Fiction?* (Wheaton, IL: Tyndale House, 2004).

Harrison, R.K. "Higher Criticism," in *Evangelical Dictionary of Theology*. Walter A. Elwell, 511–512 (Grand Rapids, MI: Baker Book House, 1984).

Kennedy, D. James. *Evangelism Explosion*. (Wheaton, IL: Tyndale House, 1977).

Kraeling, Emil G. *The Old Testament Since the Reformation*. (New York: Harper and Brothers, 1955).

Lester, Meera. *Everything Mary Magdalene*. (Avon: Adams, 2006).

Lester, Meera. *Mary Magdalene: The Modern Guide to the Bible's Most Mysterious and Misunderstood Woman*. (Avon: Adams, 2005).

Lewis, C.S. *Mere Christianity*. (New York: Macmillan, 1943).

Malet, A. *The Thought of Rudolf Bultmann*. (New York: Doubleday, 1969).

Pearcey, Nancy. *Total Truth: Liberating Christianity from Its Cultural Captivity*. (Wheaton, IL: Crossway, 2004).

Pokrovsky, Gleb. *The Way of a Pilgrim*. (Woodstock, VT: Skylight Paths Publishing, 2001).

Rice, Anne. *Christ the Lord: Out of Egypt*. (New York: Knopf, 2005).

Roberts, Robert C. "Bultmann, Rudolf," in *Evangelical Dictionary of Theology*. Edited by Walter A. Elwell, 180 (Grand Rapids, MI: Baker Book House, 1984).

Roberts, Robert C. *Rudolf Bultmann's Theology: A Critical Interpretation*. (Grand Rapids: Eerdmans, 1976).

Schaeffer, Francis, and Koop, C. Everett. *Whatever Happened to the Human Race?* (Wheaton, IL: Crossway, 1983).

Schaeffer, Francis. *Escape from Reason*. (Downers Corners, IL: InterVarsity Press, 1968).

Schaeffer, Francis. *He Is There and He Is Not Silent*. (Wheaton, IL: Tyndale House, 1980).

Schaeffer, Francis. *How Should We Then Live?* (Wheaton, IL: Crossway, 1983).

Schaeffer, Francis. *The Church Before the Watching World.* (Wheaton, IL: Crossway, 1994).

Schaeffer, Francis. *The God Who Is There.* (Downers Corners, IL: InterVarsity Press, 1998).

Schaeffer, Francis. *The Great Evangelical Disaster.* (Wheaton, IL: Crossway, 1984).

Schaeffer, Francis. *The Mark of a Christian.* (Downers Corners, IL: InterVarsity Press, 1976).

Schmithals, W. *An Introduction to the Theology of Rudolf Bultmann.* (London: SCM Press, 1968).

Thiselton, A.C. *The Two Horizons: New Testament Hermeneutics and Philosophical Description.* (Grand Rapids: Eerdmans, and Paternoster, 1980).

Ware, Kallistos, Palmer, G.E.H., and Sherrard, Philip. *The Philokalia.* (London: Faber and Faber, 2005).

Appendix C
Evangelical Christian Institutions

Evangelical Colleges and Graduate Schools

The following lists from the Council for Christian Colleges and Universities (CCCU) includes most evangelical colleges in North America.

CCCU Member Colleges

Abilene Christian University, Abilene, Texas
Anderson University, Anderson, Indiana
Asbury College, Wilmore, Kentucky
Azusa Pacific University, Azusa, California
Belhaven College, Jackson, Mississippi
Bethel College—Indiana, Mishawaka, Indiana
Bethel University, St. Paul, Minnesota
Biola University, La Mirada, California
Bluffton University, Bluffton, Ohio
Bryan College, Dayton, Tennessee
California Baptist University, Riverside, California
Calvin College, Grand Rapids, Michigan
Campbellsville University, Campbellsville, Kentucky
Carson-Newman College, Jefferson City, Tennessee
Cedarville University, Cedarville, Ohio
College of the Ozarks, Point Lookout, Missouri
Colorado Christian University, Lakewood, Colorado
Corban College, Salem, Oregon
Cornerstone University, Grand Rapids, Michigan
Covenant College, Lookout Mountain, Georgia
Crichton College, Memphis, Tennessee

Crown College, St. Bonifacius, Minnesota
Dallas Baptist University, Dallas, Texas
Dordt College, Sioux Center, Iowa
East Texas Baptist University, Marshall, Texas
Eastern Mennonite University, Harrisonburg, Virginia
Eastern Nazarene College, Quincy, Massachusetts
Eastern University, St. Davids, Pennsylvania
Erskine College, Due West, South Carolina
Evangel University, Springfield, Missouri
Fresno Pacific University, Fresno, California
Geneva College, Beaver Falls, Pennsylvania
George Fox University, Newberg, Oregon
Gordon College, Wenham, Massachusetts
Goshen College, Goshen, Indiana
Grace College & Seminary, Winona Lake, Indiana
Greenville College, Greenville, Illinois
Hardin-Simmons University, Abilene, Texas
Hope International University, Fullerton, California
Houghton College, Houghton, New York
Houston Baptist University, Houston, Texas
Howard Payne University, Brownwood, Texas
Huntington University, Huntington, Indiana
Indiana Wesleyan University, Marion, Indiana
John Brown University, Siloam Springs, Arkansas
Judson College—AL, Marion, Alabama
Judson College—IL, Elgin, Illinois
Kentucky Christian University, Grayson, Kentucky
King College, Bristol, Tennessee
King's University College, The, Edmonton, Alberta, Canada
Lee University, Cleveland, Tennessee
LeTourneau University, Longview, Texas
Lipscomb University, Nashville, Tennessee
Louisiana College, Pineville, Louisiana
Malone College, Canton, Ohio
Master's College & Seminary, The, Santa Clarita, California
Messiah College, Grantham, Pennsylvania

MidAmerica Nazarene University, Olathe, Kansas

Milligan College, Milligan College, Tennessee

Mississippi College, Clinton, Mississippi

Missouri Baptist University, St. Louis, Missouri

Montreat College, Montreat, North Carolina

Mount Vernon Nazarene University, Mount Vernon, Ohio

North Greenville College, Tigerville, South Carolina

North Park University, Chicago, Illinois

Northwest Christian College, Eugene, Oregon

Northwest Nazarene University, Nampa, Idaho

Northwest University, Kirkland, Washington

Northwestern College—IA, Orange City, Iowa

Northwestern College—MN, St. Paul, Minnesota

Nyack College, New York, New York

Nyack College, Nyack, New York

Oklahoma Baptist University, Shawnee, Oklahoma

Oklahoma Christian University, Oklahoma City, Oklahoma

Oklahoma Wesleyan University, Bartlesville, Oklahoma

Olivet Nazarene University, Bourbonnais, Illinois

Oral Roberts University, Tulsa, Oklahoma

Palm Beach Atlantic University, West Palm Beach, Florida

Point Loma Nazarene University, San Diego, California

Redeemer University College, Ancaster, Ontario, Canada

Roberts Wesleyan College, Rochester, New York

Seattle Pacific University, Seattle, Washington

Simpson University, Redding, California

Southeastern University, Lakeland, Florida

Southern Nazarene University, Bethany, Oklahoma

Southern Wesleyan University, Central, South Carolina

Southwest Baptist University, Bolivar, Missouri

Spring Arbor University, Spring Arbor, Michigan

Sterling College, Sterling, Kansas

Tabor College, Hillsboro, Kansas

Taylor University, Upland, Indiana

Trevecca Nazarene University, Nashville, Tennessee

Trinity Christian College, Palos Heights, Illinois

Trinity International University, Deerfield, Illinois
Trinity Western University, Langley, British Columbia, Canada
Union University, Jackson, Tennessee
University of Sioux Falls, Sioux Falls, South Dakota
Vanguard University of Southern California, Costa Mesa, California
Warner Pacific College, Portland, Oregon
Warner Southern College, Lake Wales, Florida
Wayland Baptist University, Plainview, Texas
Waynesburg College, Waynesburg, Pennsylvania
Westmont College, Santa Barbara, California
Wheaton College, Wheaton, Illinois
Whitworth College, Spokane, Washington
Williams Baptist College, Walnut Ridge, Arkansas

Member status in the CCCU requires that colleges be four-year undergraduate institutions that hire only professing Christian faculty members. Affiliate status is provided to institutions that want to promote Christian education but do not meet the criteria for member status. Affiliates in North America, many of which are postgraduate schools such as theological seminaries, Toronto's Institute for Christian Studies, and Regent University in Virginia, include (arranged alphabetically by province and state):

Canada

Alliance University College, Calgary, Alberta
Canadian Nazarene University College, Calgary, Alberta
Prairie Bible Institute, Three Hills, Alberta
Taylor University College & Seminary, Edmonton, Alberta
Providence College & Seminary, Otterburne, Manitoba
Atlantic Baptist University, Moncton, New Brunswick
Institute for Christian Studies, Toronto, Ontario
Tyndale University College & Seminary, North York, Ontario
Tyndale University College & Seminary, Toronto, Ontario
Briercrest College, Caronport, Saskatchewan

United States

Grand Canyon University, Phoenix, Arizona
Crestmont College, Rancho Palos Verdes, California
Fuller Theological Seminary, Pasadena, California
San Diego Christian College, El Cajon, California
William Jessup University, Rocklin, California
North Haiti Christian University, Sarasota, Florida
Emmanuel College, Franklin Springs, Georgia
Toccoa Falls College, Toccoa Falls, Georgia
Moody Bible Institute, Chicago, Illinois
Central Christian College, McPherson, Kansas
Asbury Theological Seminary, Wilmore, Kentucky
Andrews University, Berrien Springs, Michigan
Reformed Bible College, Grand Rapids, Michigan
North Central University, Minneapolis, Minnesota
Campbell University, Buies Creek, North Carolina
Franciscan University of Steubenville, Steubenville, Ohio
Mid-America Christian University, Oklahoma City, Oklahoma
Lancaster Bible College, Lancaster, Pennsylvania
Philadelphia Biblical University, Langhorne, Pennsylvania
Valley Forge Christian College, Phoenixville, Pennsylvania
Charleston Southern University, Charleston, South Carolina
Columbia International University, Columbia, South Carolina
Baylor University, Waco, Texas
Criswell College, The, Dallas, Texas
Dallas Theological Seminary, Dallas, Texas
Bluefield College, Bluefield, Virginia
Regent University, Virginia Beach, Virginia
Walla Walla College, College Place, Washington
Ohio Valley University, Vienna, West Virginia

Member Denominations of the National Association of Evangelicals

Member denominations and their year of joining the NAE are listed below.

Advent Christian General Conference (1986)
Assemblies of God (1943)
Baptist General Conference (1966)
The Brethren Church (1968)
Brethren in Christ Church (1949)
Christian Catholic Church (Evangelical Protestant) (1975)
The Christian and Missionary Alliance (1966)
Christian Church of North America (1953)
Christian Reformed Church in North America (1943–51; 1988)
Christian Union (1954)
Church of God (Cleveland) (1944)
Church of God Mountain Assembly, Inc. (1981)
Church of the Nazarene (1984)
Church of the United Brethren in Christ (1953)
Churches of Christ in Christian Union (1945)
Congregational Holiness Church (1990–92; 1994)
Conservative Baptist Association of America (1990)
Conservative Congregational Christian Conference (1951)
Conservative Lutheran Association (1984)
Elim Fellowship (1947)
Evangelical Church of North America (1969)
Evangelical Congregational Church (1962)
Evangelical Free Church of America (1943)
Evangelical Friends International of North America (1971)
Evangelical Mennonite Church (1944)
Evangelical Methodist Church (1952)
Evangelical Presbyterian Church (1982)
Evangelistic Missionary Fellowship (1982)
Fellowship of Evangelical Bible Churches (1948)
Fire Baptized Holiness Church of God of the Americas (1978)

Free Methodist Church of North America (1944)

General Association of General Baptists (1988)

International Church of the Foursquare Gospel (1952)

International Pentecostal Church of Christ (1946)

International Pentecostal Holiness Church (1943)

Mennonite Brethren Churches, USA (1946)

Midwest Congregational Christian Fellowship (1964)

Missionary Church, Inc. (1944)

Open Bible Standard Churches (1943)

Pentecostal Church of God (1954)

Pentecostal Free Will Baptist Church, Inc. (1988)

Presbyterian Church in America (1986)

Primitive Methodist Church USA (1946)

Reformed Episcopal Church (1990)

Reformed Presbyterian Church of North America (1946)

Regional Synod of Mid-America (Reformed Church in America) (1989)

The Salvation Army, National Headquarters (1990)

The Wesleyan Church (1948)

Worldwide Church of God (1997)

Index